MOCKINGBIRD

I CAN EXPLAIN

Chelsea C...
WRITER

Kate Niemczyk (#1-4) **& Ibrahim Moustafa** (#5)
ARTISTS

Sean Parsons
INKER, #4

Rachelle Rosenberg
COLOR ARTIST

VC's Joe Caramagna
LETTERER

**Joëlle Jones &
Rachelle Rosenberg**
COVER ART

**Alanna Smith &
Christina Harrington**
ASSISTANT EDITORS

Katie Kubert
EDITOR

Tom Brevoort
EXECUTIVE EDITOR

MOCKINGBIRD: S.H.I.E.L.D. 50TH ANNIVERSARY #1

Chelsea Cain
WRITER

Joëlle Jones
ARTIST

Rachelle Rosenberg
COLOR ARTIST

VC's Joe Caramagna
LETTERER

Paul Renaud
COVER ART

Jon Moisan
EDITOR

COLLECTION EDITOR: JENNIFER GRÜNWALD
ASSOCIATE MANAGING EDITOR: KATERI WOODY
ASSOCIATE EDITOR: SARAH BRUNSTAD
EDITOR, SPECIAL PROJECTS: MARK D. BEAZLEY
VP PRODUCTION & SPECIAL PROJECTS: JEFF YOUNGQUIST
SVP PRINT, SALES & MARKETING: DAVID GABRIEL
BOOK DESIGNER: JAY BOWEN

EDITOR IN CHIEF: AXEL ALONSO
CHIEF CREATIVE OFFICER: JOE QUESADA
PUBLISHER: DAN BUCKLEY
EXECUTIVE PRODUCER: ALAN FINE

MOCKINGBIRD VOL. 1: I CAN EXPLAIN. Contains material originally published in magazine form as MOCKINGBIRD: S.H.I.E.L.D. #50TH ANNIVERSARY #1 and MOCKINGBIRD #1-5. Second printing 2016. ISBN# 978-1-302-90122-6. Published by MARVEL WORLDWIDE, INC., a subsidiary of MARVEL ENTERTAINMENT, LLC. OFFICE OF PUBLICATION... MARVEL No similarity between any of the names, characters, persons, and/or institutions in this magazine with those of any living or dead ... ist is purely coincidental. **Printed in Canada.** ALAN FINE, President, Marvel Entertainment; DAN BUCKLEY, President, TV, Publishing & Brand ... VP of Publishing; DAVID BOGART, SVP of Business Affairs & Operations, Publishing & Partnership; C.B. CEBULSKI, VP of Brand Management ... ing; JEFF YOUNGQUIST, VP of Production & Special Projects; DAN CARR, Executive Director of Publishing Technology; ALEX MORALES, Direc... LEE, Chairman Emeritus. For information regarding advertising in Marvel Comics or on Marvel.com, please contact Vit DeBellis, Integrated ... ries, please call 888-511-5480. **Manufactured between 11/2/2016 and 11/21/2016 by SOLISCO PRINTERS, SCOTT, QC, CANADA.**

1098765432

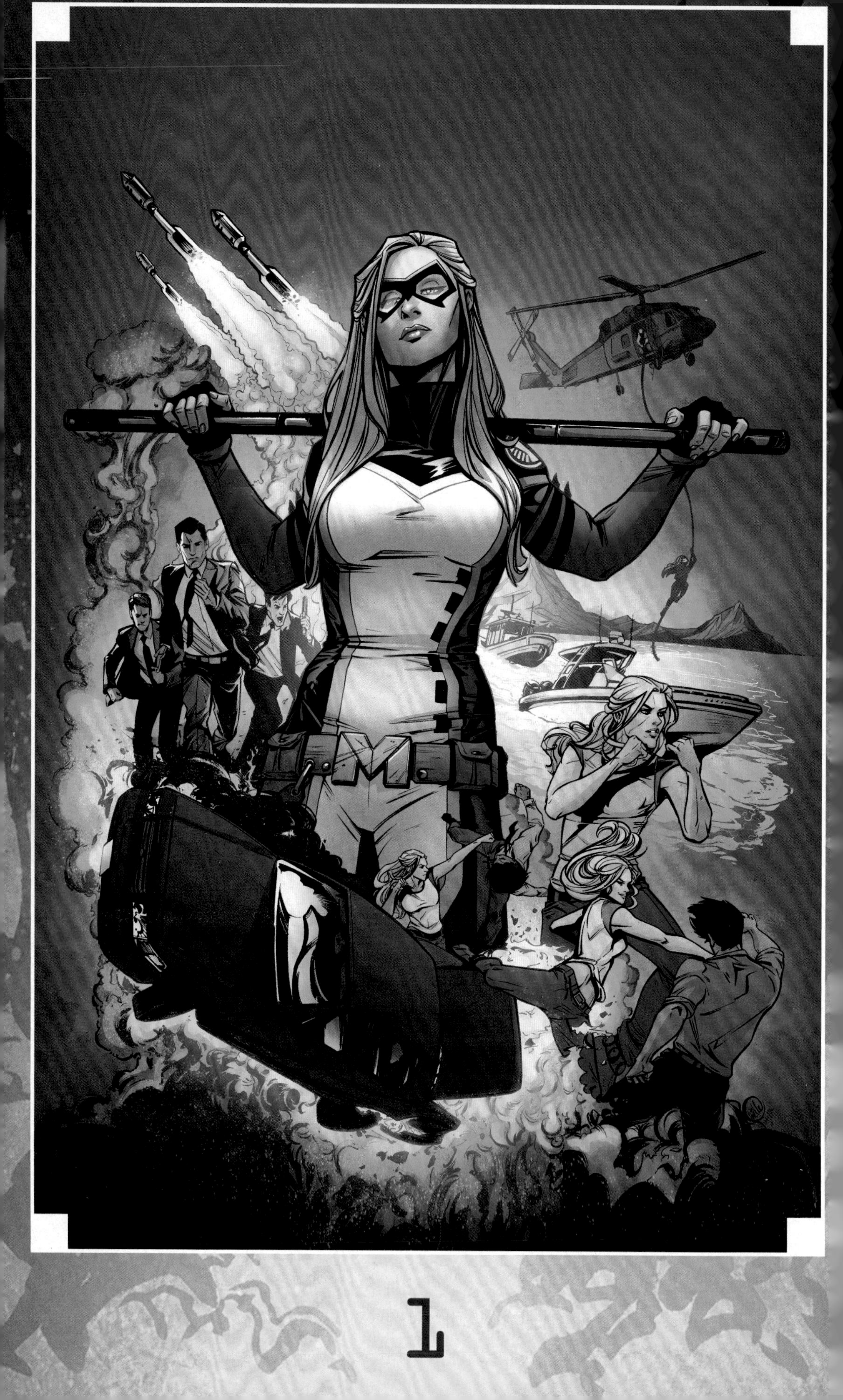

1

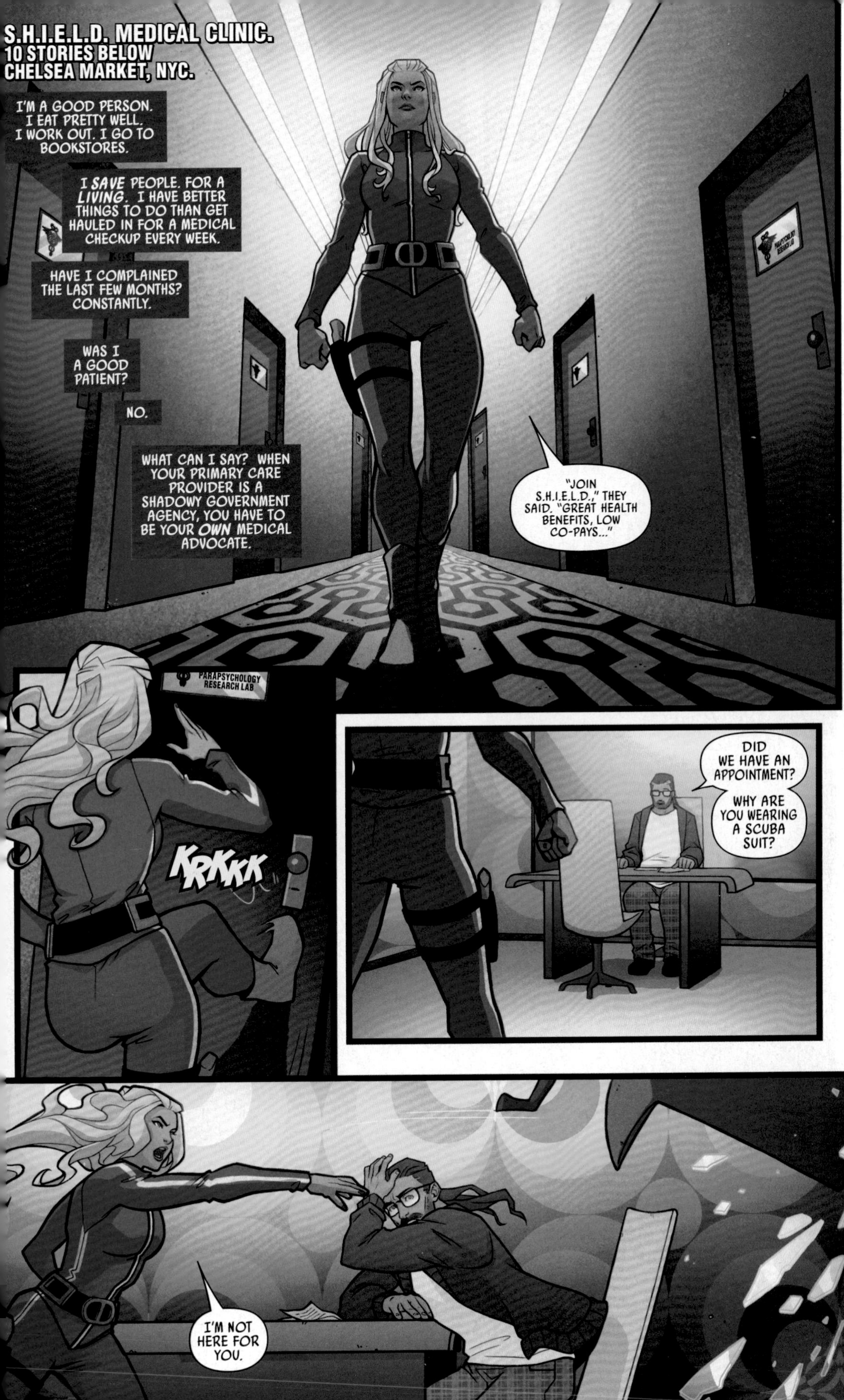
S.H.I.E.L.D. MEDICAL CLINIC. 10 STORIES BELOW CHELSEA MARKET, NYC.
I'M A GOOD PERSON. I EAT PRETTY WELL. I WORK OUT. I GO TO BOOKSTORES.
I SAVE PEOPLE. FOR A LIVING. I HAVE BETTER THINGS TO DO THAN GET HAULED IN FOR A MEDICAL CHECKUP EVERY WEEK.
HAVE I COMPLAINED THE LAST FEW MONTHS? CONSTANTLY.
WAS I A GOOD PATIENT?
NO.
WHAT CAN I SAY? WHEN YOUR PRIMARY CARE PROVIDER IS A SHADOWY GOVERNMENT AGENCY, YOU HAVE TO BE YOUR OWN MEDICAL ADVOCATE.
"JOIN S.H.I.E.L.D.," THEY SAID. "GREAT HEALTH BENEFITS, LOW CO-PAYS..."
PARAPSYCHOLOGY RESEARCH LAB
KRKKK
DID WE HAVE AN APPOINTMENT?
WHY ARE YOU WEARING A SCUBA SUIT?
I'M NOT HERE FOR YOU.

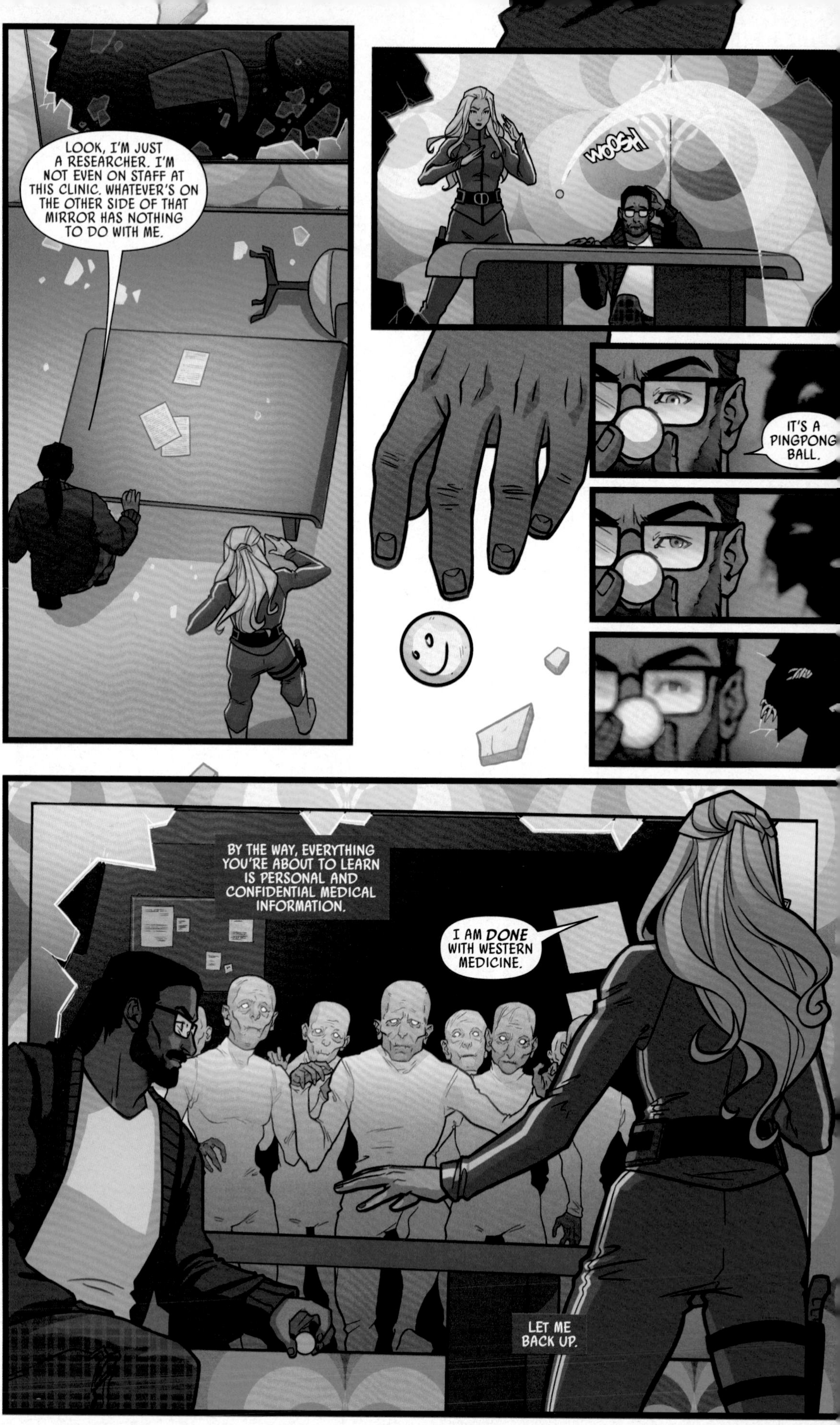
LOOK, I'M JUST A RESEARCHER. I'M NOT EVEN ON STAFF AT THIS CLINIC. WHATEVER'S ON THE OTHER SIDE OF THAT MIRROR HAS NOTHING TO DO WITH ME.
WOOSH
IT'S A PINGPONG BALL.
BY THE WAY, EVERYTHING YOU'RE ABOUT TO LEARN IS PERSONAL AND CONFIDENTIAL MEDICAL INFORMATION.
I AM DONE WITH WESTERN MEDICINE.
LET ME BACK UP.

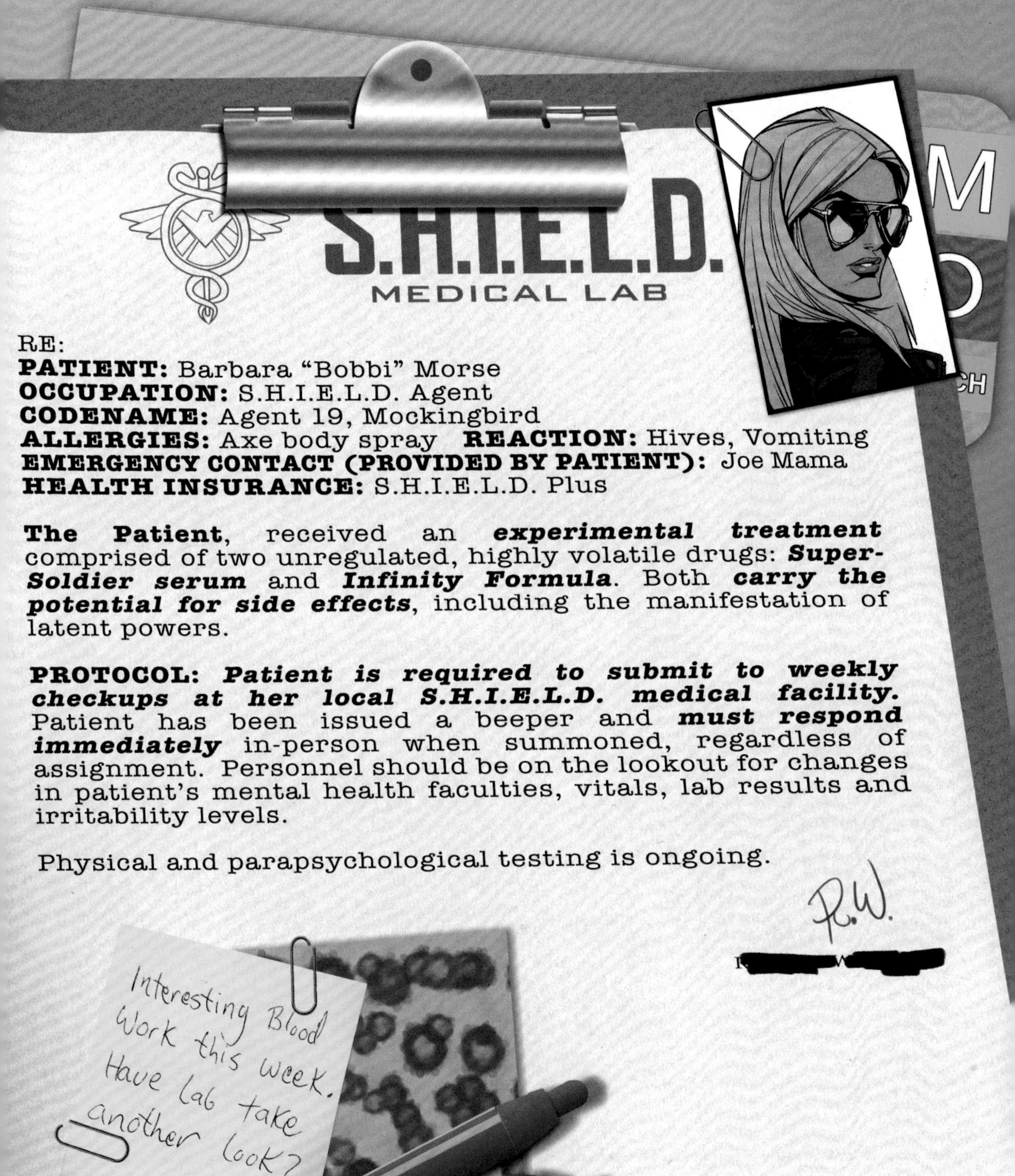

S.H.I.E.L.D.
MEDICAL LAB

RE:
PATIENT: Barbara "Bobbi" Morse
OCCUPATION: S.H.I.E.L.D. Agent
CODENAME: Agent 19, Mockingbird
ALLERGIES: Axe body spray **REACTION:** Hives, Vomiting
EMERGENCY CONTACT (PROVIDED BY PATIENT): Joe Mama
HEALTH INSURANCE: S.H.I.E.L.D. Plus

The Patient, received an ***experimental treatment*** comprised of two unregulated, highly volatile drugs: ***Super-Soldier serum*** and ***Infinity Formula***. Both ***carry the potential for side effects***, including the manifestation of latent powers.

PROTOCOL: *Patient is required to submit to weekly checkups at her local S.H.I.E.L.D. medical facility.* Patient has been issued a beeper and ***must respond immediately*** in-person when summoned, regardless of assignment. Personnel should be on the lookout for changes in patient's mental health faculties, vitals, lab results and irritability levels.

Physical and parapsychological testing is ongoing.

R.W.

[redacted]

Interesting Blood Work this week. Have lab take another look?
Extremis
BUILD BETTER ORGANS TODAY
Extremis
BUILD BETTER ORGANS TODAY

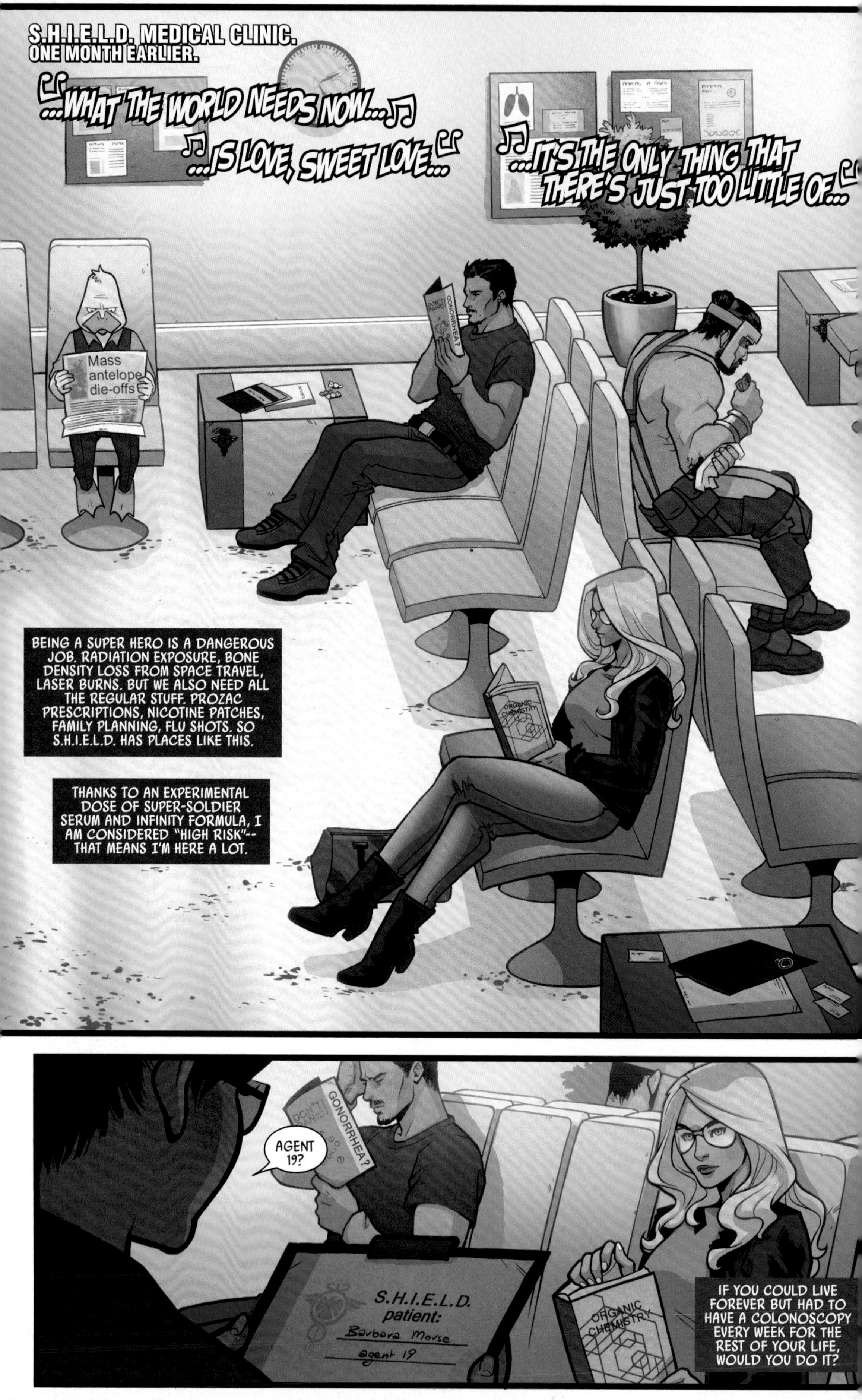

S.H.I.E.L.D. MEDICAL CLINIC.
ONE MONTH EARLIER.
♫...WHAT THE WORLD NEEDS NOW...♫
♫...IS LOVE, SWEET LOVE...♫
♫...IT'S THE ONLY THING THAT THERE'S JUST TOO LITTLE OF...♫
Mass antelope die-offs
DON'T PANIC!
GONORRHEA?
ORGANIC CHEMISTRY
BEING A SUPER HERO IS A DANGEROUS JOB. RADIATION EXPOSURE, BONE DENSITY LOSS FROM SPACE TRAVEL, LASER BURNS. BUT WE ALSO NEED ALL THE REGULAR STUFF. PROZAC PRESCRIPTIONS, NICOTINE PATCHES, FAMILY PLANNING, FLU SHOTS. SO S.H.I.E.L.D. HAS PLACES LIKE THIS.
THANKS TO AN EXPERIMENTAL DOSE OF SUPER-SOLDIER SERUM AND INFINITY FORMULA, I AM CONSIDERED "HIGH RISK"-- THAT MEANS I'M HERE A LOT.
AGENT 19?
DON'T PANIC!
GONORRHEA?
S.H.I.E.L.D.
patient:
Barbara Morse
agent 19
ORGANIC CHEMISTRY
IF YOU COULD LIVE FOREVER BUT HAD TO HAVE A COLONOSCOPY EVERY WEEK FOR THE REST OF YOUR LIFE, WOULD YOU DO IT?

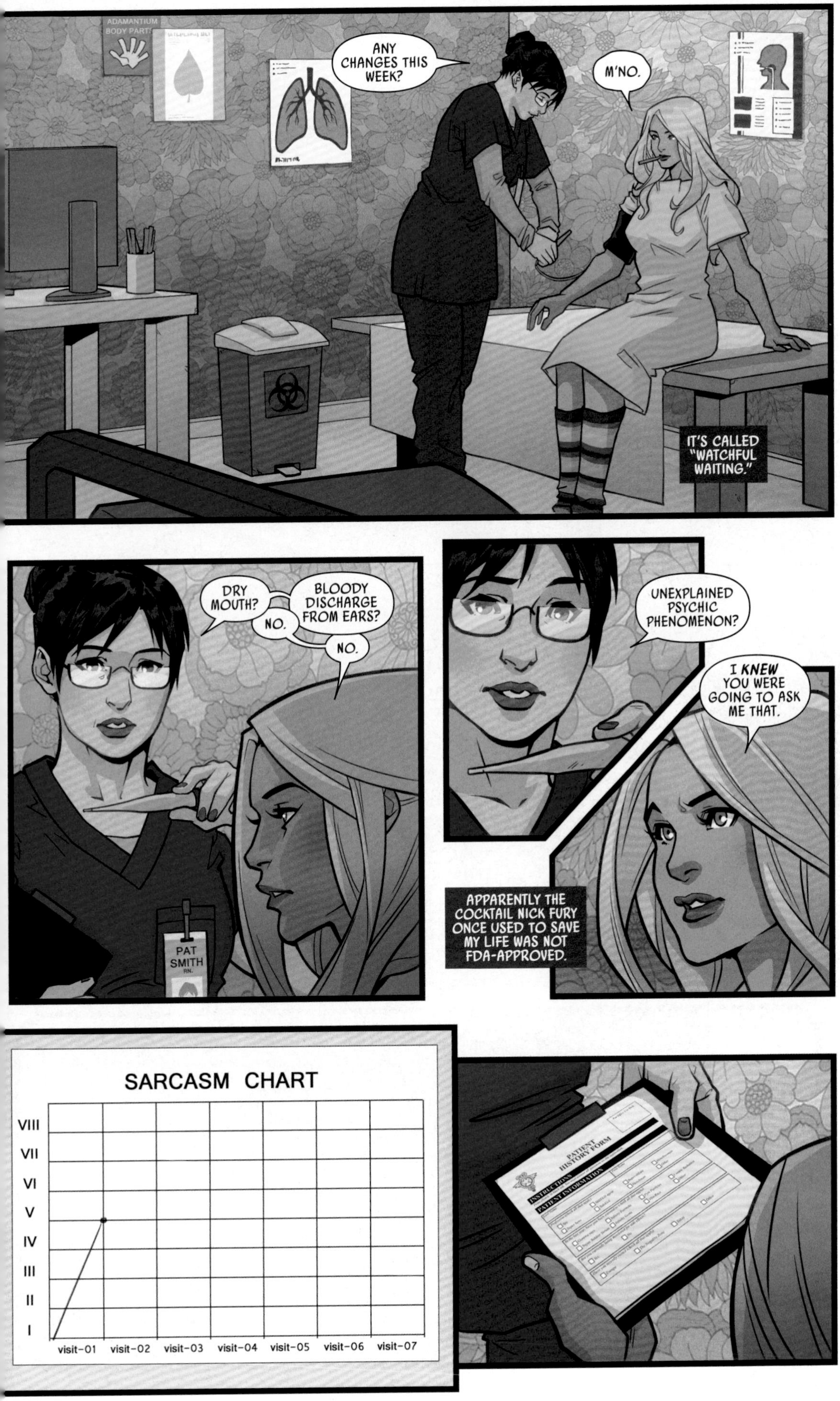

ADAMANTIUM BODY PARTS
ANY CHANGES THIS WEEK?
M'NO.
IT'S CALLED "WATCHFUL WAITING."
DRY MOUTH?
NO.
BLOODY DISCHARGE FROM EARS?
NO.
PAT SMITH RN.
UNEXPLAINED PSYCHIC PHENOMENON?
I KNEW YOU WERE GOING TO ASK ME THAT.
APPARENTLY THE COCKTAIL NICK FURY ONCE USED TO SAVE MY LIFE WAS NOT FDA-APPROVED.
SARCASM CHART
VIII
VII
VI
V
IV
III
II
I
visit-01 visit-02 visit-03 visit-04 visit-05 visit-06 visit-07
PATIENT HISTORY FORM
INSTRUCTIONS
PATIENT INFORMATION

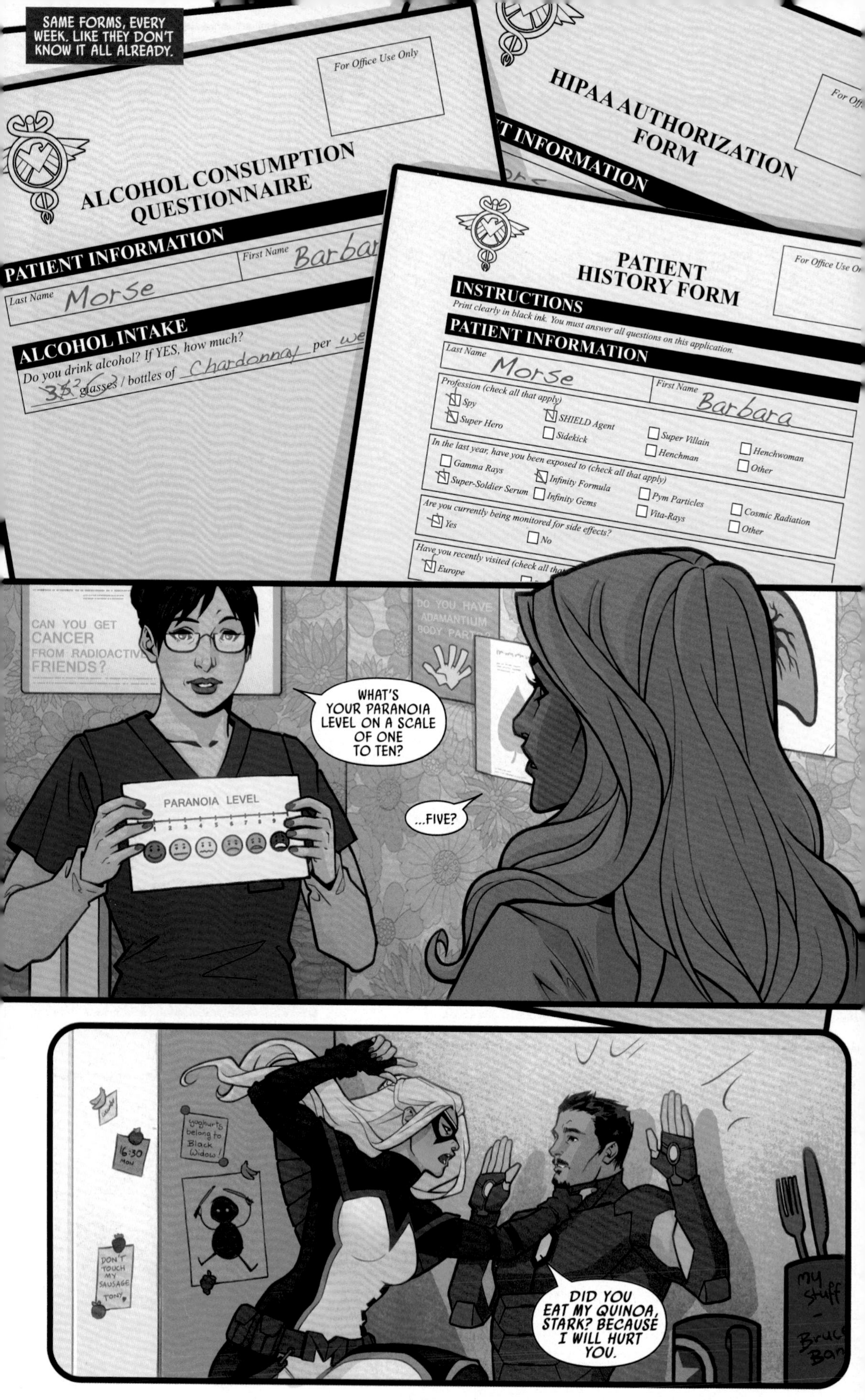

SAME FORMS, EVERY WEEK. LIKE THEY DON'T KNOW IT ALL ALREADY.
For Office Use Only
ALCOHOL CONSUMPTION QUESTIONNAIRE
PATIENT INFORMATION
First Name Barbar
Last Name Morse
ALCOHOL INTAKE
Do you drink alcohol? If YES, how much?
glasses / bottles of Chardonnay per we
HIPAA AUTHORIZATION FORM
For Office Use Only
PATIENT HISTORY FORM
INSTRUCTIONS
Print clearly in black ink. You must answer all questions on this application.
PATIENT INFORMATION
Last Name Morse
First Name Barbara
Profession (check all that apply)
Spy
Super Hero
SHIELD Agent
Sidekick
Super Villain
Henchman
Henchwoman
Other
In the last year, have you been exposed to (check all that apply)
Gamma Rays
Super-Soldier Serum
Infinity Formula
Infinity Gems
Pym Particles
Vita-Rays
Cosmic Radiation
Other
Are you currently being monitored for side effects?
Yes
No
Have you recently visited (check all that
Europe
CAN YOU GET CANCER FROM RADIOACTIVE FRIENDS?
DO YOU HAVE ADAMANTIUM BODY PARTS?
WHAT'S YOUR PARANOIA LEVEL ON A SCALE OF ONE TO TEN?
PARANOIA LEVEL
...FIVE?
yoghurts belong to Black Widow!
16:30 MON
DON'T TOUCH MY SAUSAGE TONY
DID YOU EAT MY QUINOA, STARK? BECAUSE I WILL HURT YOU.

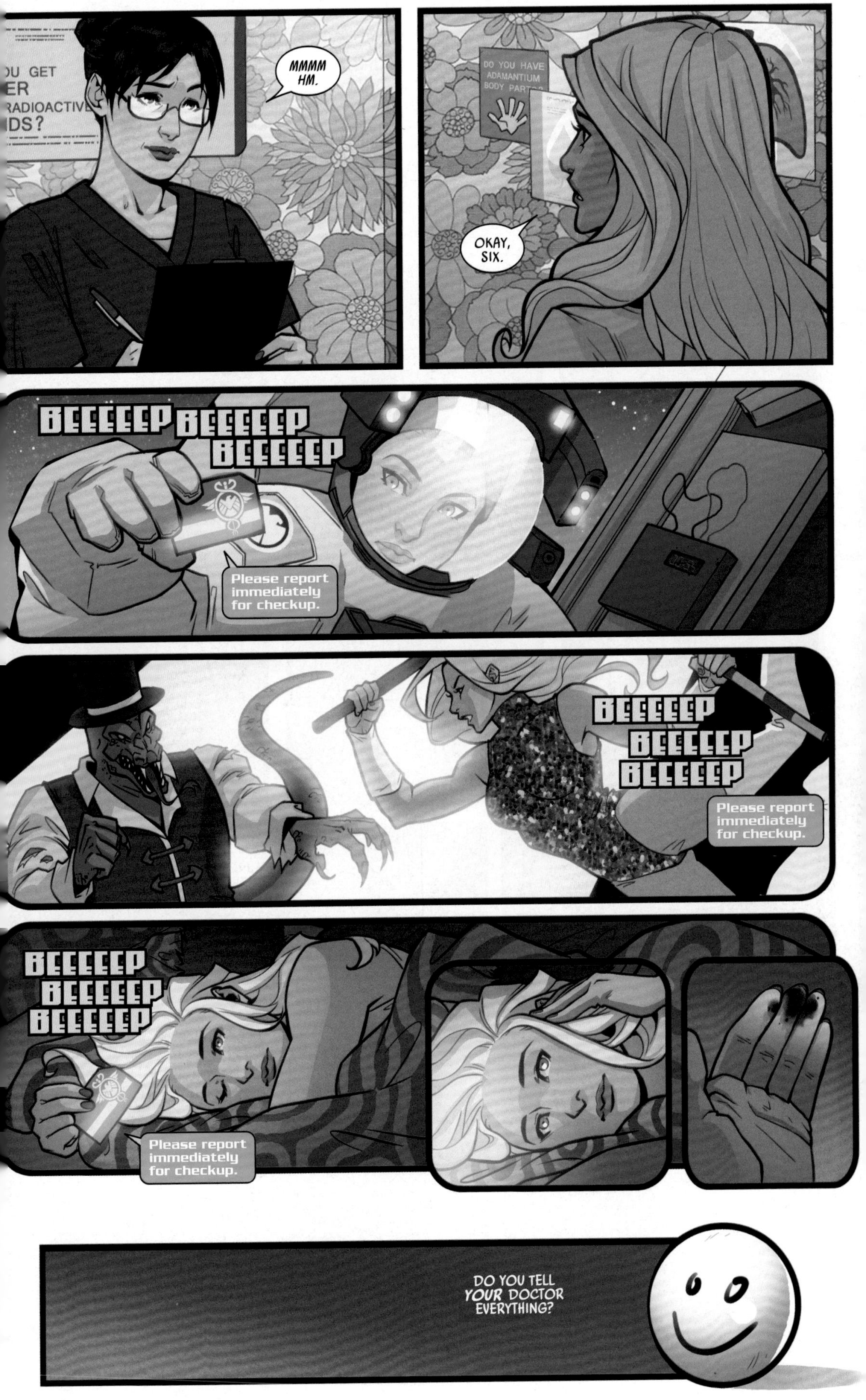

...U GET
...ER
...RADIOACTIVE
...DS?
MMMM HM.
DO YOU HAVE ADAMANTIUM BODY PART...
OKAY, SIX.
BEEEEEP BEEEEEP BEEEEEP
Please report immediately for checkup.
BEEEEEP BEEEEEP BEEEEEP
Please report immediately for checkup.
BEEEEEP BEEEEEP BEEEEEP
Please report immediately for checkup.
DO YOU TELL YOUR DOCTOR EVERYTHING?

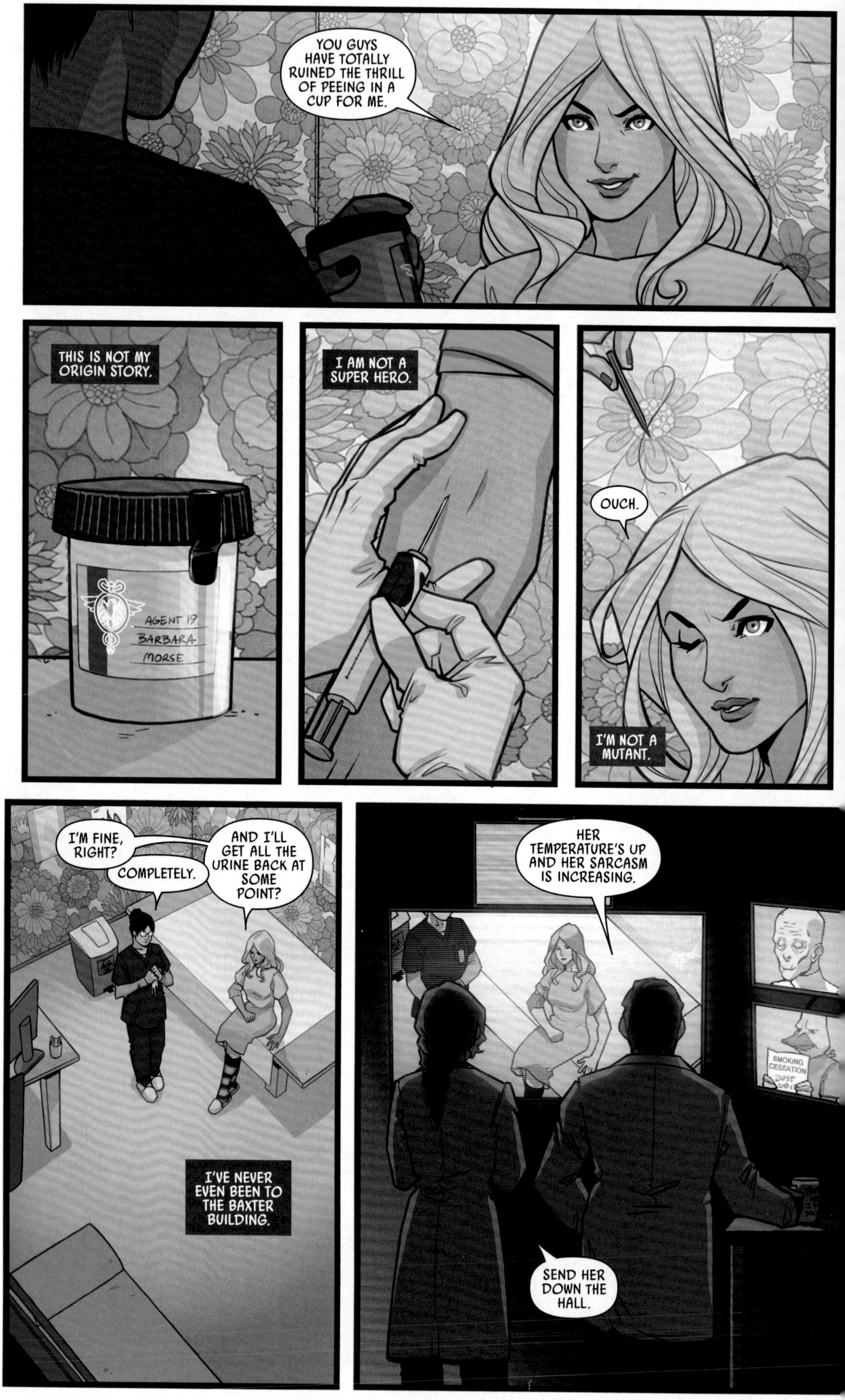
YOU GUYS HAVE TOTALLY RUINED THE THRILL OF PEEING IN A CUP FOR ME.
THIS IS NOT MY ORIGIN STORY.
AGENT 19
BARBARA
MORSE
I AM NOT A SUPER HERO.
OUCH.
I'M NOT A MUTANT.
I'M FINE, RIGHT?
COMPLETELY.
AND I'LL GET ALL THE URINE BACK AT SOME POINT?
I'VE NEVER EVEN BEEN TO THE BAXTER BUILDING.
HER TEMPERATURE'S UP AND HER SARCASM IS INCREASING.
SMOKING CESSATION
SEND HER DOWN THE HALL.

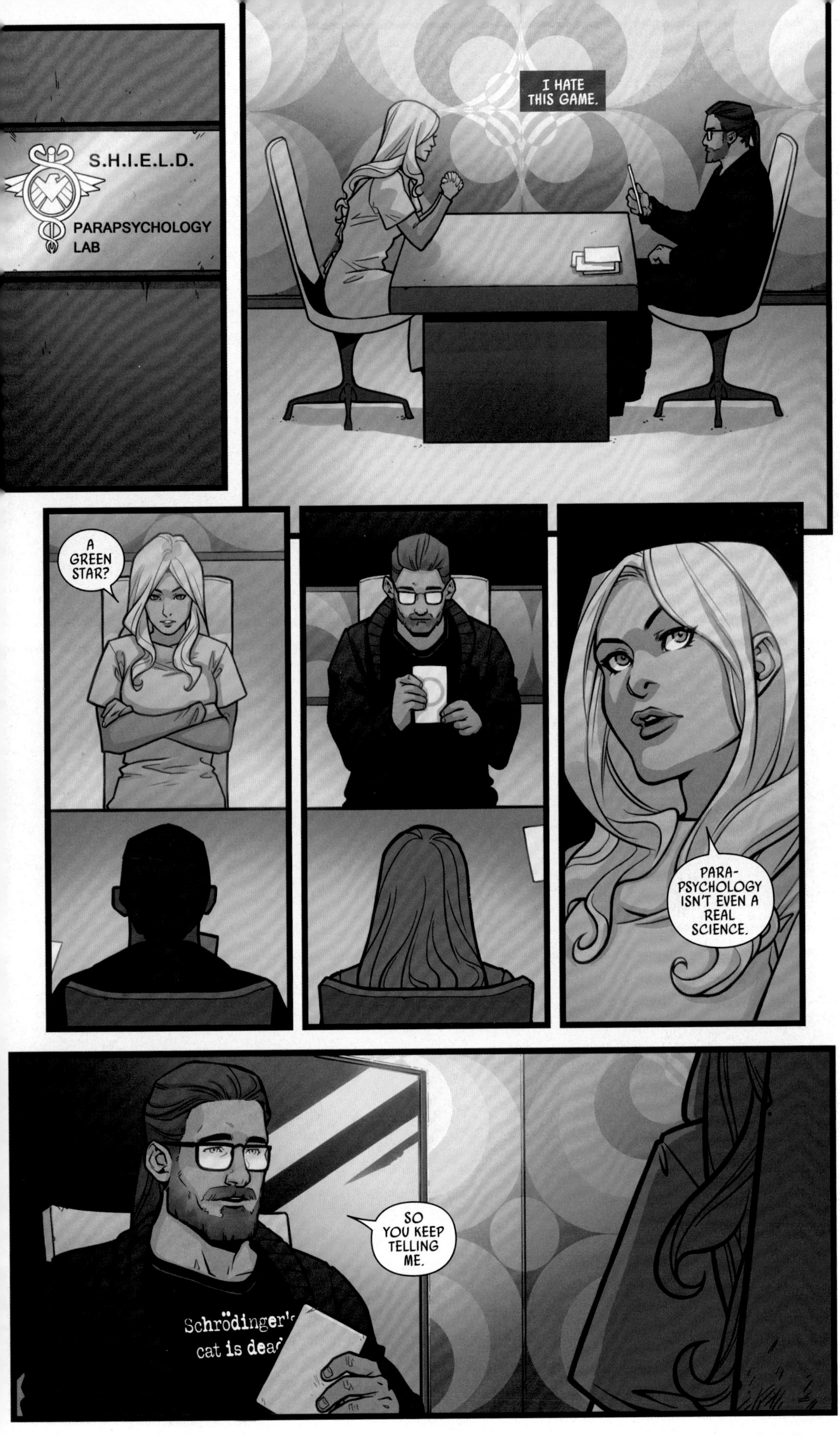
S.H.I.E.L.D.
PARAPSYCHOLOGY LAB
I HATE THIS GAME.
A GREEN STAR?
PARAPSYCHOLOGY ISN'T EVEN A REAL SCIENCE.
SO YOU KEEP TELLING ME.
Schrödinger's cat is dead

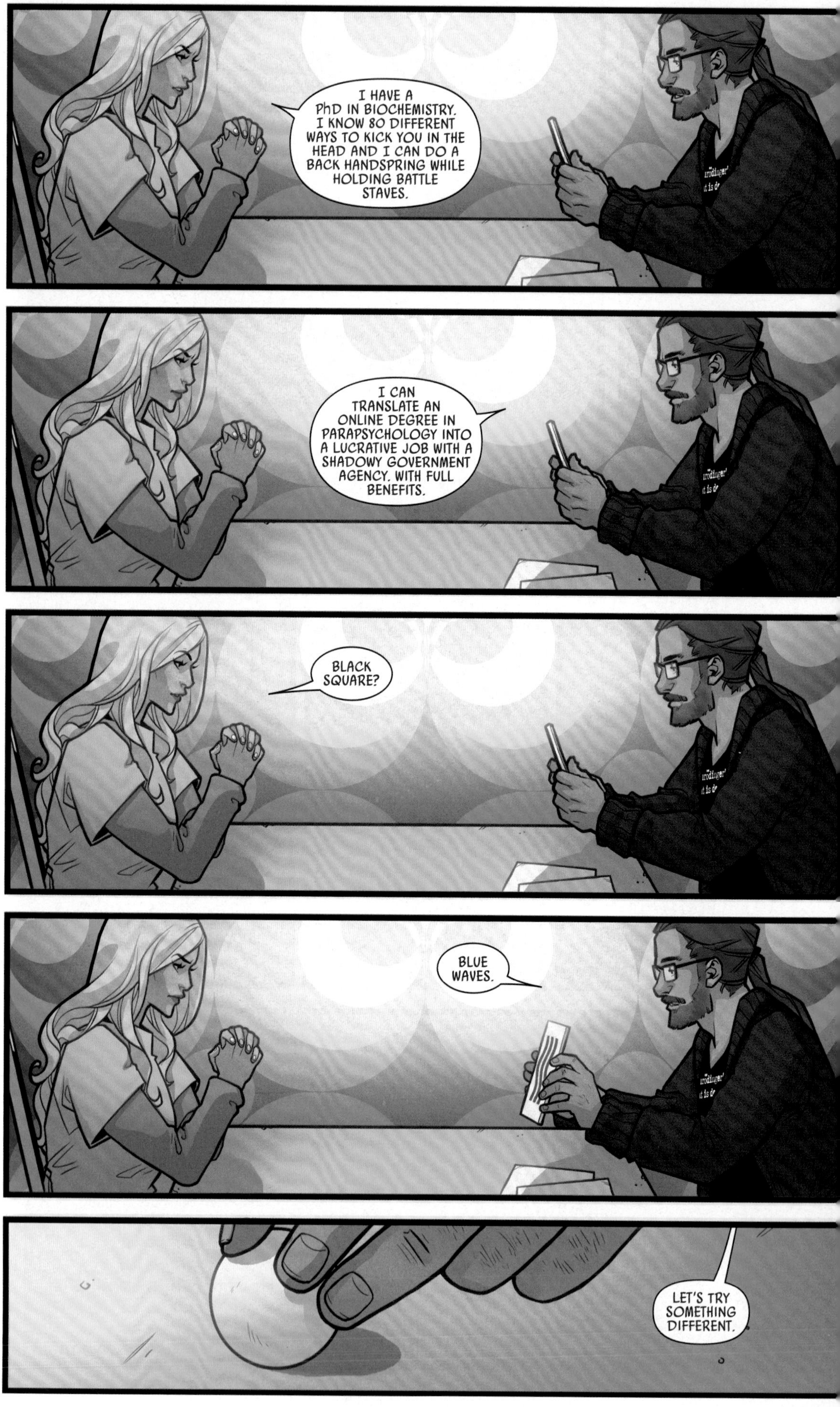
I HAVE A PhD IN BIOCHEMISTRY. I KNOW 80 DIFFERENT WAYS TO KICK YOU IN THE HEAD AND I CAN DO A BACK HANDSPRING WHILE HOLDING BATTLE STAVES.
I CAN TRANSLATE AN ONLINE DEGREE IN PARAPSYCHOLOGY INTO A LUCRATIVE JOB WITH A SHADOWY GOVERNMENT AGENCY. WITH FULL BENEFITS.
BLACK SQUARE?
BLUE WAVES.
LET'S TRY SOMETHING DIFFERENT.

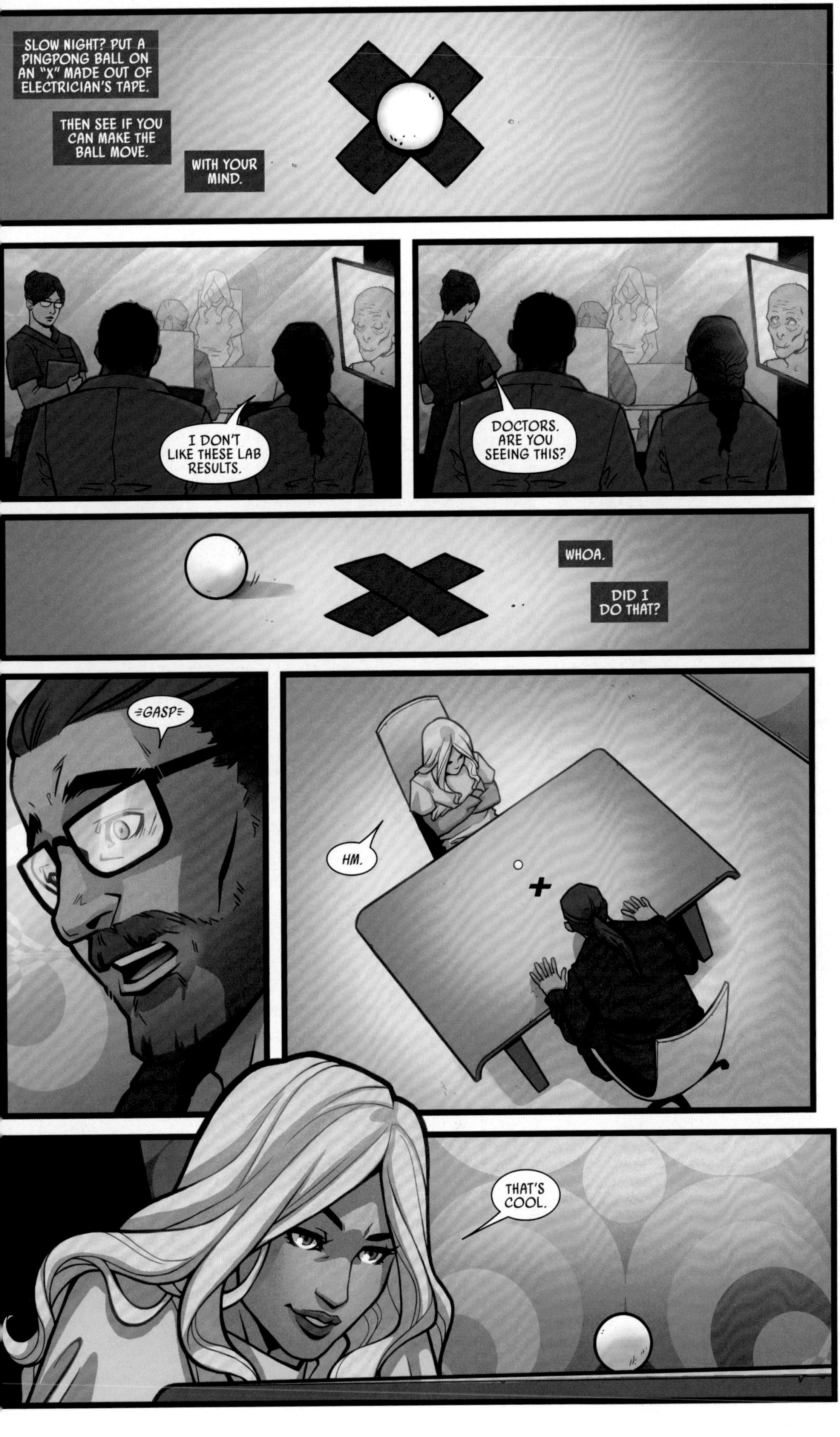
SLOW NIGHT? PUT A PINGPONG BALL ON AN "X" MADE OUT OF ELECTRICIAN'S TAPE.
THEN SEE IF YOU CAN MAKE THE BALL MOVE.
WITH YOUR MIND.
I DON'T LIKE THESE LAB RESULTS.
DOCTORS. ARE YOU SEEING THIS?
WHOA.
DID I DO THAT?
GASP
HM.
THAT'S COOL.

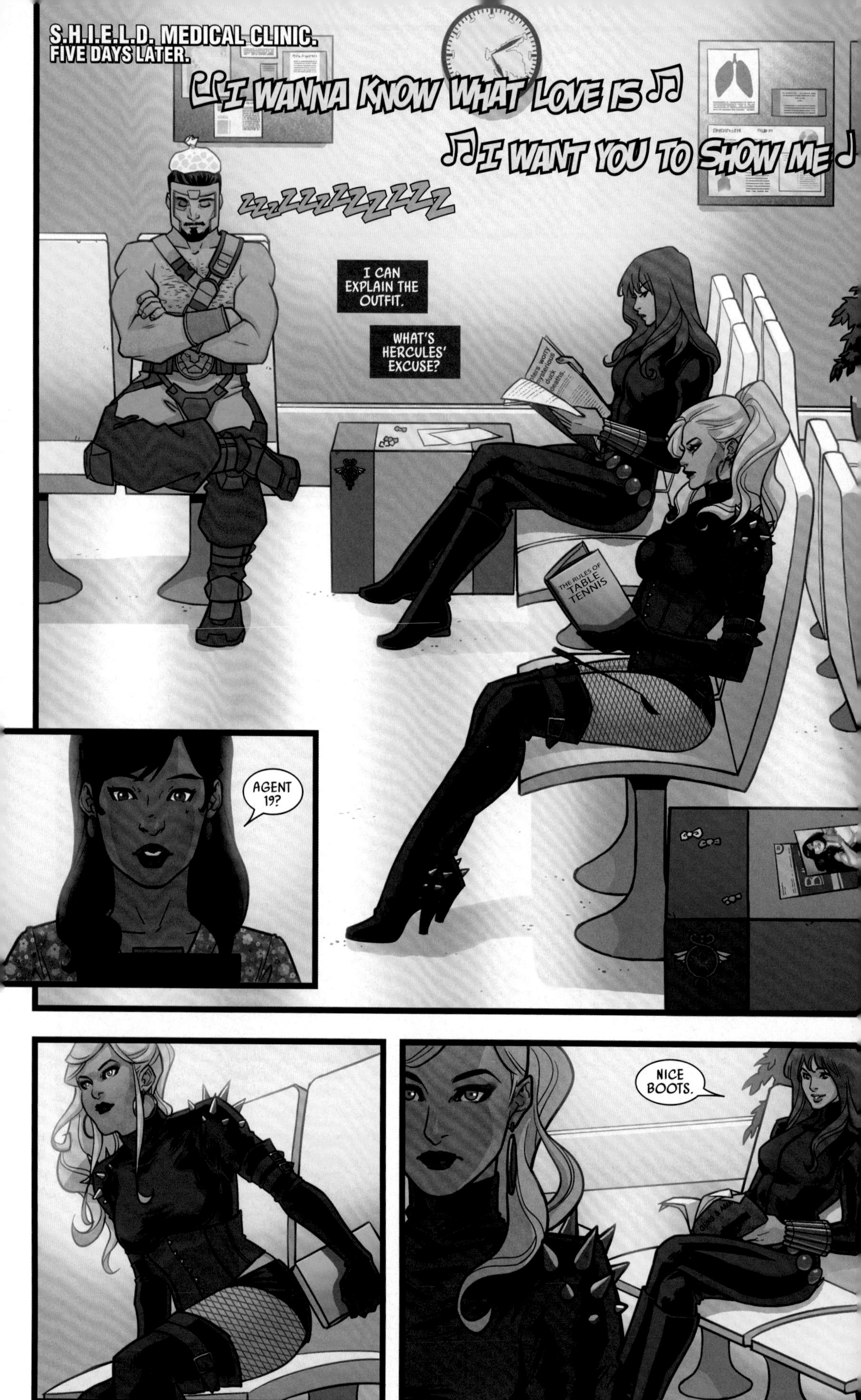
S.H.I.E.L.D. MEDICAL CLINIC. FIVE DAYS LATER.
♫I WANNA KNOW WHAT LOVE IS♫
♫I WANT YOU TO SHOW ME♩
ZzzZZZZZZZZZ
I CAN EXPLAIN THE OUTFIT.
WHAT'S HERCULES' EXCUSE?
mysterious duck deaths.
THE RULES OF TABLE TENNIS
AGENT 19?
NICE BOOTS.

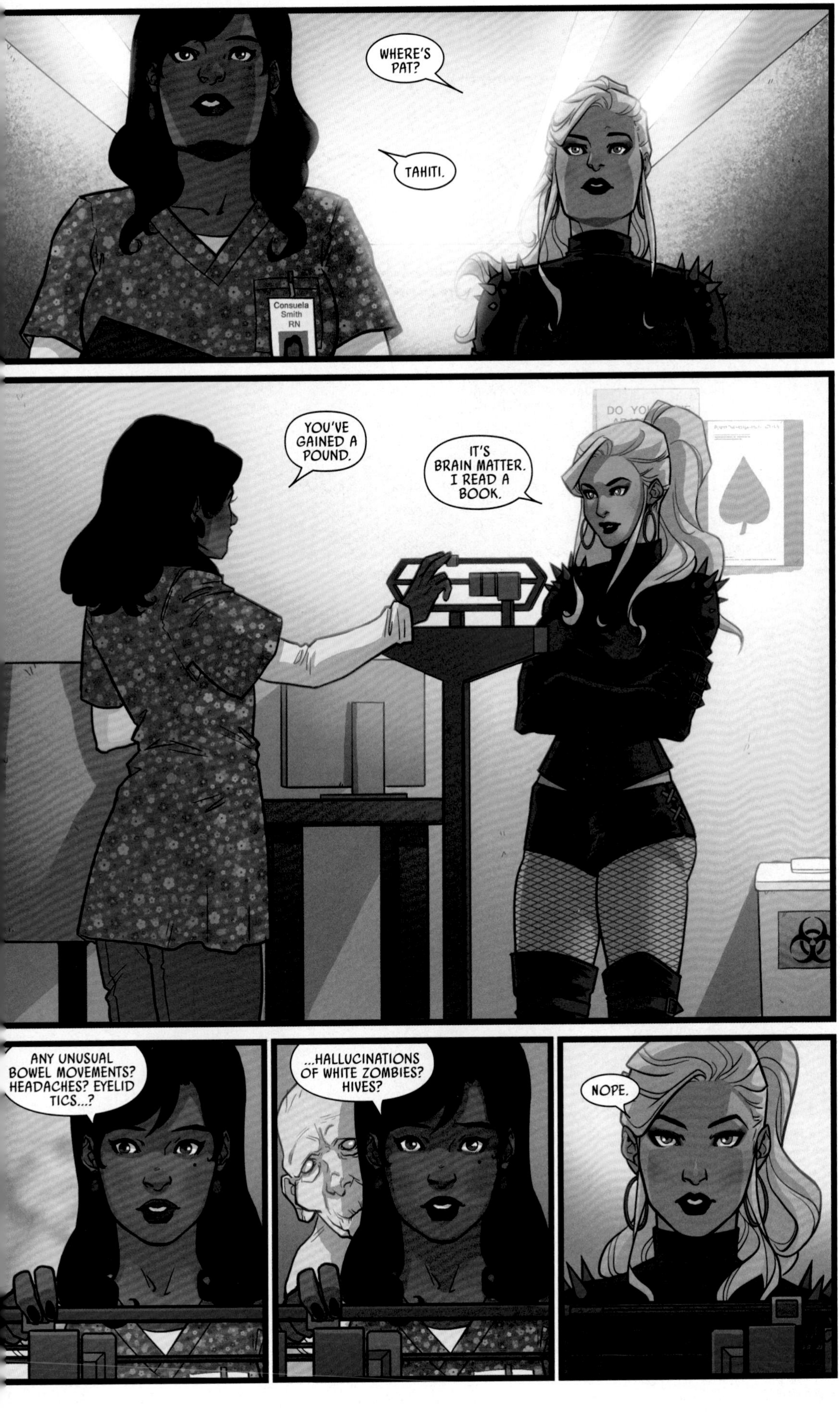
WHERE'S PAT?
TAHITI.
Consuela Smith RN
YOU'VE GAINED A POUND.
IT'S BRAIN MATTER. I READ A BOOK.
DO YOU
ANY UNUSUAL BOWEL MOVEMENTS? HEADACHES? EYELID TICS...?
...HALLUCINATIONS OF WHITE ZOMBIES? HIVES?
NOPE.

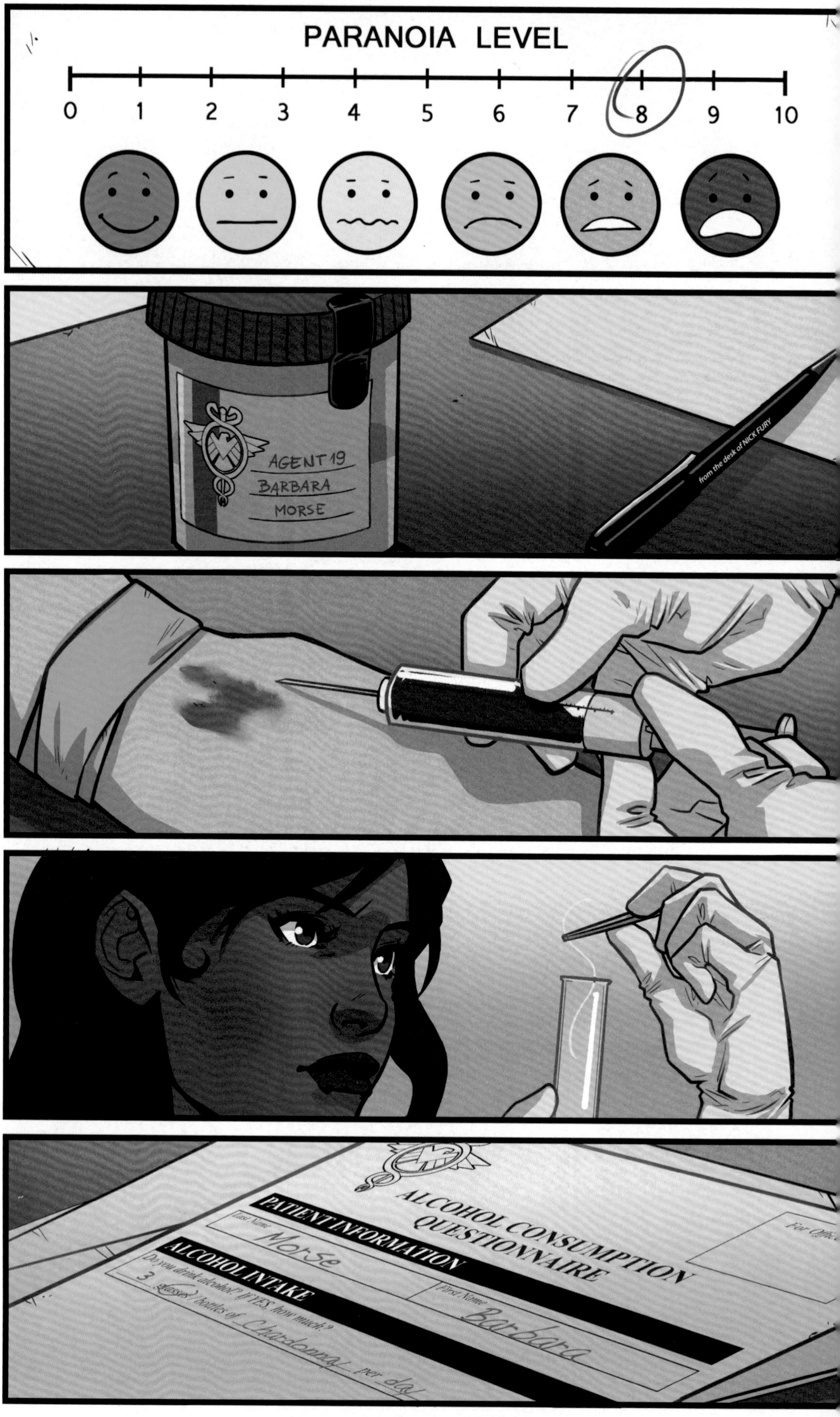

PARANOIA LEVEL
0 1 2 3 4 5 6 7 8 9 10
AGENT 19
BARBARA
MORSE
from the desk of NICK FURY
ALCOHOL CONSUMPTION QUESTIONNAIRE
PATIENT INFORMATION
Last Name Morse
First Name Barbara
ALCOHOL INTAKE
Do you drink alcohol? If YES, how much?
3 glasses / bottles of Chardonnay per day

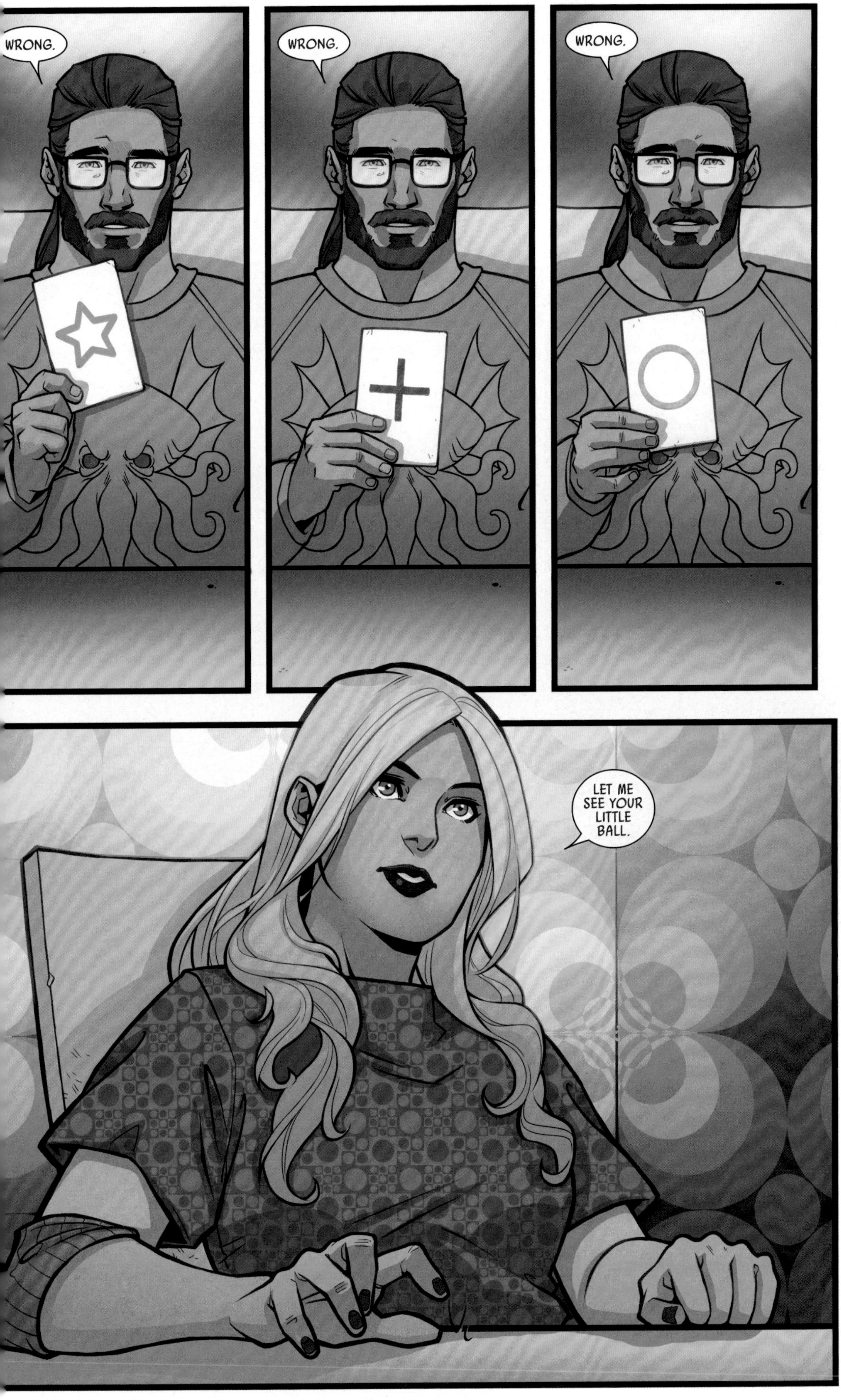
WRONG.
WRONG.
WRONG.
LET ME SEE YOUR LITTLE BALL.

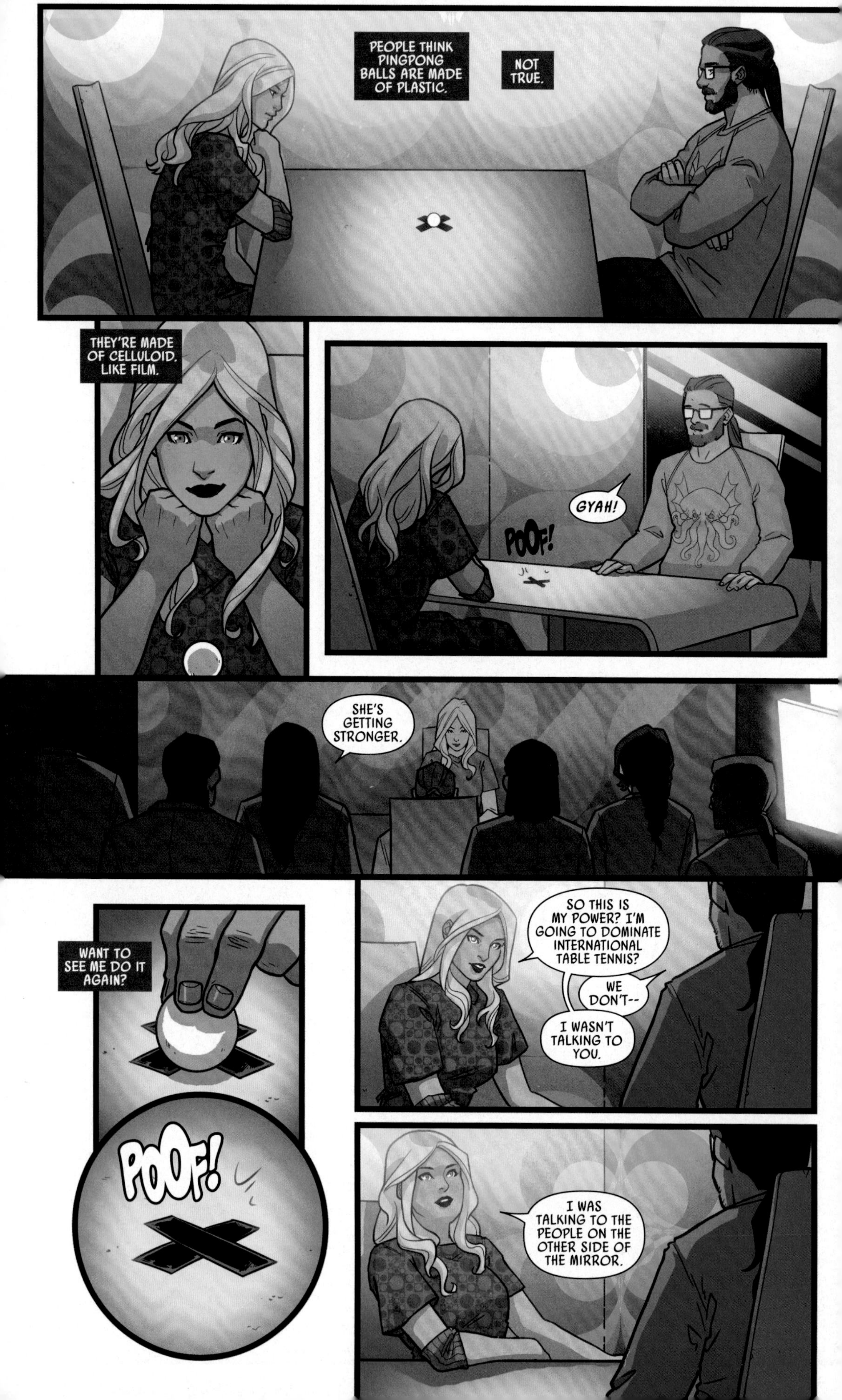
PEOPLE THINK PINGPONG BALLS ARE MADE OF PLASTIC.
NOT TRUE.
THEY'RE MADE OF CELLULOID. LIKE FILM.
GYAH!
POOF!
SHE'S GETTING STRONGER.
WANT TO SEE ME DO IT AGAIN?
POOF!
SO THIS IS MY POWER? I'M GOING TO DOMINATE INTERNATIONAL TABLE TENNIS?
WE DON'T--
I WASN'T TALKING TO YOU.
I WAS TALKING TO THE PEOPLE ON THE OTHER SIDE OF THE MIRROR.

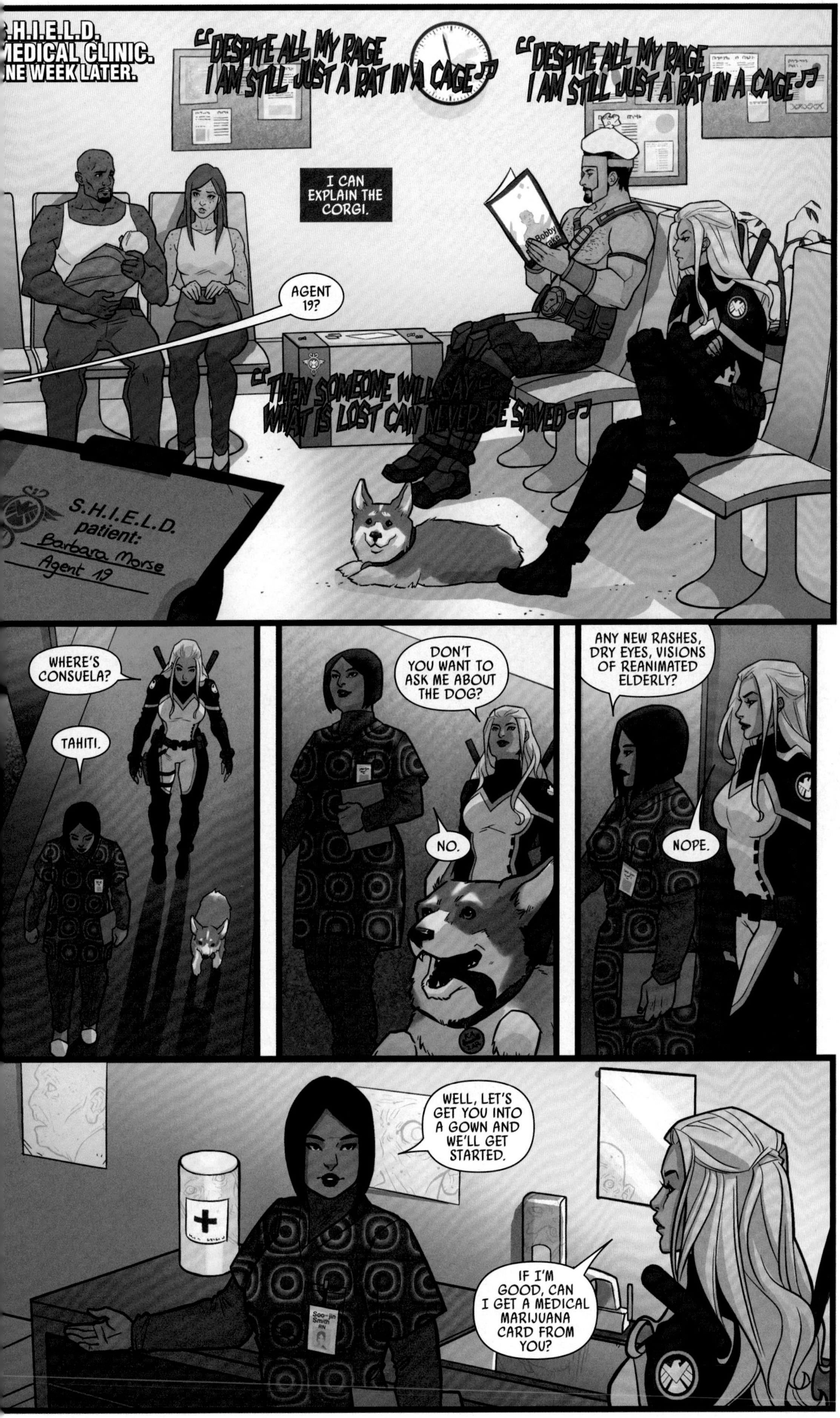
S.H.I.E.L.D.
MEDICAL CLINIC.
NE WEEK LATER.
"DESPITE ALL MY RAGE I AM STILL JUST A RAT IN A CAGE ♪"
"DESPITE ALL MY RAGE I AM STILL JUST A RAT IN A CAGE ♪"
I CAN EXPLAIN THE CORGI.
AGENT 19?
"THEN SOMEONE WILL SAY WHAT IS LOST CAN NEVER BE SAVED ♪"
S.H.I.E.L.D.
patient:
Barbara Morse
Agent 19
WHERE'S CONSUELA?
TAHITI.
DON'T YOU WANT TO ASK ME ABOUT THE DOG?
NO.
ANY NEW RASHES, DRY EYES, VISIONS OF REANIMATED ELDERLY?
NOPE.
WELL, LET'S GET YOU INTO A GOWN AND WE'LL GET STARTED.
Soo-jin Smith RN
IF I'M GOOD, CAN I GET A MEDICAL MARIJUANA CARD FROM YOU?

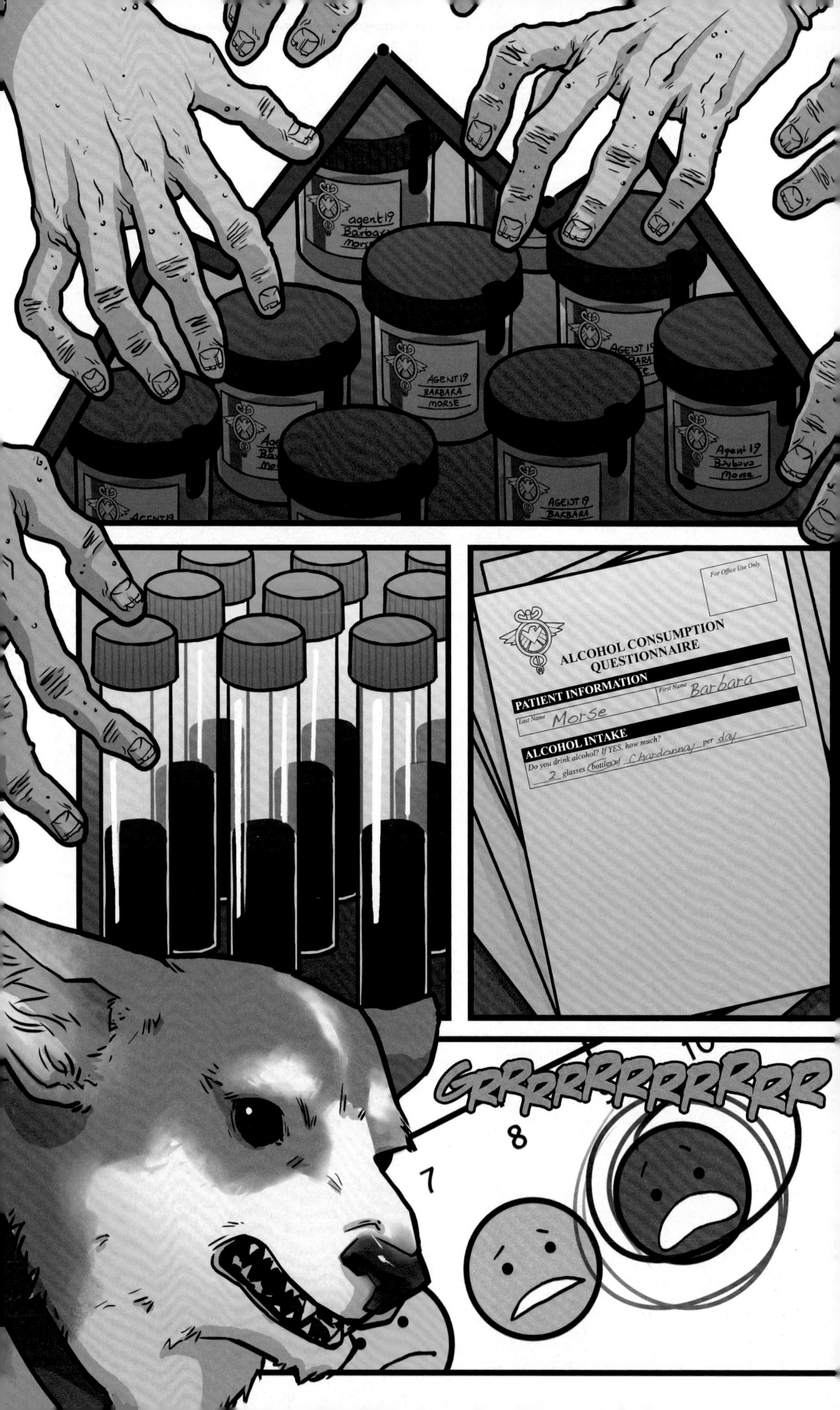

agent 19
Barbara
Morse
AGENT 19
BARBARA
MORSE
Agent 19
Barbara
Morse
For Office Use Only
ALCOHOL CONSUMPTION
QUESTIONNAIRE
PATIENT INFORMATION
Last Name Morse
First Name Barbara
ALCOHOL INTAKE
Do you drink alcohol? If YES, how much?
2 glasses bottles of Chardonnay per day
GRRRRRRRRRRR
10
8
7

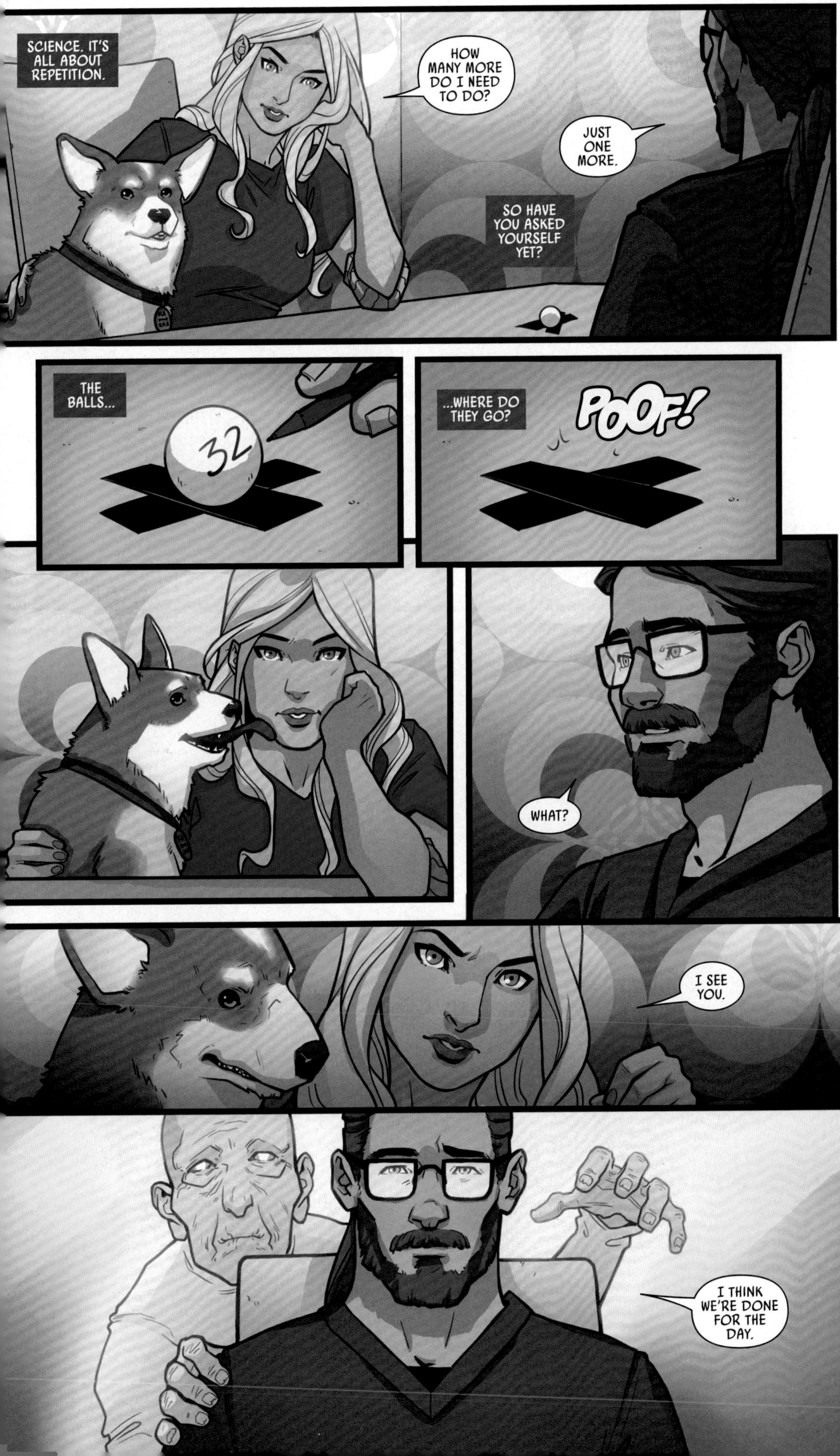

SCIENCE. IT'S ALL ABOUT REPETITION.
HOW MANY MORE DO I NEED TO DO?
JUST ONE MORE.
SO HAVE YOU ASKED YOURSELF YET?
THE BALLS...
32
...WHERE DO THEY GO?
POOF!
WHAT?
I SEE YOU.
I THINK WE'RE DONE FOR THE DAY.

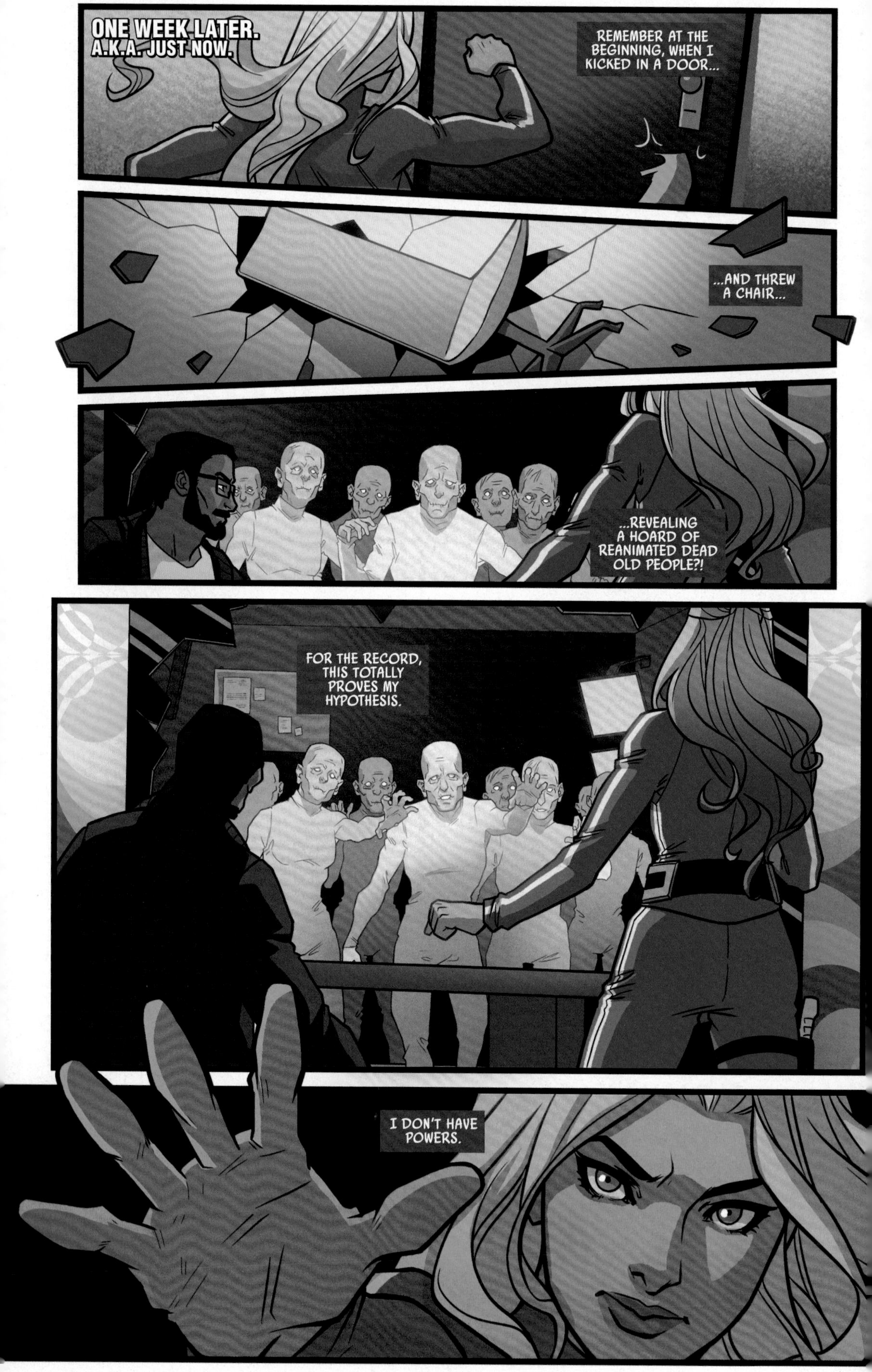
ONE WEEK LATER.
A.K.A. JUST NOW.
REMEMBER AT THE BEGINNING, WHEN I KICKED IN A DOOR...
...AND THREW A CHAIR...
...REVEALING A HOARD OF REANIMATED DEAD OLD PEOPLE?!
FOR THE RECORD, THIS TOTALLY PROVES MY HYPOTHESIS.
I DON'T HAVE POWERS.

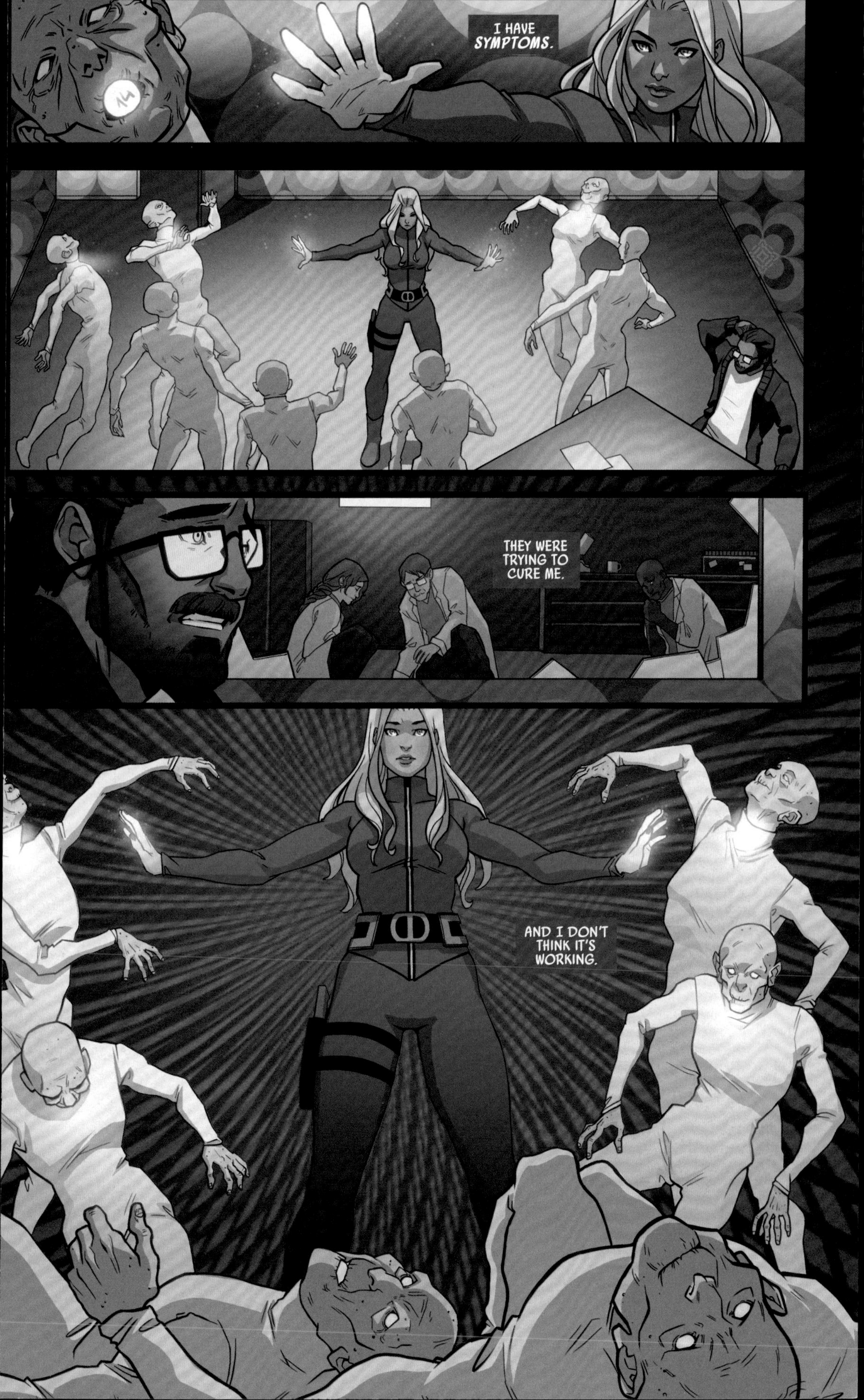
I HAVE SYMPTOMS.
THEY WERE TRYING TO CURE ME.
AND I DON'T THINK IT'S WORKING.

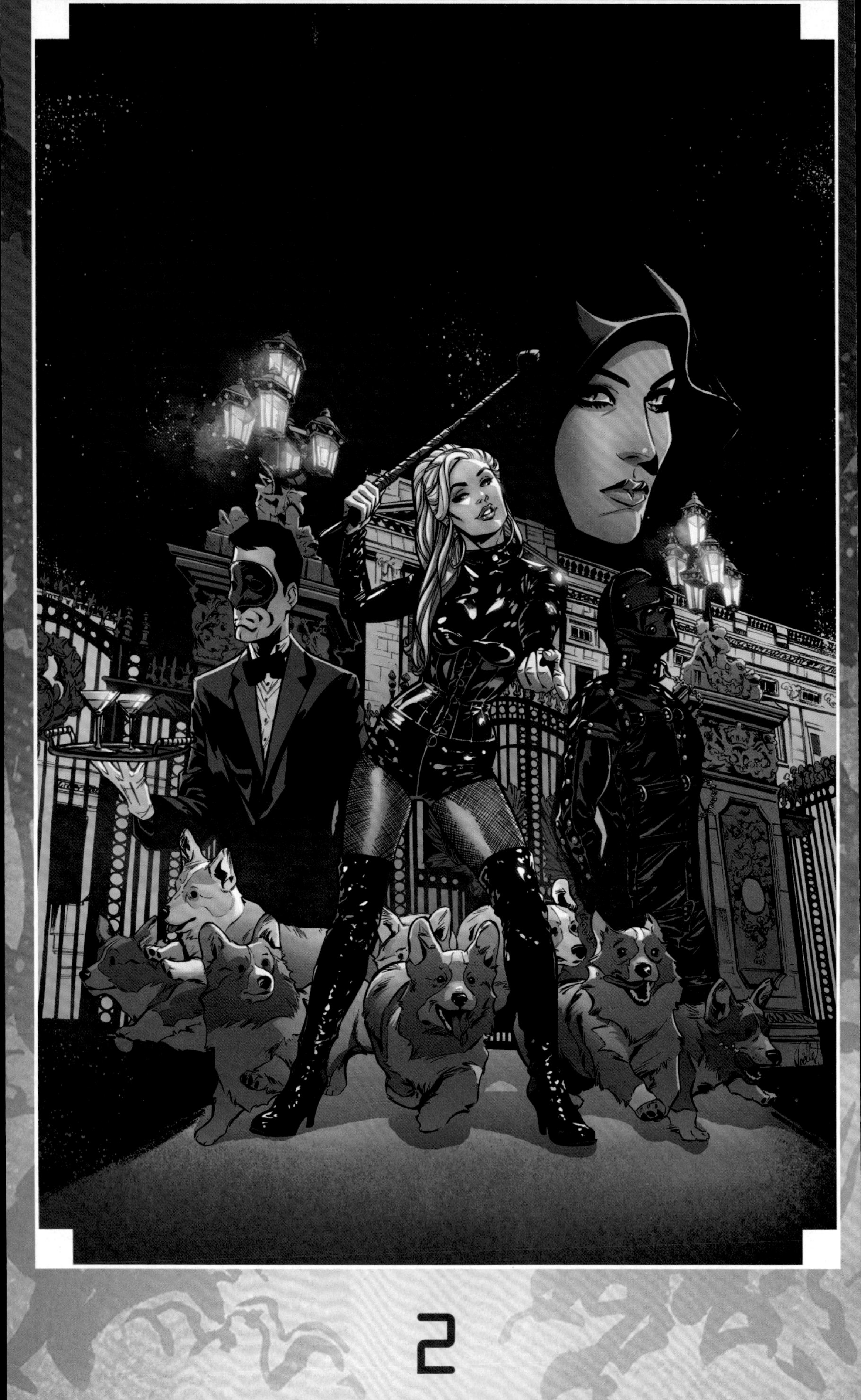

2

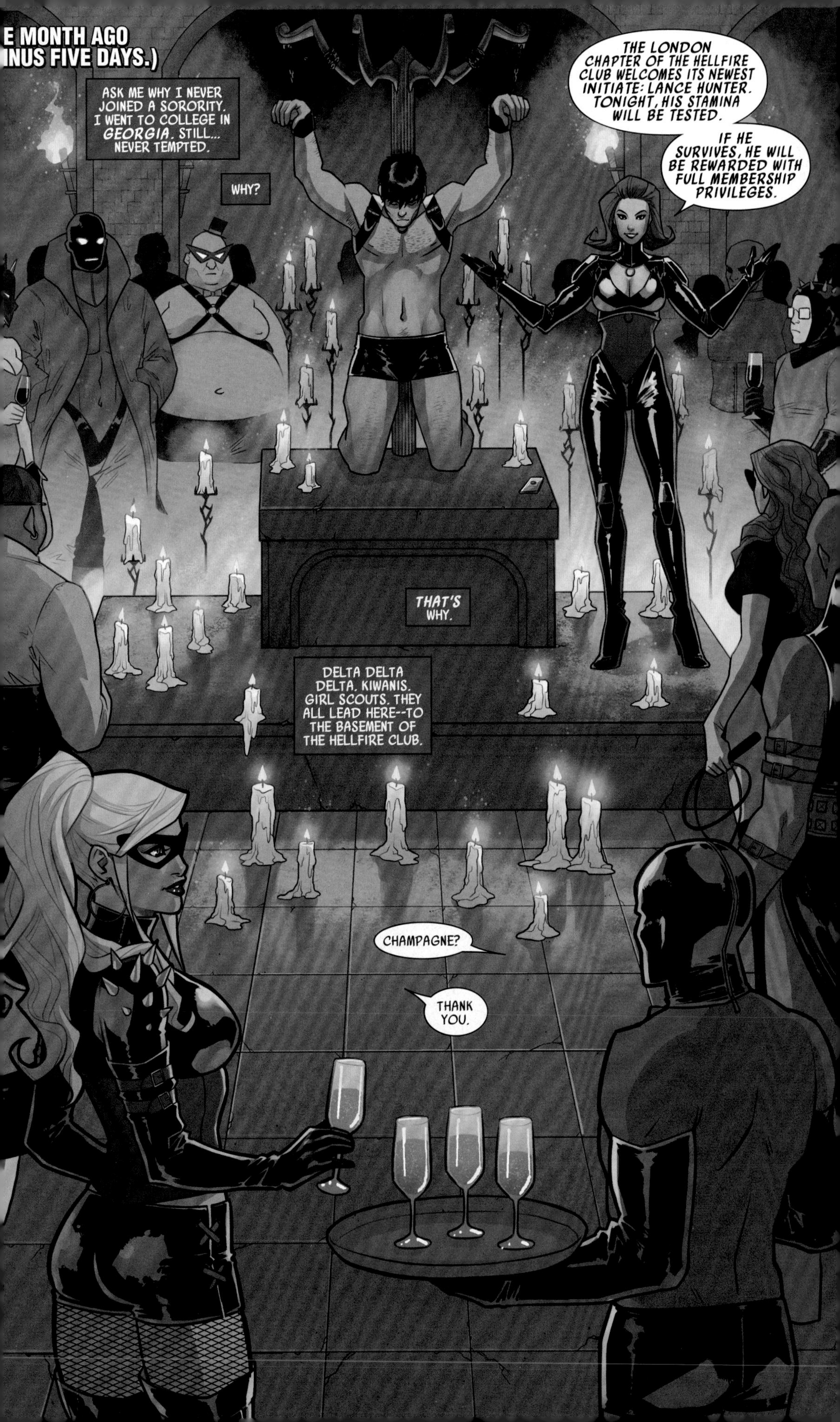
E MONTH AGO
INUS FIVE DAYS.)
ASK ME WHY I NEVER JOINED A SORORITY. I WENT TO COLLEGE IN GEORGIA. STILL... NEVER TEMPTED.
WHY?
THE LONDON CHAPTER OF THE HELLFIRE CLUB WELCOMES ITS NEWEST INITIATE: LANCE HUNTER. TONIGHT, HIS STAMINA WILL BE TESTED.
IF HE SURVIVES, HE WILL BE REWARDED WITH FULL MEMBERSHIP PRIVILEGES.
THAT'S WHY.
DELTA DELTA DELTA. KIWANIS. GIRL SCOUTS. THEY ALL LEAD HERE--TO THE BASEMENT OF THE HELLFIRE CLUB.
CHAMPAGNE?
THANK YOU.

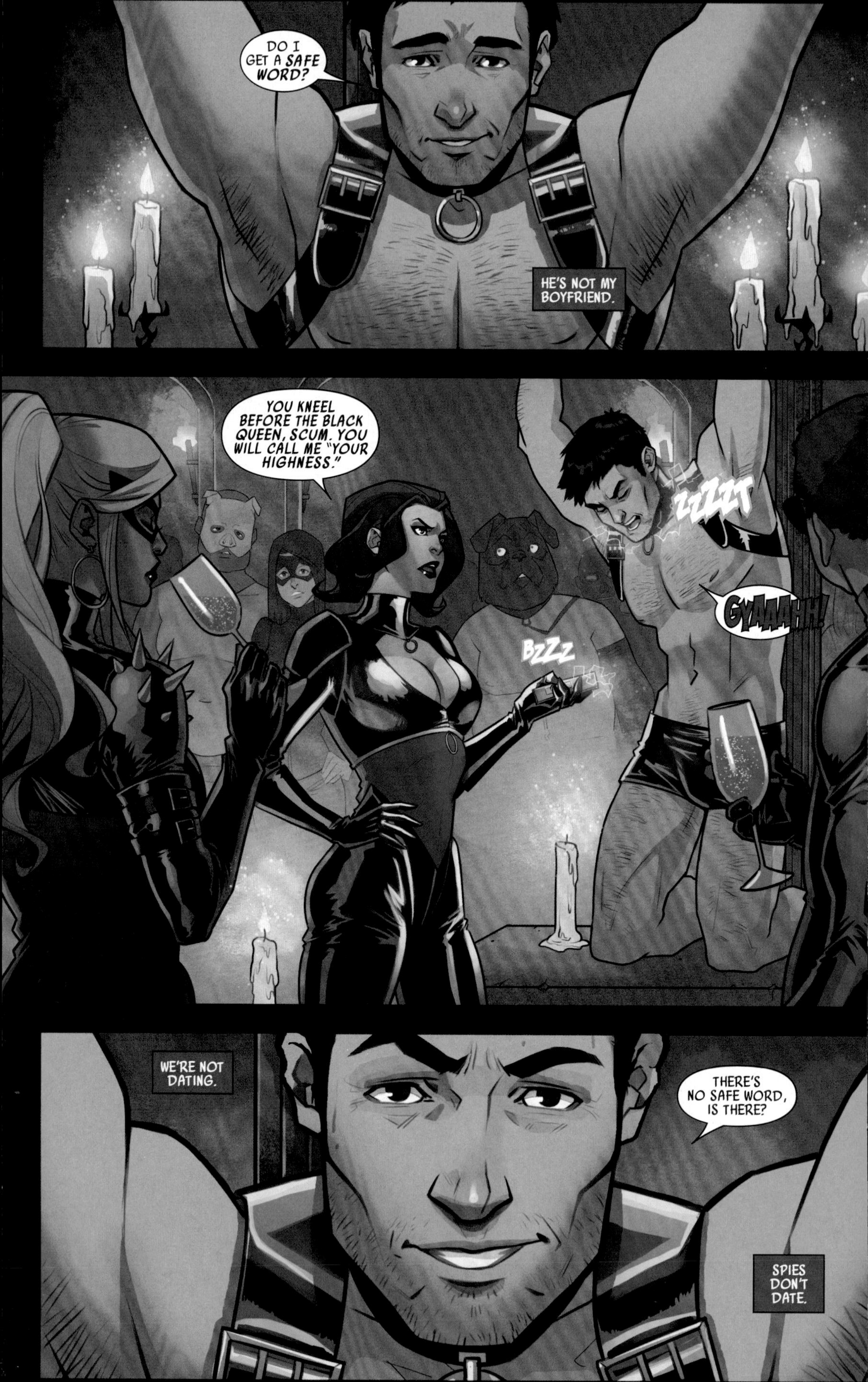
DO I GET A SAFE WORD?
HE'S NOT MY BOYFRIEND.
YOU KNEEL BEFORE THE BLACK QUEEN, SCUM. YOU WILL CALL ME "YOUR HIGHNESS."
ZZZZZT
GYAAAHH!
BZZZ
WE'RE NOT DATING.
THERE'S NO SAFE WORD, IS THERE?
SPIES DON'T DATE.

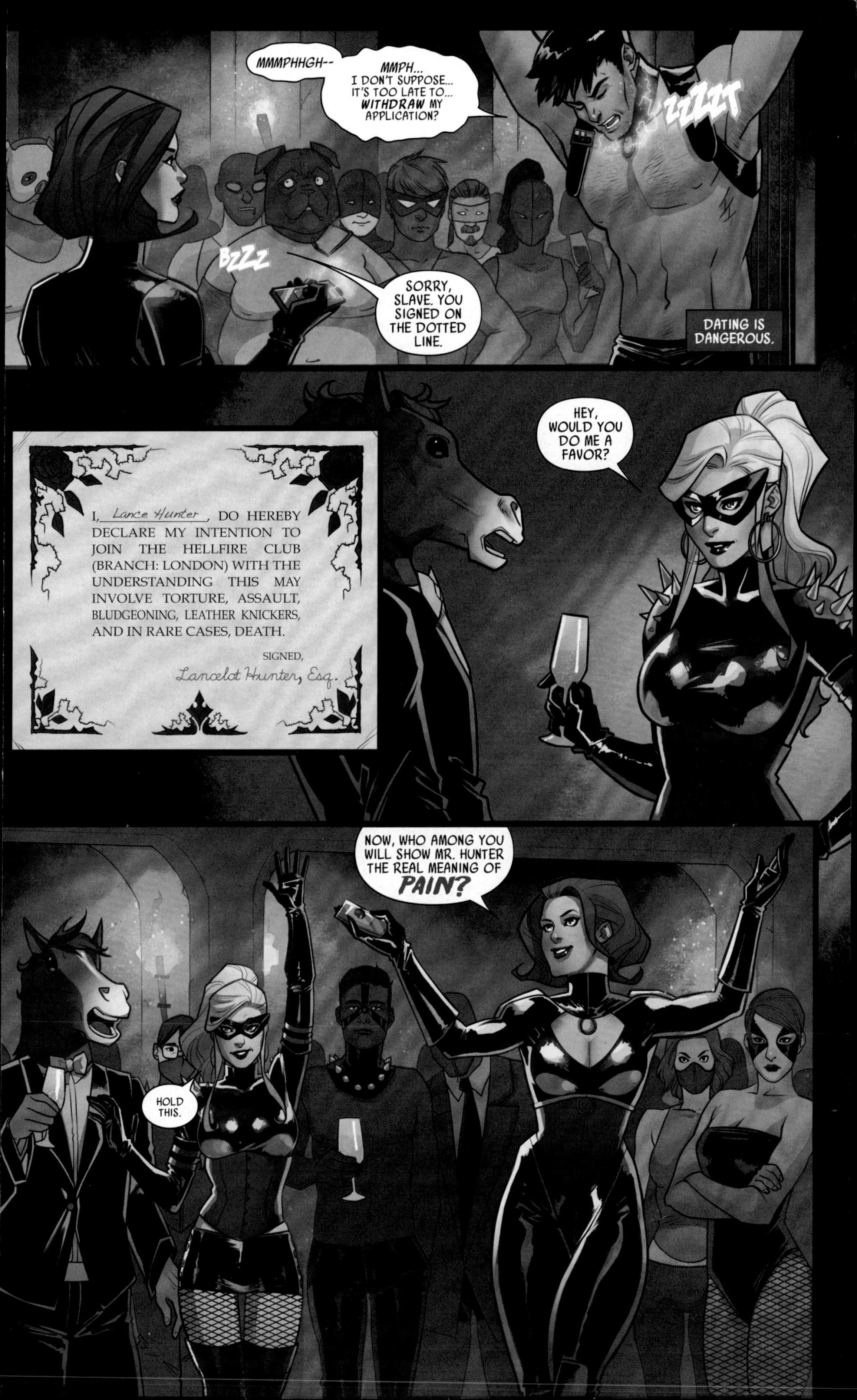
MMMPHHGH--
MMPH... I DON'T SUPPOSE... IT'S TOO LATE TO... WITHDRAW MY APPLICATION?
ZZZZT
BZZZ
SORRY, SLAVE. YOU SIGNED ON THE DOTTED LINE.
DATING IS DANGEROUS.
I, Lance Hunter, DO HEREBY DECLARE MY INTENTION TO JOIN THE HELLFIRE CLUB (BRANCH: LONDON) WITH THE UNDERSTANDING THIS MAY INVOLVE TORTURE, ASSAULT, BLUDGEONING, LEATHER KNICKERS, AND IN RARE CASES, DEATH.
SIGNED,
Lancelot Hunter, Esq.
HEY, WOULD YOU DO ME A FAVOR?
NOW, WHO AMONG YOU WILL SHOW MR. HUNTER THE REAL MEANING OF PAIN?
HOLD THIS.

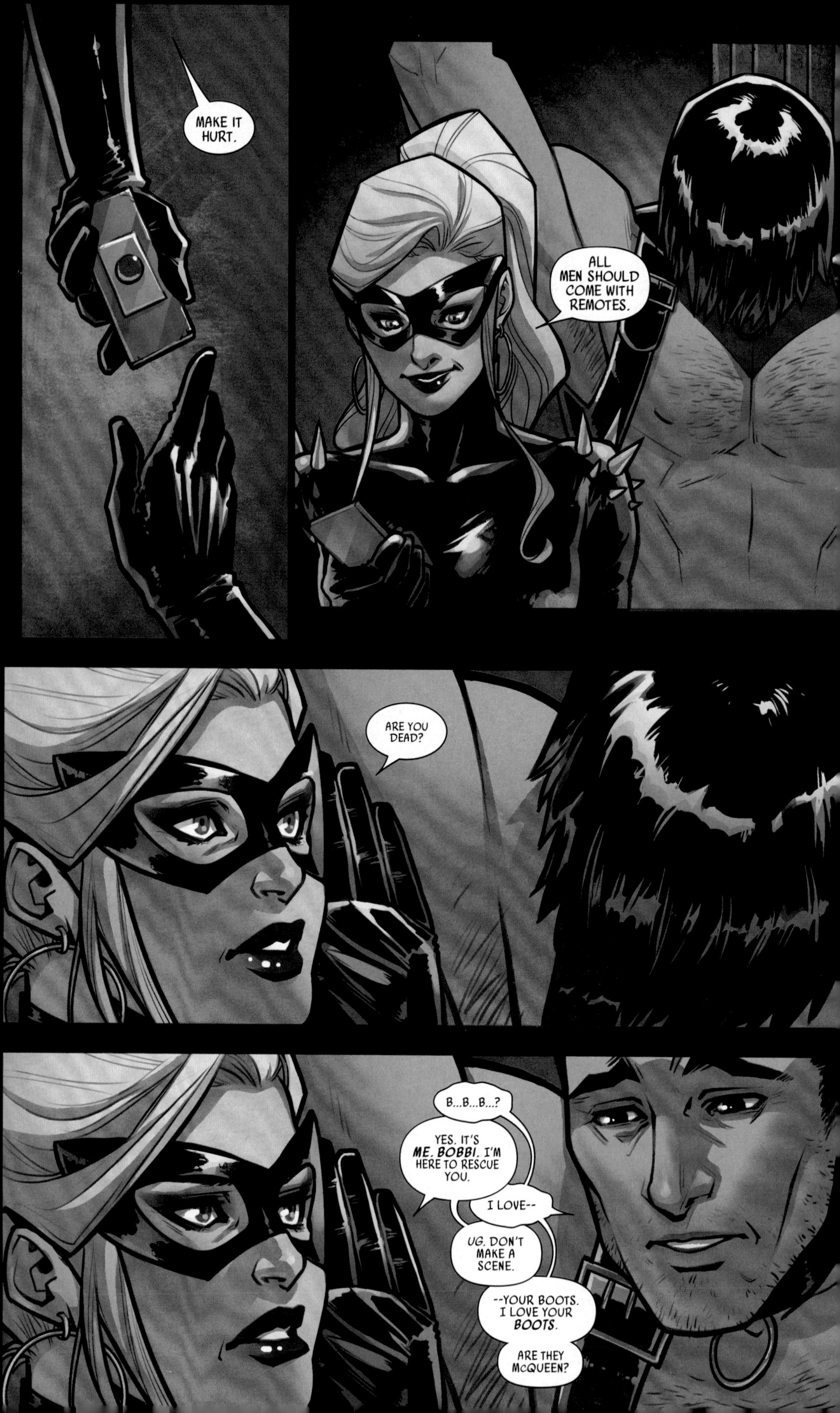

MAKE IT HURT.
ALL MEN SHOULD COME WITH REMOTES.
ARE YOU DEAD?
B...B...B...?
YES. IT'S ME. BOBBI. I'M HERE TO RESCUE YOU.
I LOVE--
UG. DON'T MAKE A SCENE.
--YOUR BOOTS. I LOVE YOUR BOOTS.
ARE THEY McQUEEN?

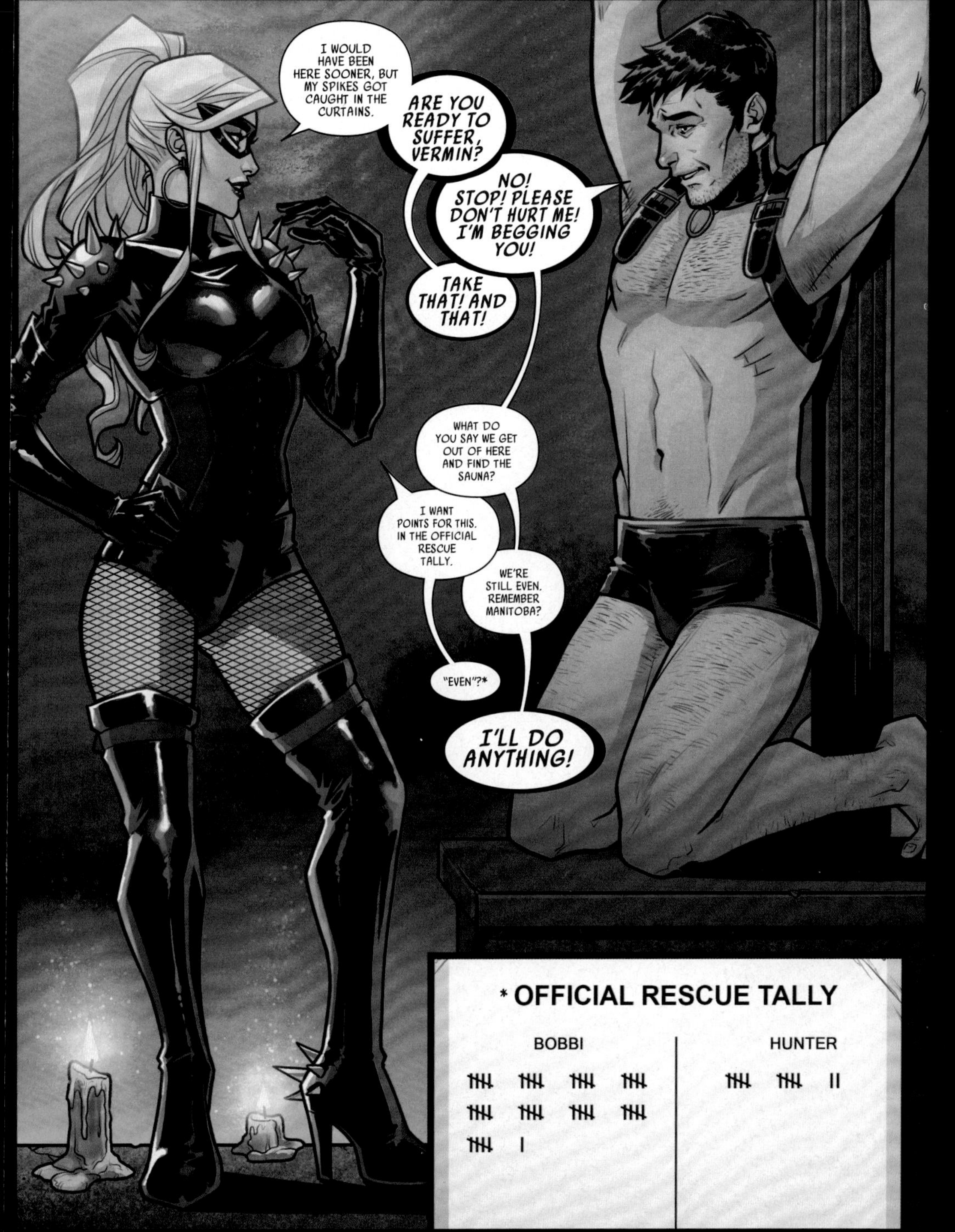
I WOULD HAVE BEEN HERE SOONER, BUT MY SPIKES GOT CAUGHT IN THE CURTAINS.
ARE YOU READY TO SUFFER, VERMIN?
NO! STOP! PLEASE DON'T HURT ME! I'M BEGGING YOU!
TAKE THAT! AND THAT!
WHAT DO YOU SAY WE GET OUT OF HERE AND FIND THE SAUNA?
I WANT POINTS FOR THIS. IN THE OFFICIAL RESCUE TALLY.
WE'RE STILL EVEN. REMEMBER MANITOBA?
"EVEN"?*
I'LL DO ANYTHING!
* OFFICIAL RESCUE TALLY
BOBBI
HUNTER

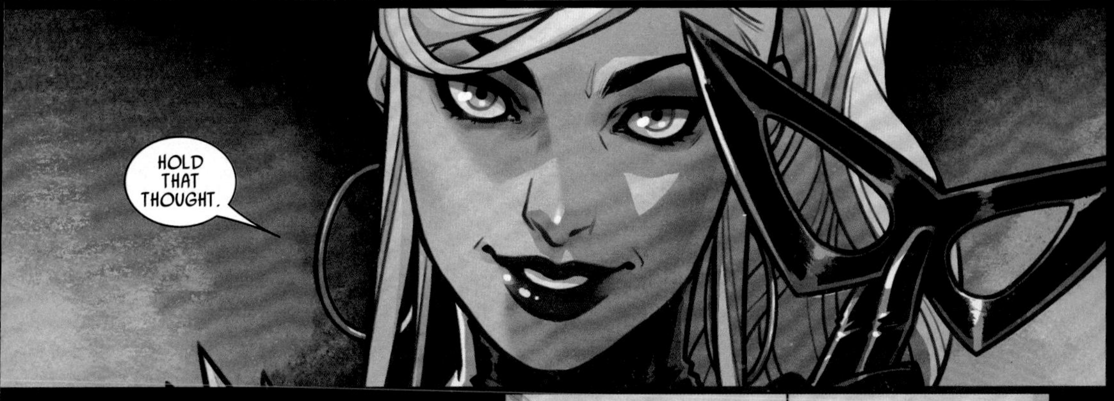
HOLD THAT THOUGHT.

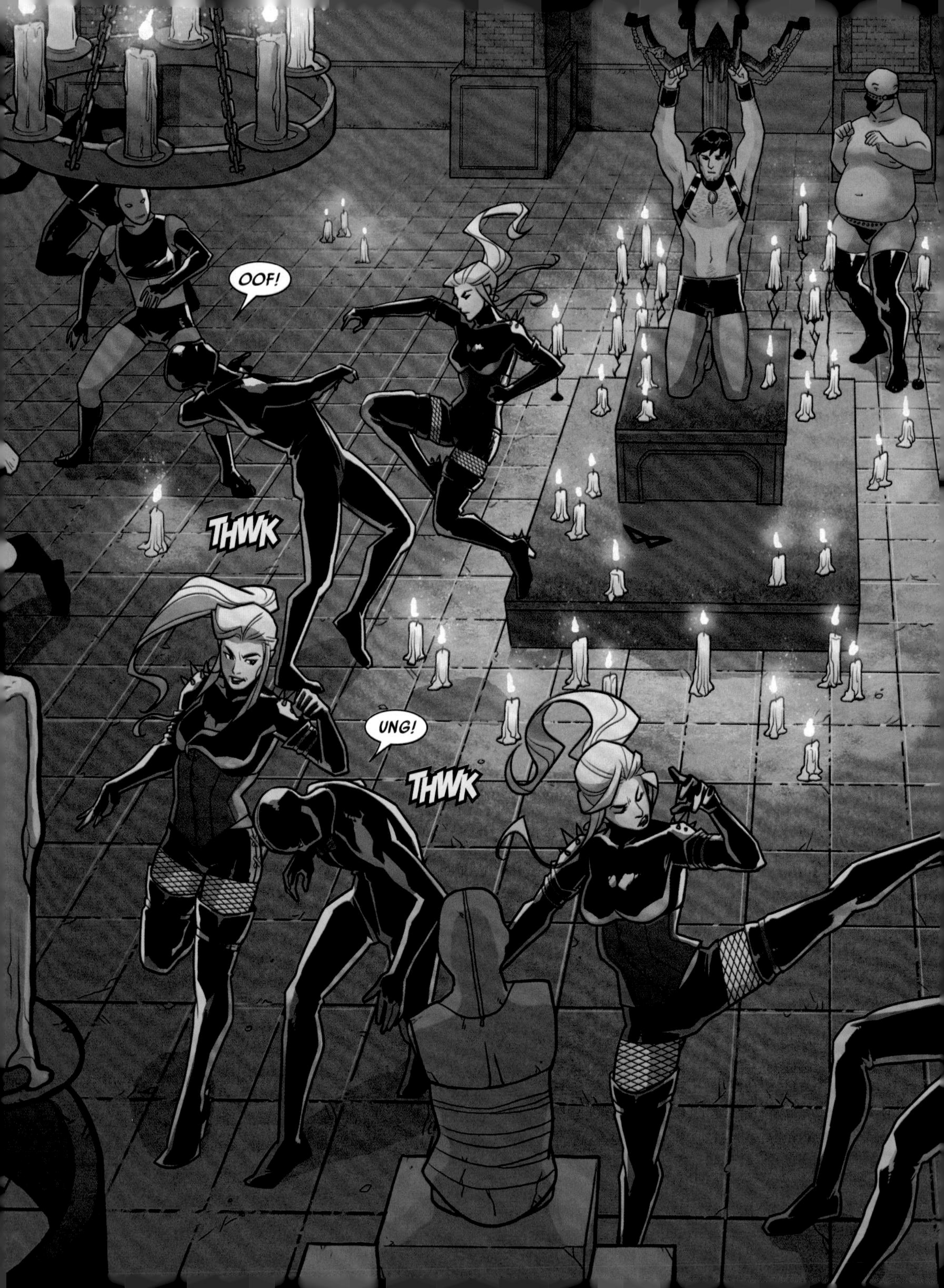
OOF!
THWK
UNG!
THWK

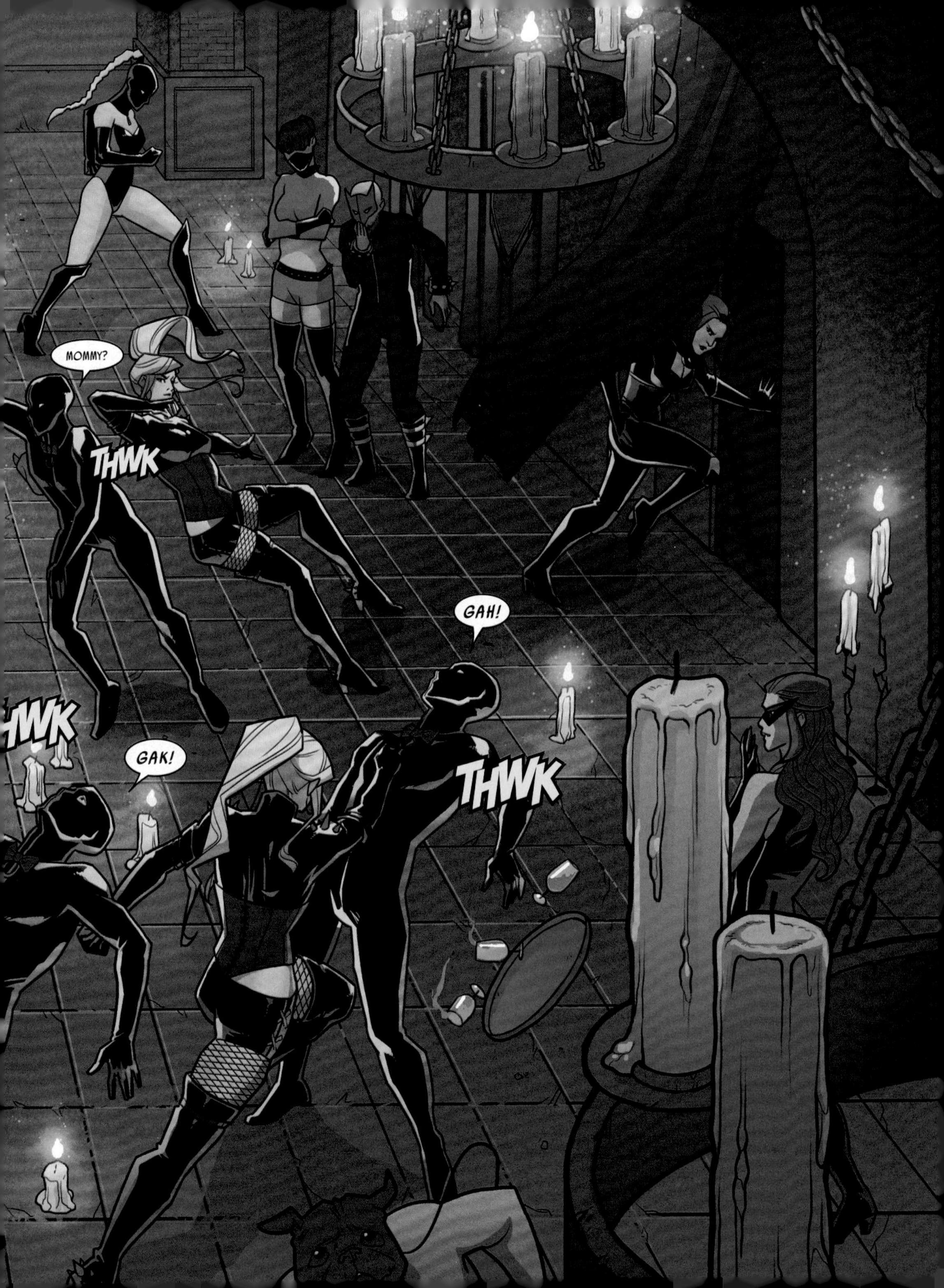
MOMMY?
THWK
GAH!
THWK
GAK!
THWK

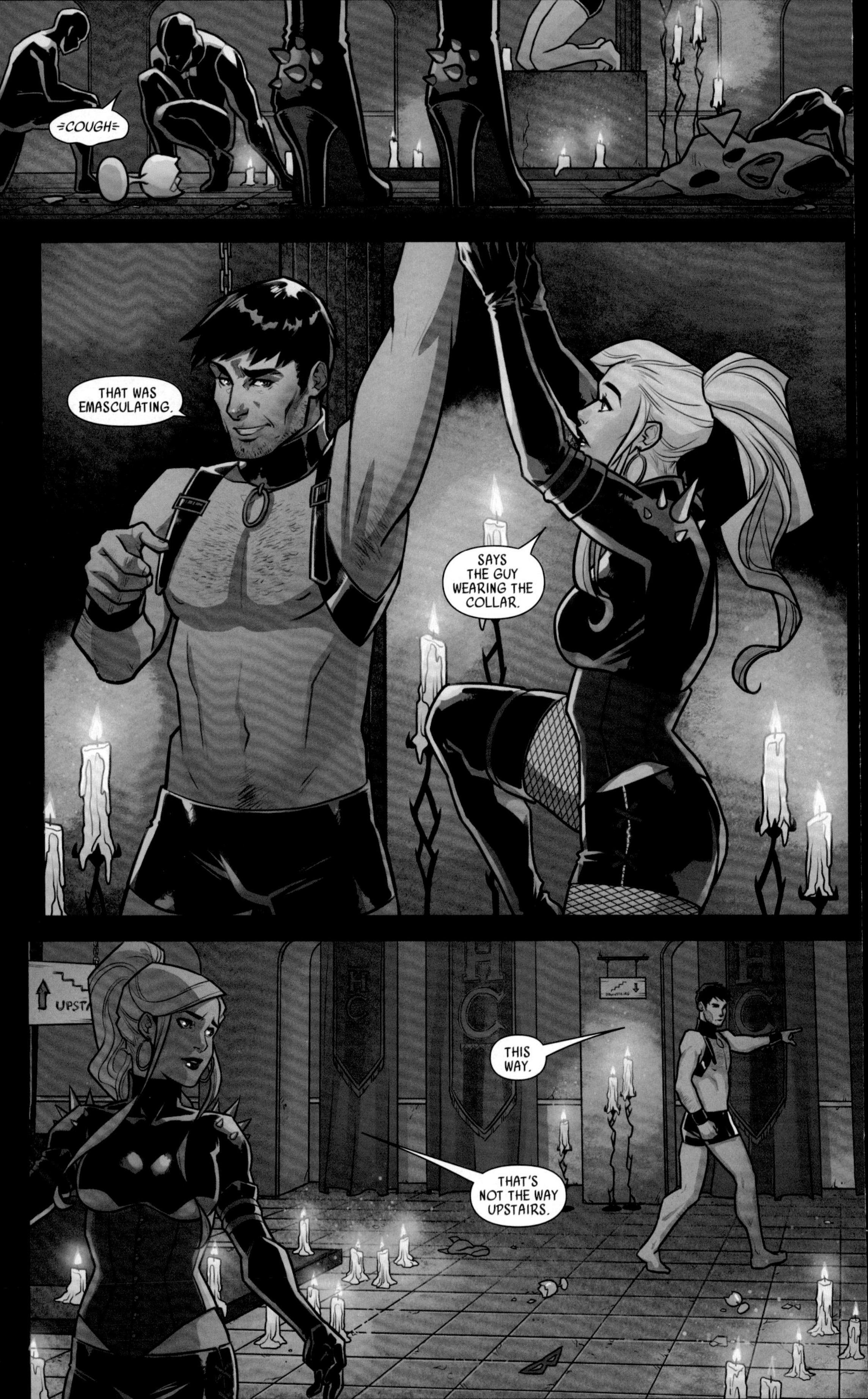
COUGH
THAT WAS EMASCULATING.
SAYS THE GUY WEARING THE COLLAR.
THIS WAY.
THAT'S NOT THE WAY UPSTAIRS.

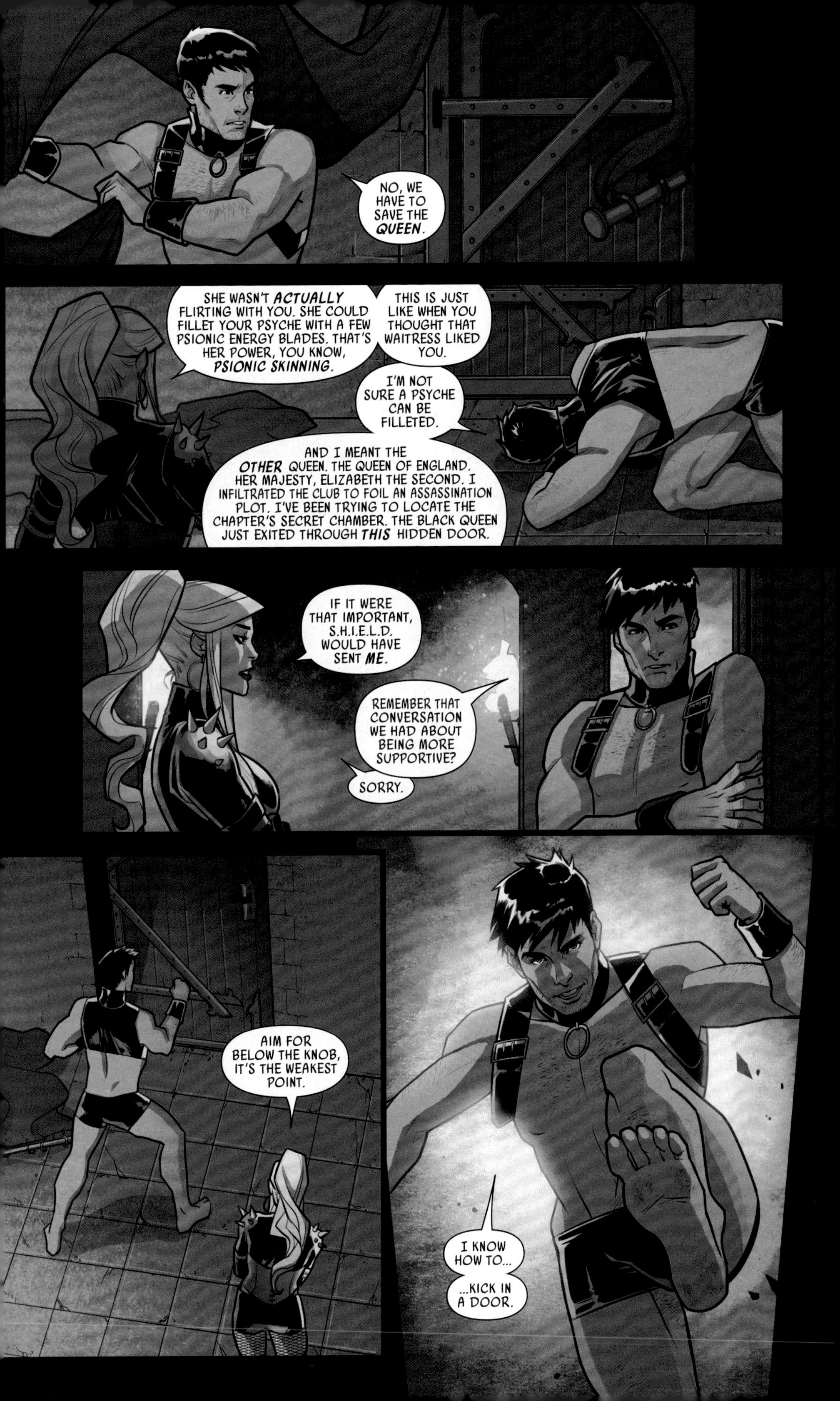
NO, WE HAVE TO SAVE THE QUEEN.
SHE WASN'T ACTUALLY FLIRTING WITH YOU. SHE COULD FILLET YOUR PSYCHE WITH A FEW PSIONIC ENERGY BLADES. THAT'S HER POWER, YOU KNOW, PSIONIC SKINNING.
THIS IS JUST LIKE WHEN YOU THOUGHT THAT WAITRESS LIKED YOU.
I'M NOT SURE A PSYCHE CAN BE FILLETED.
AND I MEANT THE OTHER QUEEN. THE QUEEN OF ENGLAND. HER MAJESTY, ELIZABETH THE SECOND. I INFILTRATED THE CLUB TO FOIL AN ASSASSINATION PLOT. I'VE BEEN TRYING TO LOCATE THE CHAPTER'S SECRET CHAMBER. THE BLACK QUEEN JUST EXITED THROUGH THIS HIDDEN DOOR.
IF IT WERE THAT IMPORTANT, S.H.I.E.L.D. WOULD HAVE SENT ME.
REMEMBER THAT CONVERSATION WE HAD ABOUT BEING MORE SUPPORTIVE?
SORRY.
AIM FOR BELOW THE KNOB, IT'S THE WEAKEST POINT.
I KNOW HOW TO...
...KICK IN A DOOR.

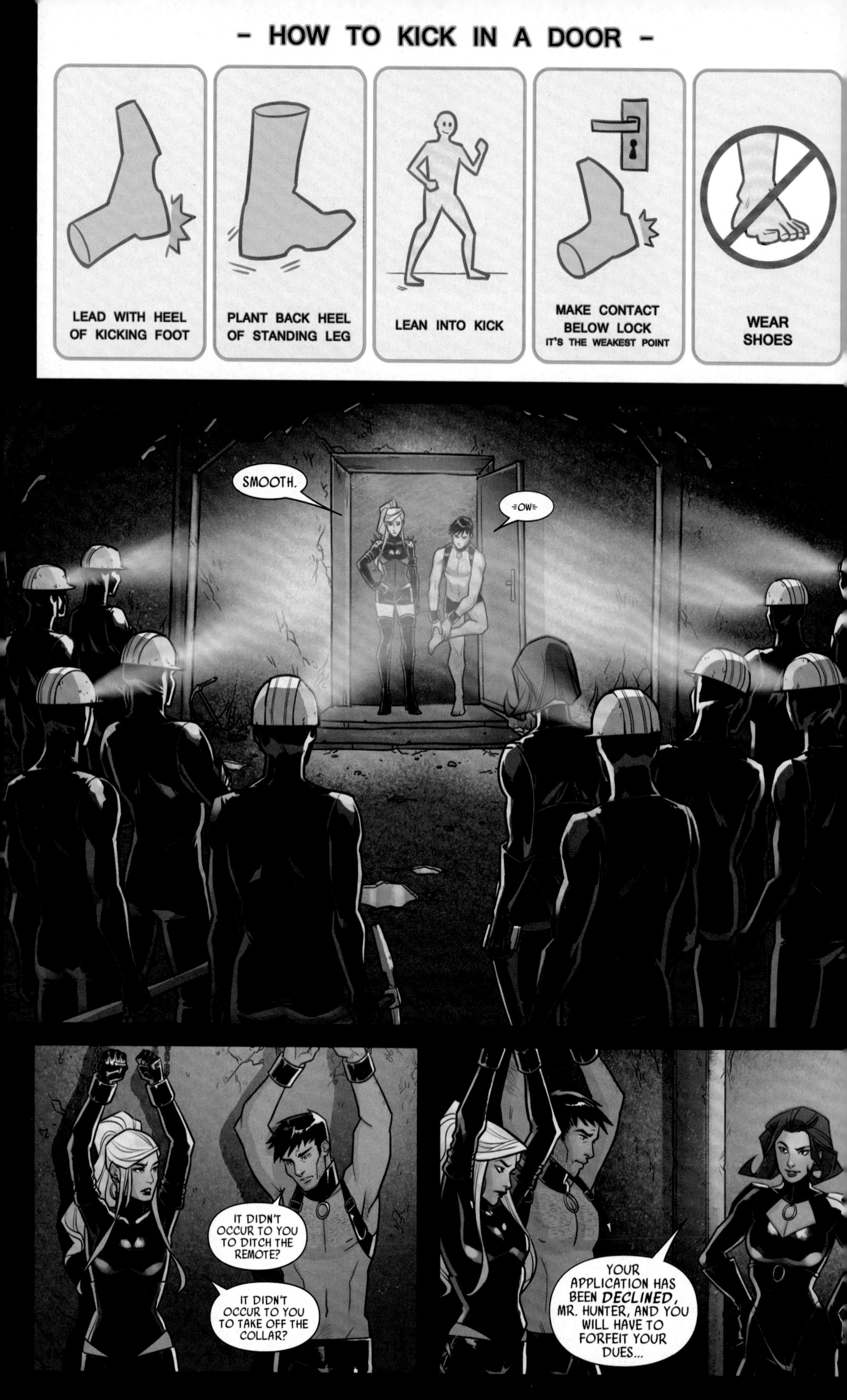
- HOW TO KICK IN A DOOR -
LEAD WITH HEEL OF KICKING FOOT
PLANT BACK HEEL OF STANDING LEG
LEAN INTO KICK
MAKE CONTACT BELOW LOCK
IT'S THE WEAKEST POINT
WEAR SHOES
SMOOTH.
OW
IT DIDN'T OCCUR TO YOU TO DITCH THE REMOTE?
IT DIDN'T OCCUR TO YOU TO TAKE OFF THE COLLAR?
YOUR APPLICATION HAS BEEN DECLINED, MR. HUNTER, AND YOU WILL HAVE TO FORFEIT YOUR DUES...

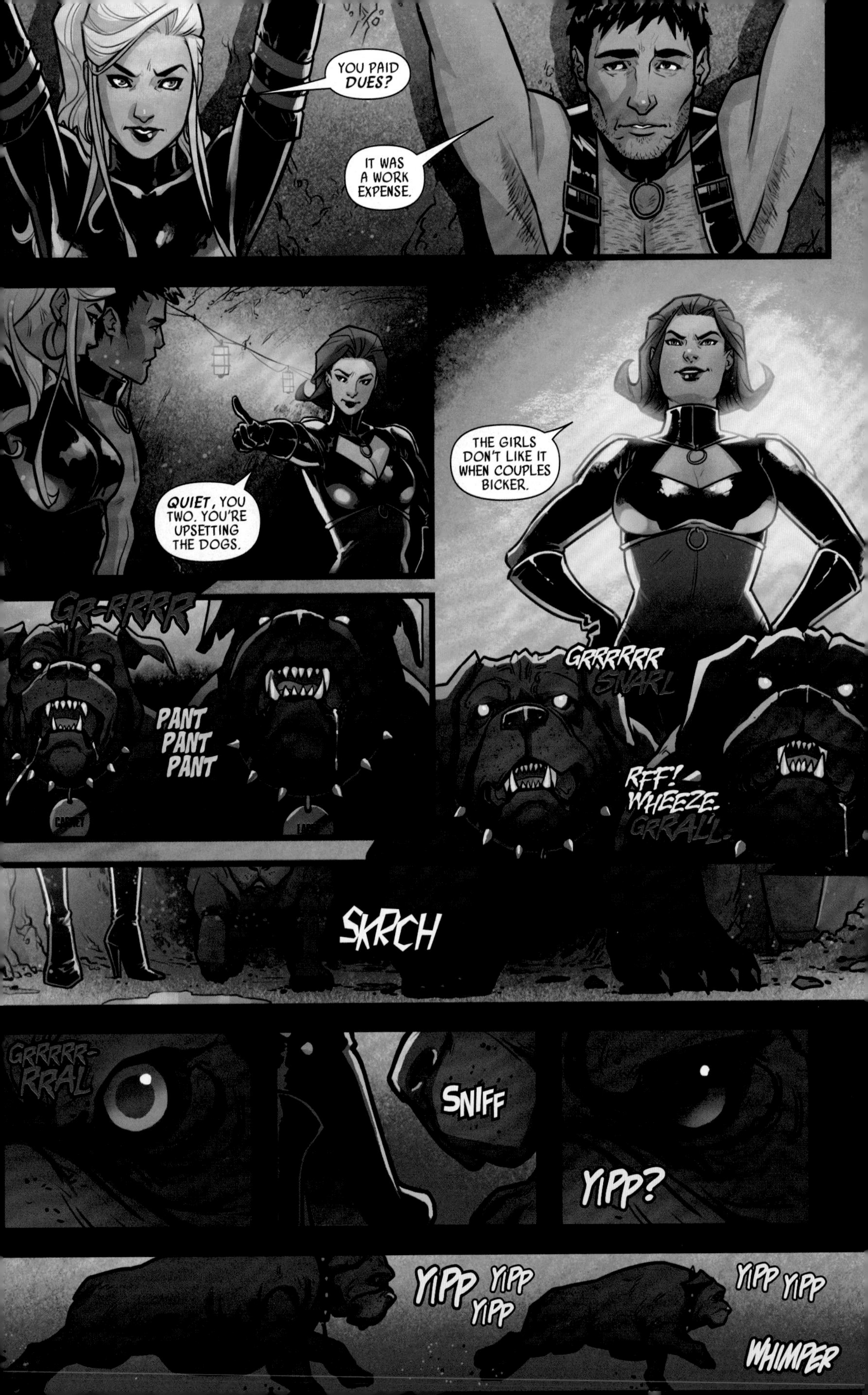

YOU PAID DUES?
IT WAS A WORK EXPENSE.
QUIET, YOU TWO. YOU'RE UPSETTING THE DOGS.
THE GIRLS DON'T LIKE IT WHEN COUPLES BICKER.
GR-RRRR
PANT PANT PANT
GRRRRRR SNARL
RFF! WHEEZE. GRRALL.
SKRCH
GRRRRR-RRAL
SNIFF
YIPP?
YIPP YIPP YIPP
YIPP YIPP
WHIMPER

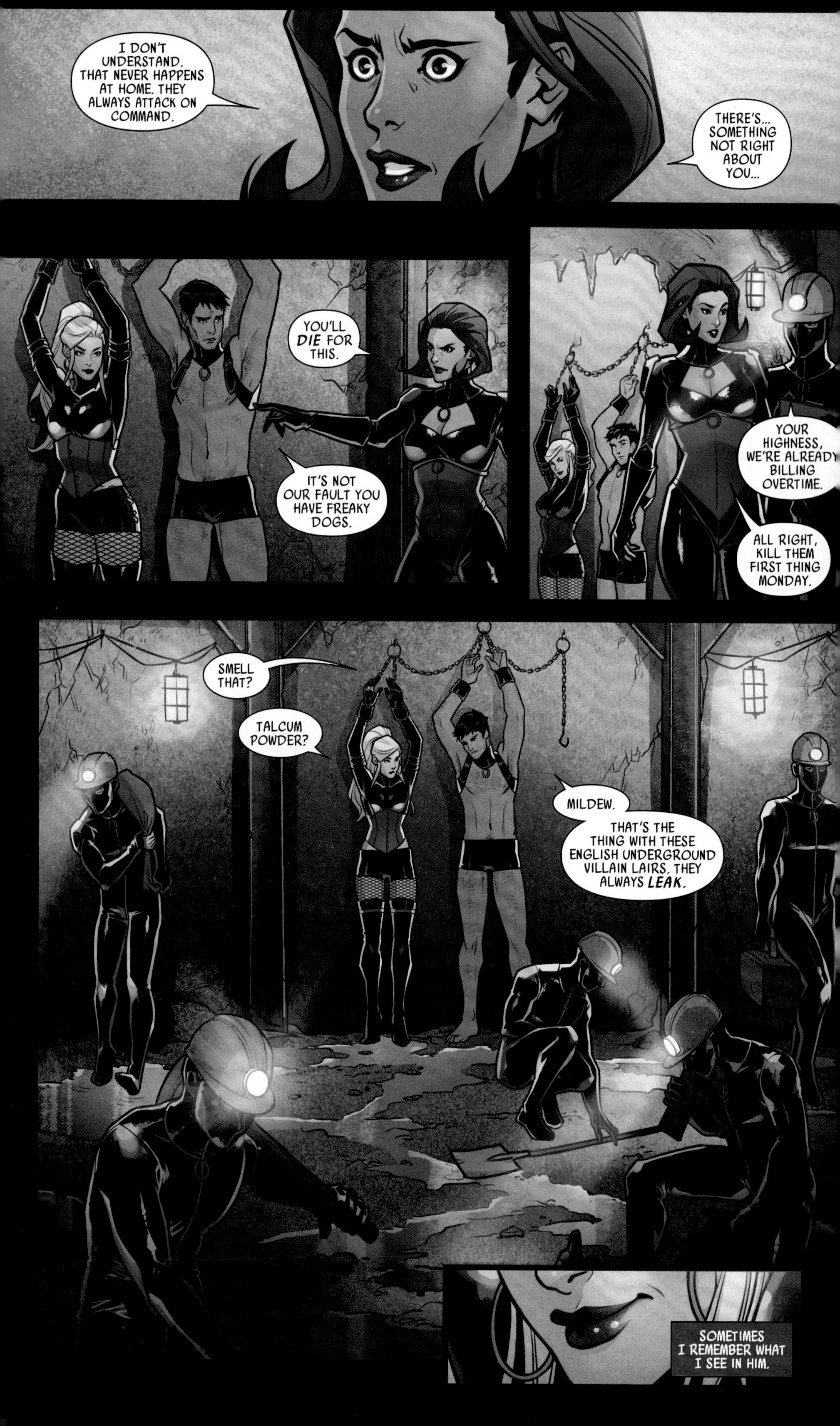
I DON'T UNDERSTAND. THAT NEVER HAPPENS AT HOME. THEY ALWAYS ATTACK ON COMMAND.
THERE'S... SOMETHING NOT RIGHT ABOUT YOU...
YOU'LL DIE FOR THIS.
IT'S NOT OUR FAULT YOU HAVE FREAKY DOGS.
YOUR HIGHNESS, WE'RE ALREADY BILLING OVERTIME.
ALL RIGHT, KILL THEM FIRST THING MONDAY.
SMELL THAT?
TALCUM POWDER?
MILDEW.
THAT'S THE THING WITH THESE ENGLISH UNDERGROUND VILLAIN LAIRS. THEY ALWAYS LEAK.
SOMETIMES I REMEMBER WHAT I SEE IN HIM.

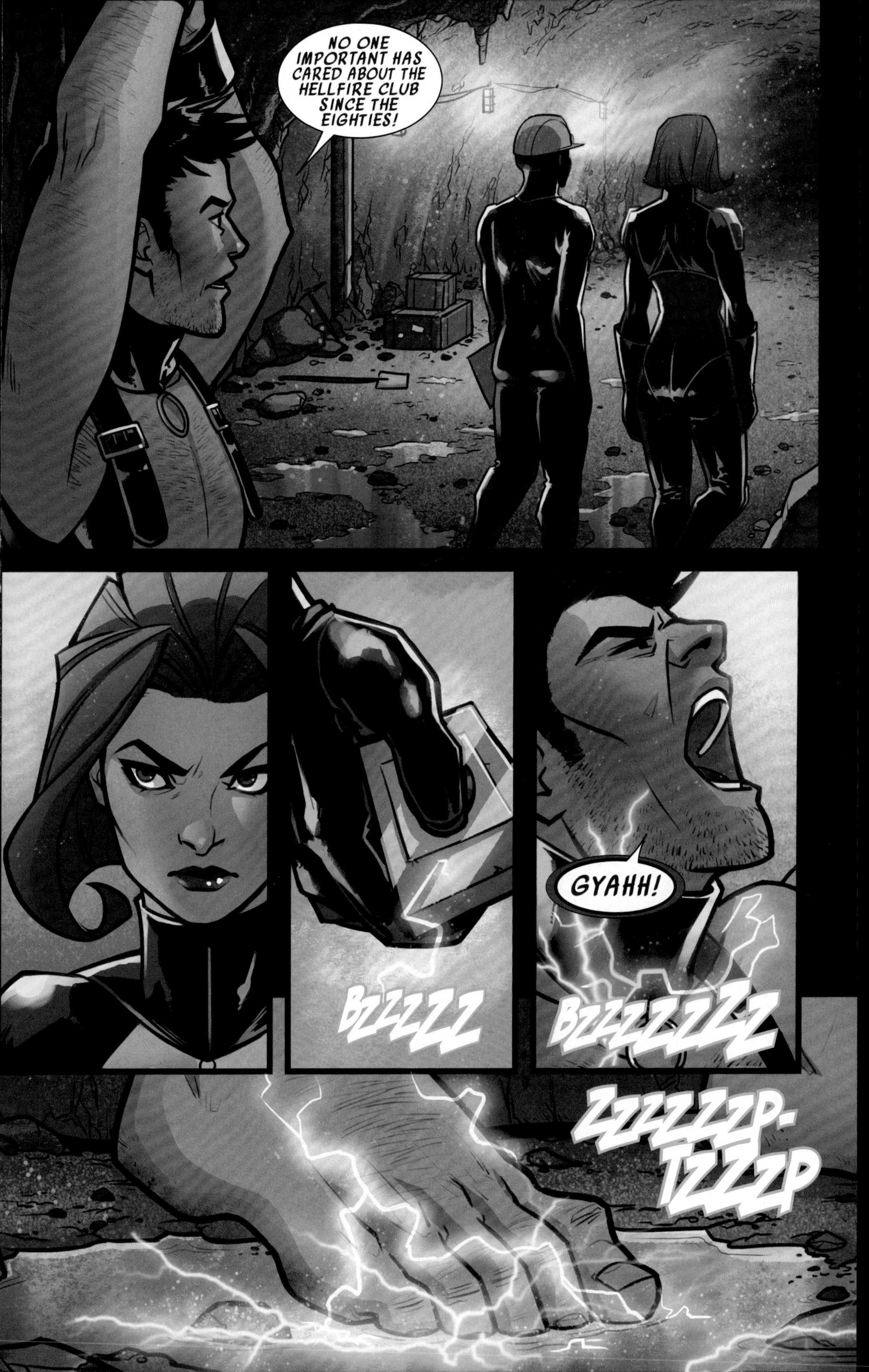
NO ONE IMPORTANT HAS CARED ABOUT THE HELLFIRE CLUB SINCE THE EIGHTIES!
BZZZZZ
GYAHH!
BZZZZZZZZ
ZZZZZZP-TZZZP

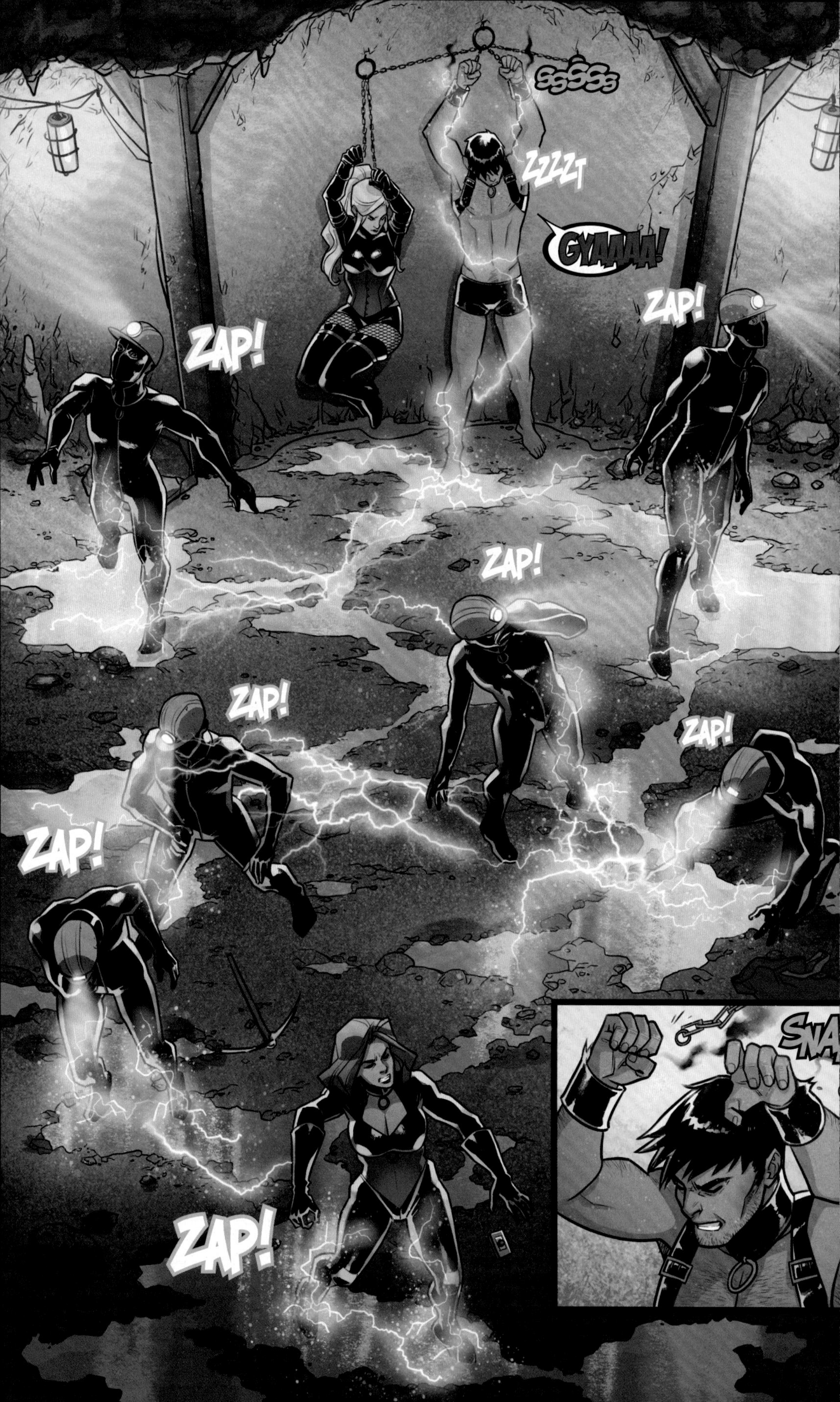
SSSSS
ZZZZT
GYAAAA!
ZAP!
ZAP!
ZAP!
ZAP!
ZAP!
ZAP!
ZAP!
SNA

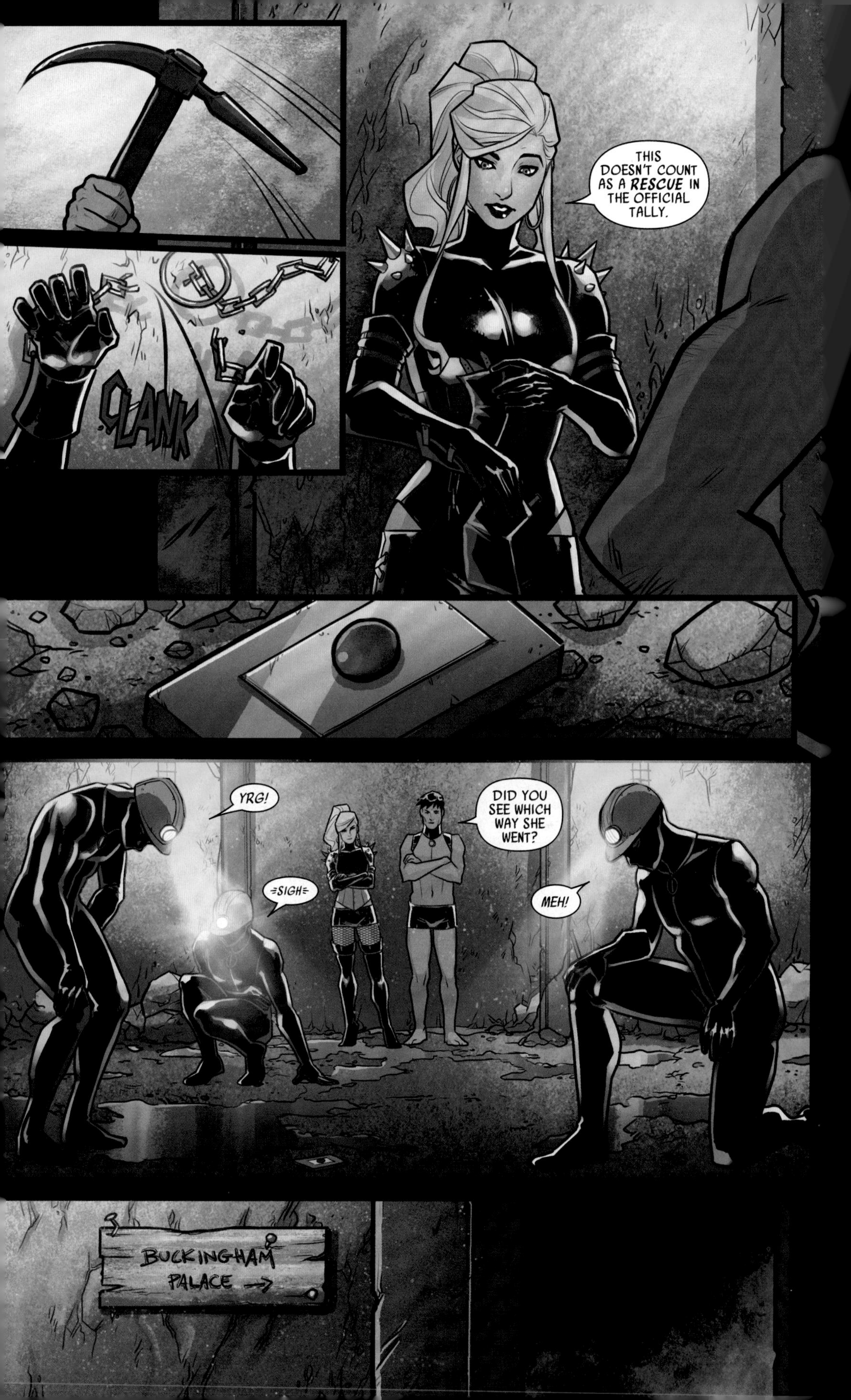
CLANK
THIS DOESN'T COUNT AS A *RESCUE* IN THE OFFICIAL TALLY.
YRG!
=SIGH=
DID YOU SEE WHICH WAY SHE WENT?
MEH!
BUCKINGHAM PALACE →

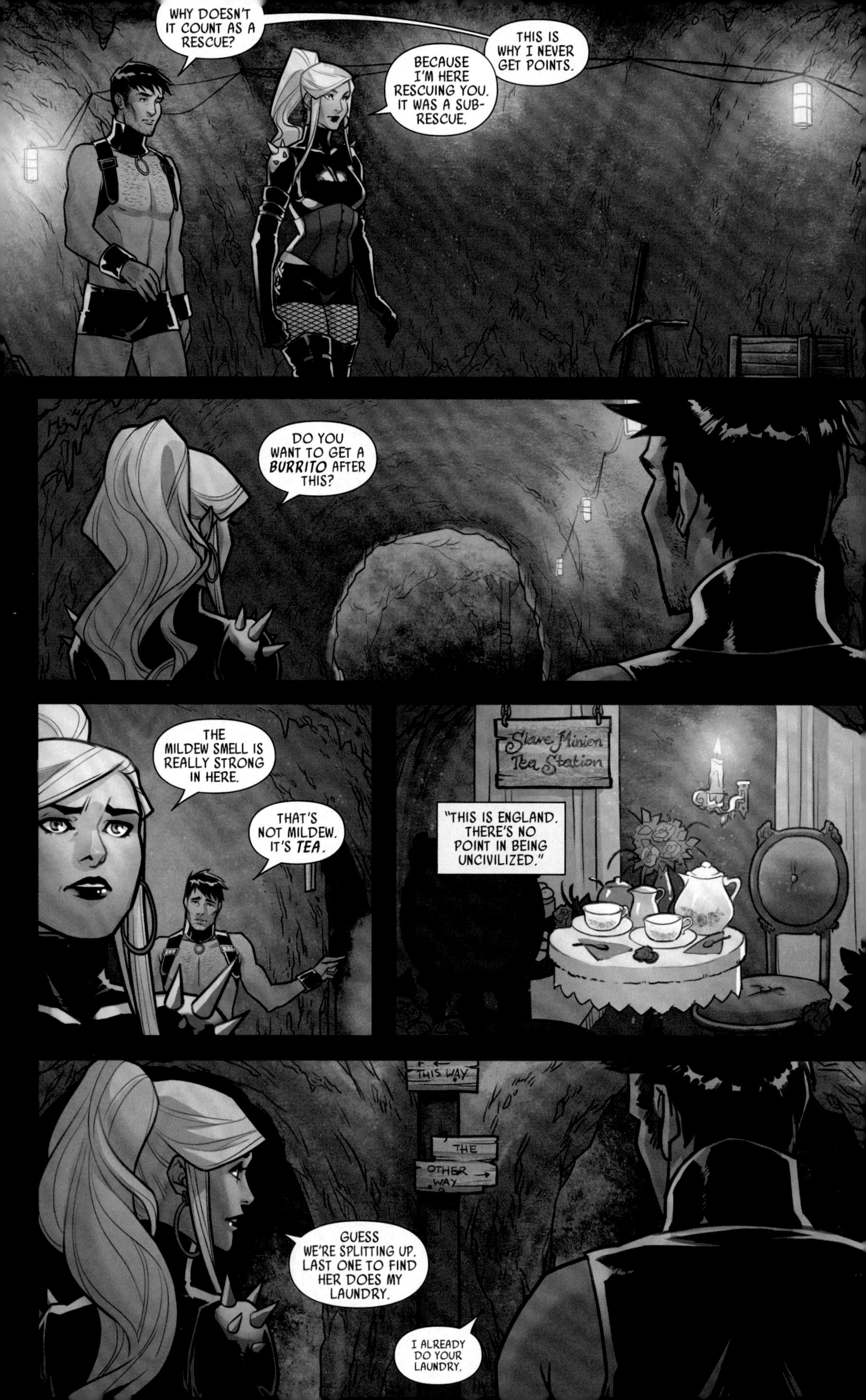
WHY DOESN'T IT COUNT AS A RESCUE?
BECAUSE I'M HERE RESCUING YOU. IT WAS A SUB-RESCUE.
THIS IS WHY I NEVER GET POINTS.
DO YOU WANT TO GET A BURRITO AFTER THIS?
THE MILDEW SMELL IS REALLY STRONG IN HERE.
THAT'S NOT MILDEW. IT'S TEA.
Slave Minion Tea Station
"THIS IS ENGLAND. THERE'S NO POINT IN BEING UNCIVILIZED."
THIS WAY
THE OTHER WAY
GUESS WE'RE SPLITTING UP. LAST ONE TO FIND HER DOES MY LAUNDRY.
I ALREADY DO YOUR LAUNDRY.

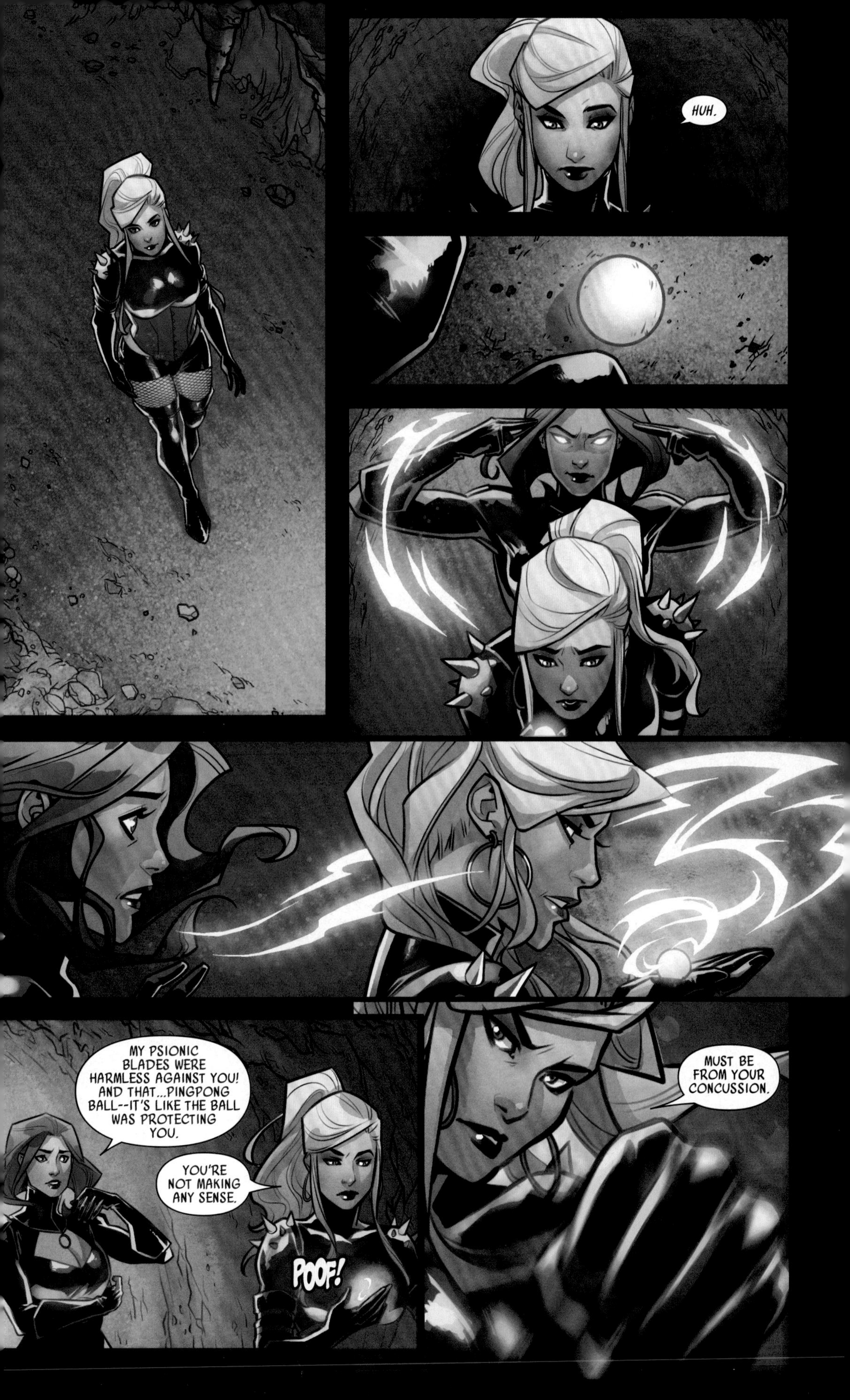
HUH.
MY PSIONIC BLADES WERE HARMLESS AGAINST YOU! AND THAT...PINGPONG BALL--IT'S LIKE THE BALL WAS PROTECTING YOU.
YOU'RE NOT MAKING ANY SENSE.
POOF!
MUST BE FROM YOUR CONCUSSION.

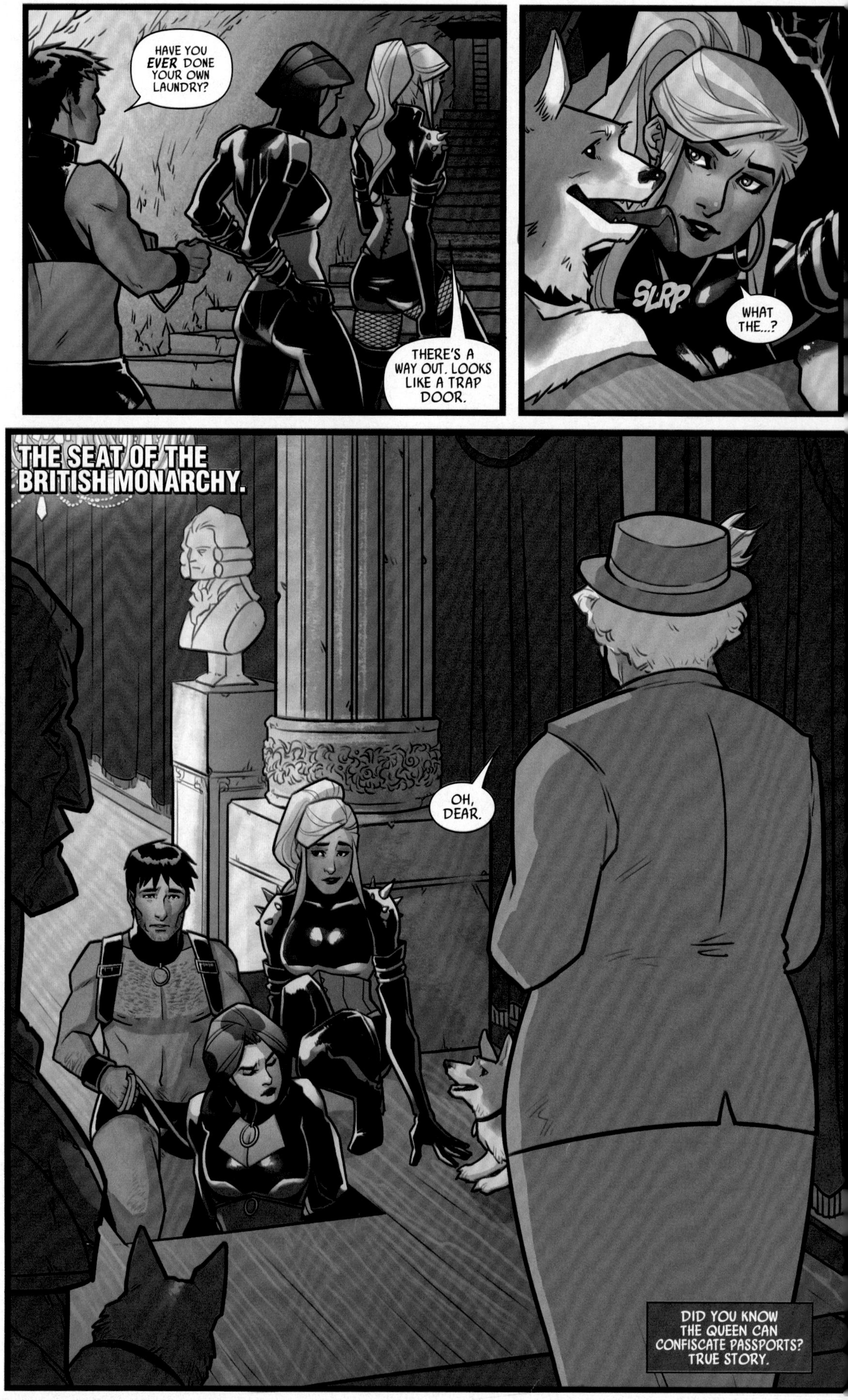

HAVE YOU EVER DONE YOUR OWN LAUNDRY?
THERE'S A WAY OUT. LOOKS LIKE A TRAP DOOR.
SLRP
WHAT THE...?
THE SEAT OF THE BRITISH MONARCHY.
OH, DEAR.
DID YOU KNOW THE QUEEN CAN CONFISCATE PASSPORTS? TRUE STORY.

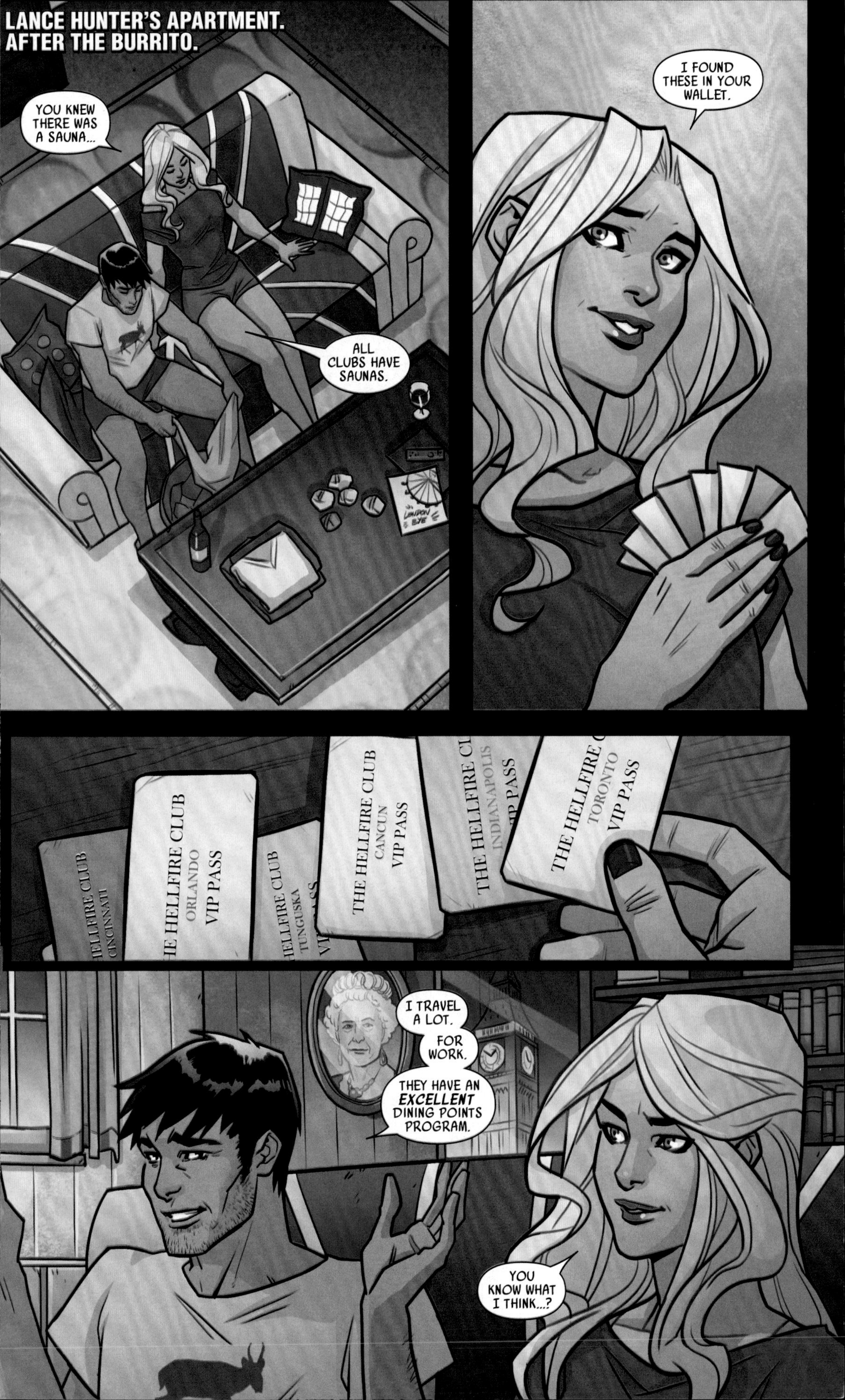

LANCE HUNTER'S APARTMENT. AFTER THE BURRITO.
YOU KNEW THERE WAS A SAUNA...
ALL CLUBS HAVE SAUNAS.
LONDON EYE
I FOUND THESE IN YOUR WALLET.
CINCINNATI
ORLANDO VIP PASS
TUNGUSKA
THE HELLFIRE CLUB CANCUN VIP PASS
THE HELLFIRE CLUB INDIANAPOLIS
TORONTO VIP PASS
I TRAVEL A LOT.
FOR WORK.
THEY HAVE AN EXCELLENT DINING POINTS PROGRAM.
YOU KNOW WHAT I THINK...?

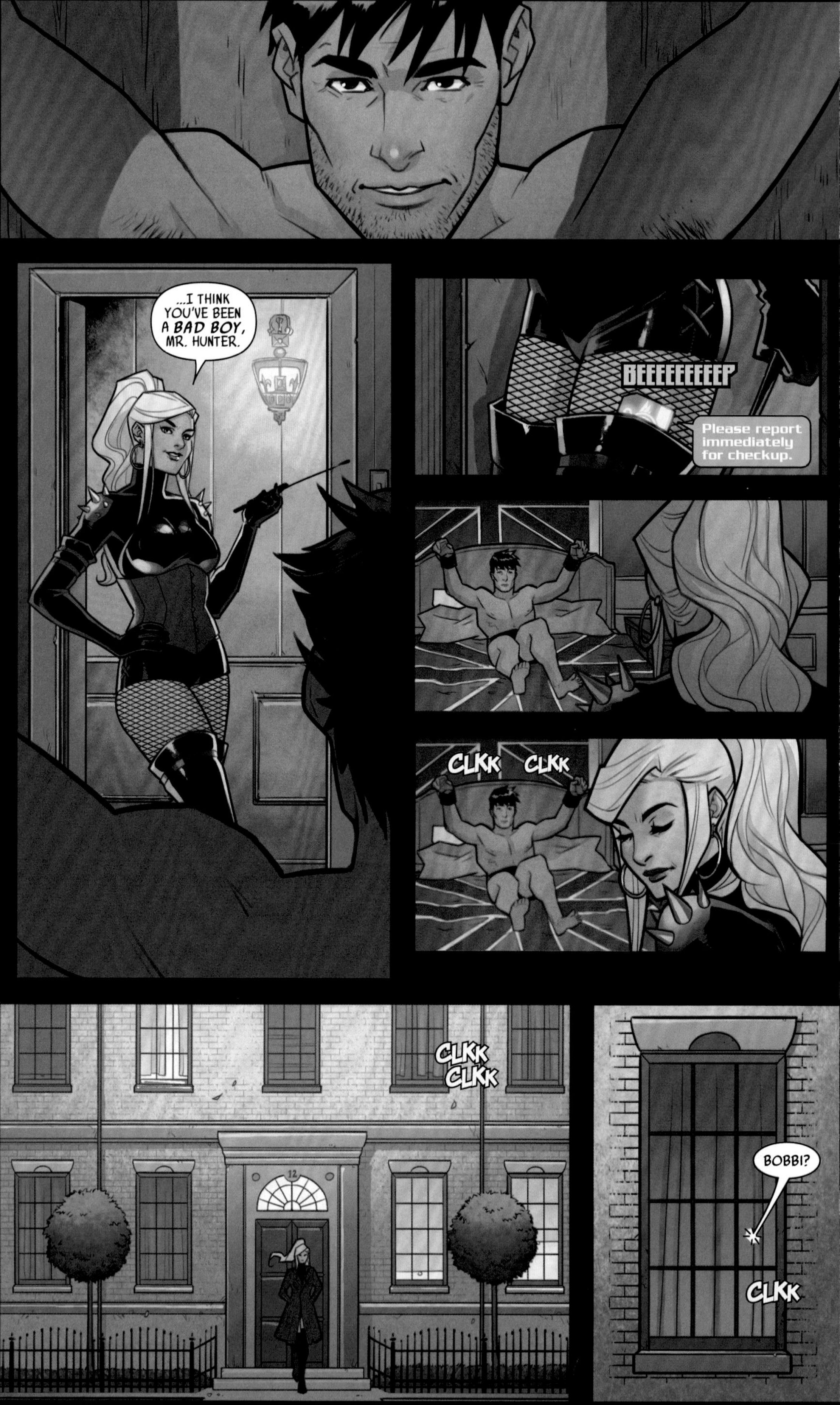
...I THINK YOU'VE BEEN A *BAD BOY*, MR. HUNTER.
BEEEEEEEEEP
Please report immediately for checkup.
CLKK CLKK
CLKK CLKK
BOBBI?
CLKK

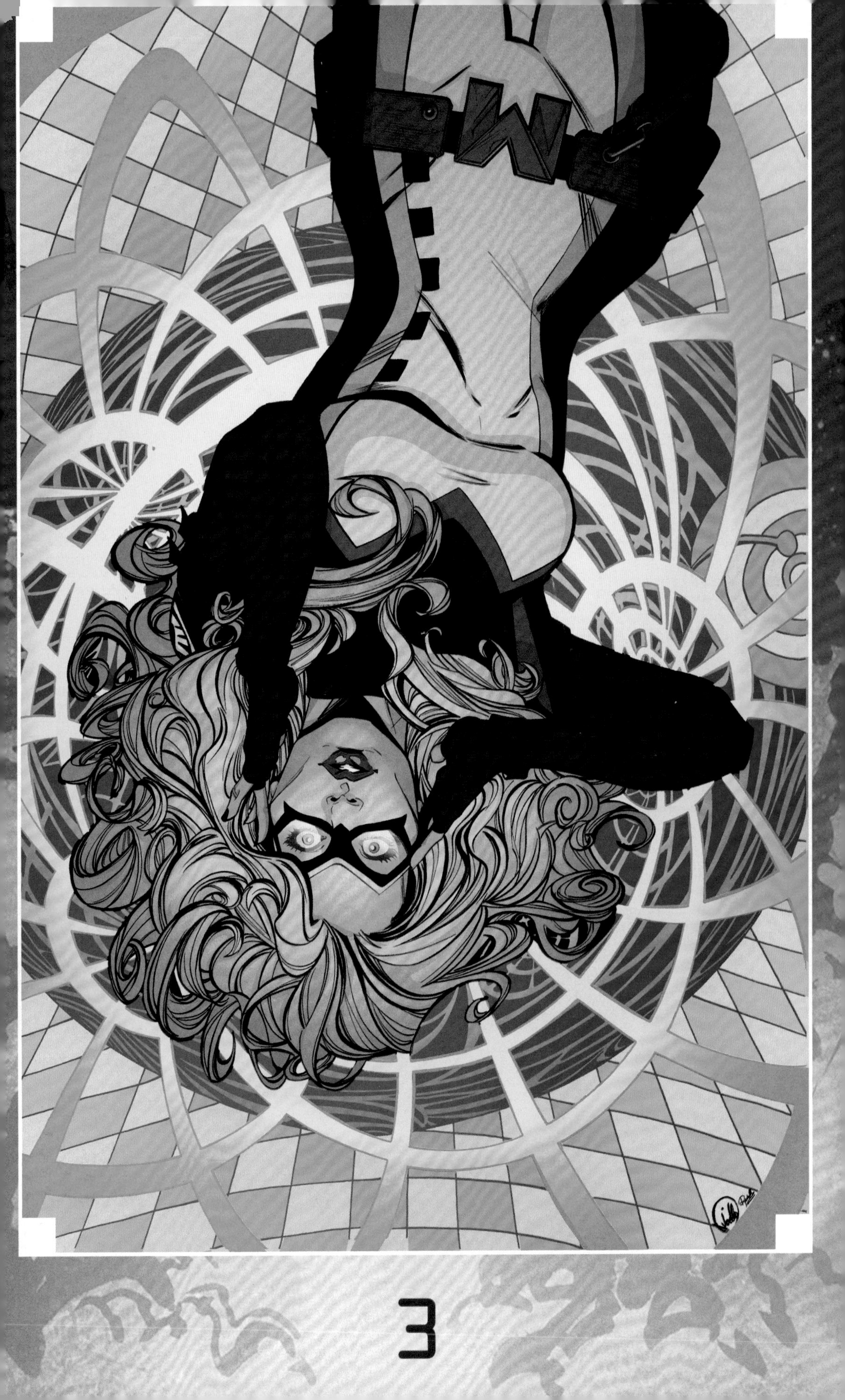

3

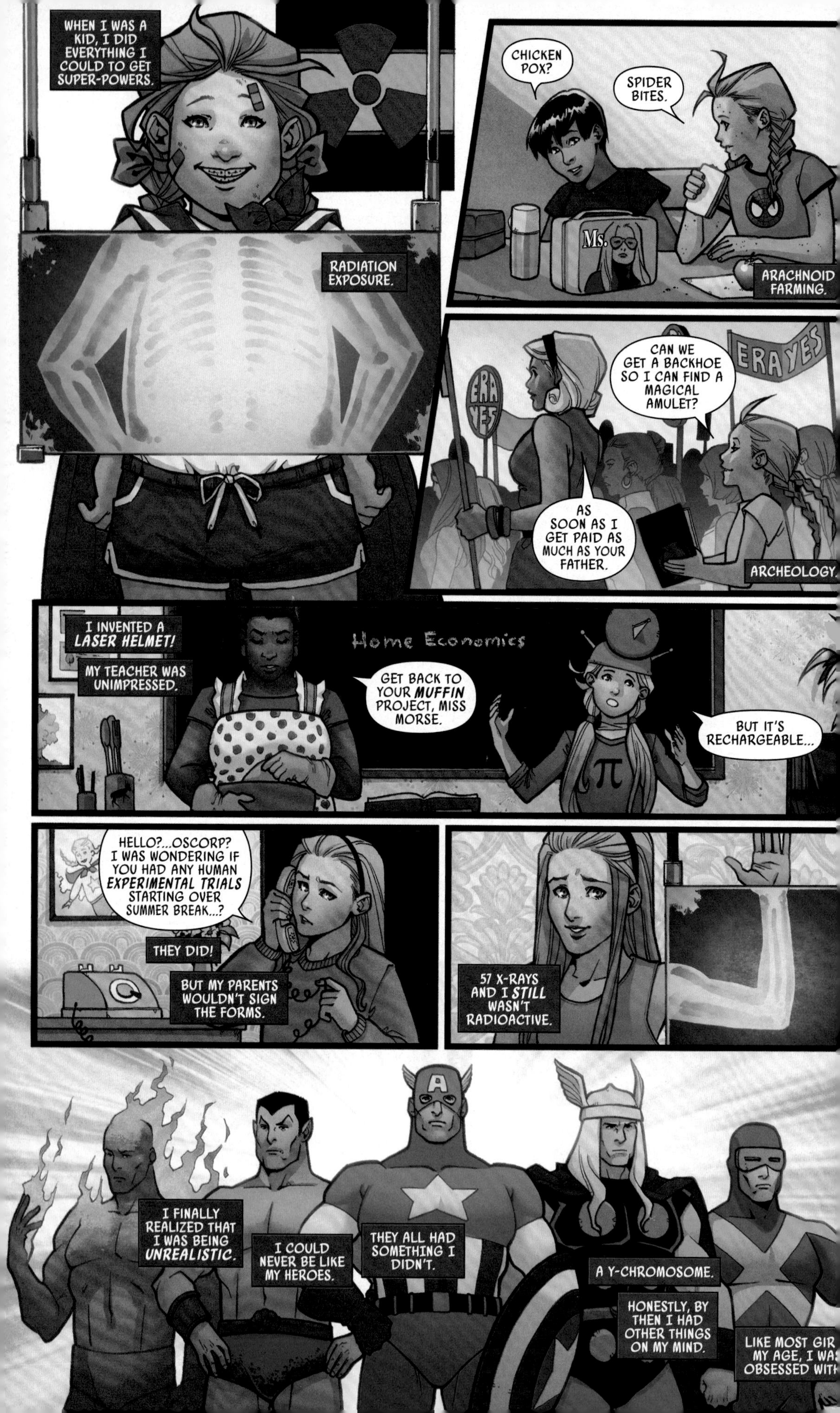
WHEN I WAS A KID, I DID EVERYTHING I COULD TO GET SUPER-POWERS.
RADIATION EXPOSURE.
CHICKEN POX?
SPIDER BITES.
Ms.
ARACHNOID FARMING.
ERA YES
CAN WE GET A BACKHOE SO I CAN FIND A MAGICAL AMULET?
AS SOON AS I GET PAID AS MUCH AS YOUR FATHER.
ARCHEOLOGY.
I INVENTED A LASER HELMET!
MY TEACHER WAS UNIMPRESSED.
Home Economics
GET BACK TO YOUR MUFFIN PROJECT, MISS MORSE.
BUT IT'S RECHARGEABLE...
HELLO?...OSCORP? I WAS WONDERING IF YOU HAD ANY HUMAN EXPERIMENTAL TRIALS STARTING OVER SUMMER BREAK...?
THEY DID!
BUT MY PARENTS WOULDN'T SIGN THE FORMS.
57 X-RAYS AND I STILL WASN'T RADIOACTIVE.
I FINALLY REALIZED THAT I WAS BEING UNREALISTIC.
I COULD NEVER BE LIKE MY HEROES.
THEY ALL HAD SOMETHING I DIDN'T.
A Y-CHROMOSOME.
HONESTLY, BY THEN I HAD OTHER THINGS ON MY MIND.
LIKE MOST GIR MY AGE, I WA OBSESSED WITH

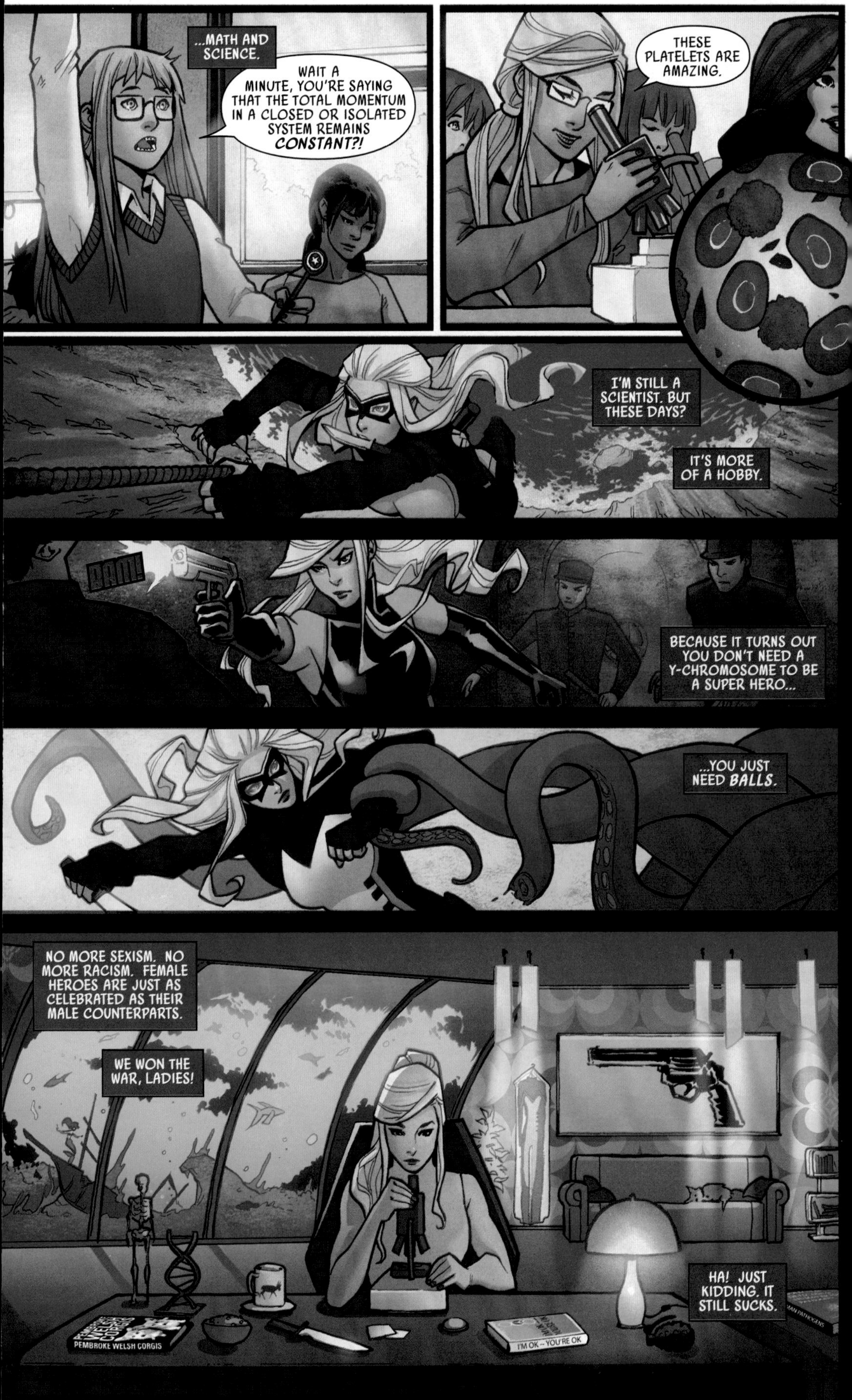

...MATH AND SCIENCE.
WAIT A MINUTE, YOU'RE SAYING THAT THE TOTAL MOMENTUM IN A CLOSED OR ISOLATED SYSTEM REMAINS CONSTANT?!
THESE PLATELETS ARE AMAZING.
I'M STILL A SCIENTIST. BUT THESE DAYS?
IT'S MORE OF A HOBBY.
BAM!
BECAUSE IT TURNS OUT YOU DON'T NEED A Y-CHROMOSOME TO BE A SUPER HERO...
...YOU JUST NEED BALLS.
NO MORE SEXISM. NO MORE RACISM. FEMALE HEROES ARE JUST AS CELEBRATED AS THEIR MALE COUNTERPARTS.
WE WON THE WAR, LADIES!
HA! JUST KIDDING. IT STILL SUCKS.
PEMBROKE WELSH CORGIS
I'M OK ~ YOU'RE OK

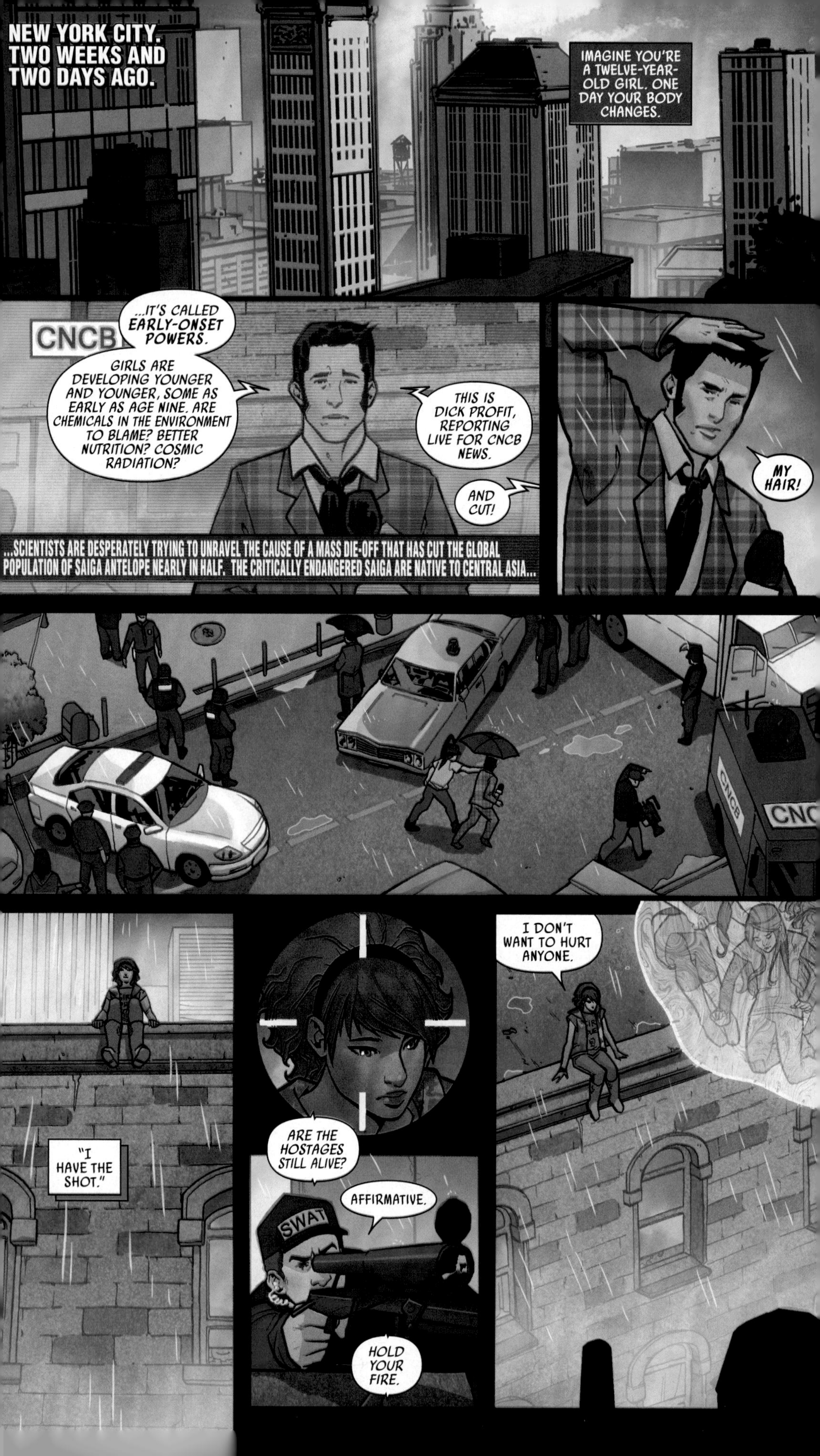
NEW YORK CITY. TWO WEEKS AND TWO DAYS AGO.
IMAGINE YOU'RE A TWELVE-YEAR-OLD GIRL. ONE DAY YOUR BODY CHANGES.
CNCB
...IT'S CALLED EARLY-ONSET POWERS.
GIRLS ARE DEVELOPING YOUNGER AND YOUNGER, SOME AS EARLY AS AGE NINE. ARE CHEMICALS IN THE ENVIRONMENT TO BLAME? BETTER NUTRITION? COSMIC RADIATION?
THIS IS DICK PROFIT, REPORTING LIVE FOR CNCB NEWS.
AND CUT!
...SCIENTISTS ARE DESPERATELY TRYING TO UNRAVEL THE CAUSE OF A MASS DIE-OFF THAT HAS CUT THE GLOBAL POPULATION OF SAIGA ANTELOPE NEARLY IN HALF. THE CRITICALLY ENDANGERED SAIGA ARE NATIVE TO CENTRAL ASIA...
MY HAIR!
CNCB
"I HAVE THE SHOT."
ARE THE HOSTAGES STILL ALIVE?
AFFIRMATIVE.
SWAT
HOLD YOUR FIRE.
I DON'T WANT TO HURT ANYONE.

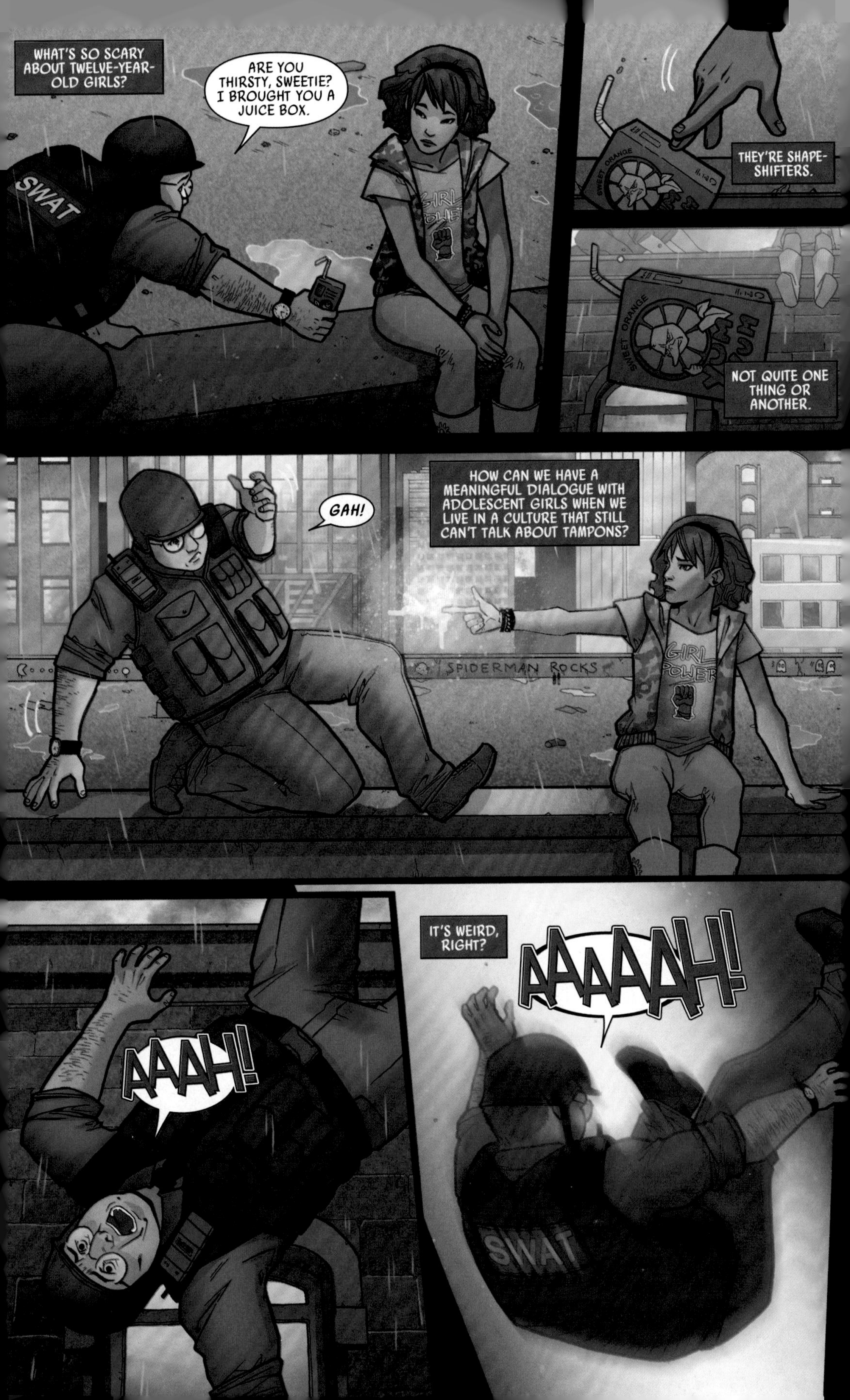

WHAT'S SO SCARY ABOUT TWELVE-YEAR-OLD GIRLS?
ARE YOU THIRSTY, SWEETIE? I BROUGHT YOU A JUICE BOX.
SWAT
GIRL POWER
SWEET ORANGE
THEY'RE SHAPE-SHIFTERS.
NOT QUITE ONE THING OR ANOTHER.
GAH!
HOW CAN WE HAVE A MEANINGFUL DIALOGUE WITH ADOLESCENT GIRLS WHEN WE LIVE IN A CULTURE THAT STILL CAN'T TALK ABOUT TAMPONS?
SPIDERMAN ROCKS
AAAH!
IT'S WEIRD, RIGHT?
AAAAAH!
SWAT

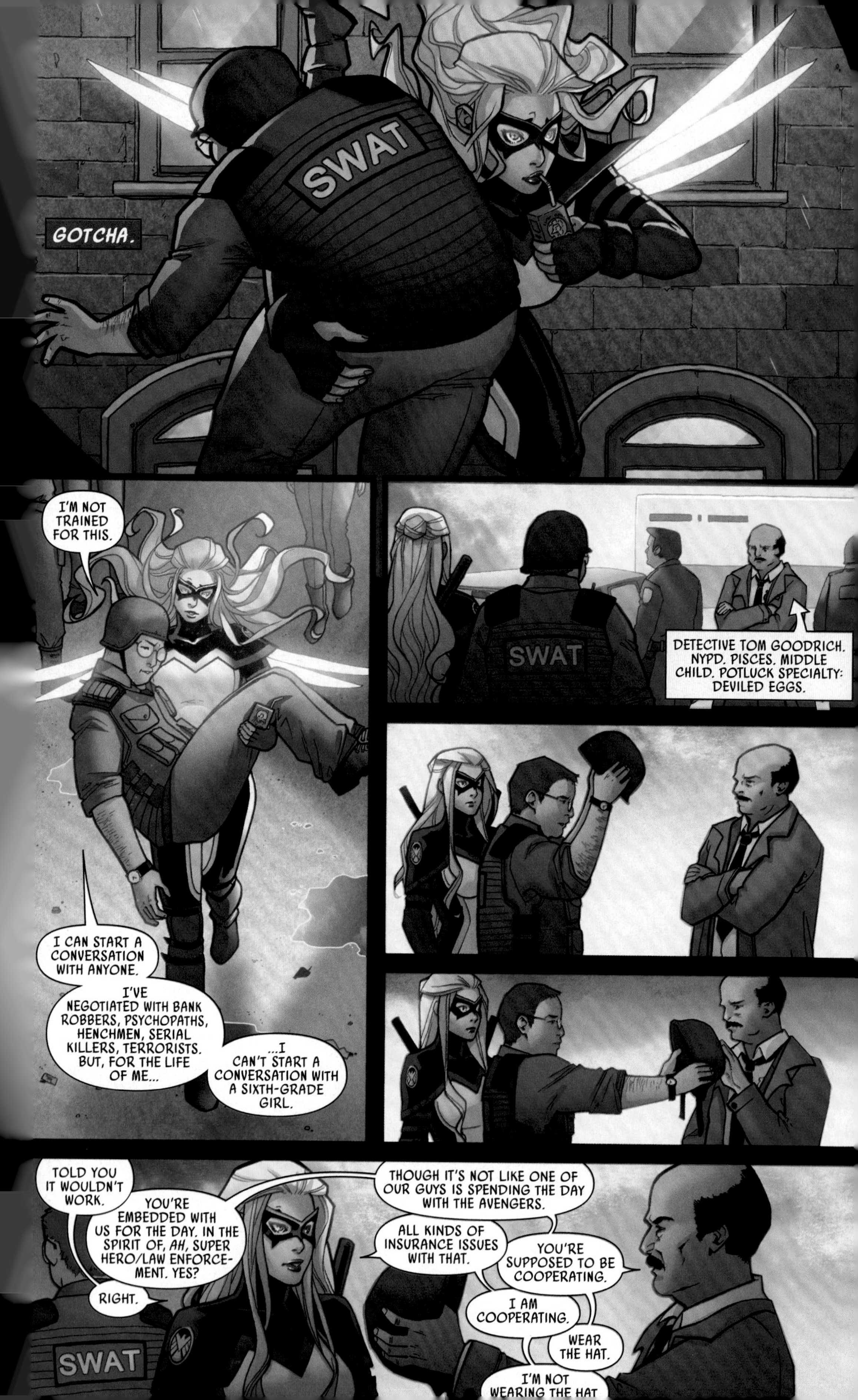

GOTCHA.
I'M NOT TRAINED FOR THIS.
DETECTIVE TOM GOODRICH. NYPD. PISCES. MIDDLE CHILD. POTLUCK SPECIALTY: DEVILED EGGS.
I CAN START A CONVERSATION WITH ANYONE.
I'VE NEGOTIATED WITH BANK ROBBERS, PSYCHOPATHS, HENCHMEN, SERIAL KILLERS, TERRORISTS. BUT, FOR THE LIFE OF ME...
...I CAN'T START A CONVERSATION WITH A SIXTH-GRADE GIRL.
TOLD YOU IT WOULDN'T WORK.
YOU'RE EMBEDDED WITH US FOR THE DAY. IN THE SPIRIT OF, AH, SUPER HERO/LAW ENFORCEMENT. YES?
RIGHT.
THOUGH IT'S NOT LIKE ONE OF OUR GUYS IS SPENDING THE DAY WITH THE AVENGERS.
ALL KINDS OF INSURANCE ISSUES WITH THAT.
YOU'RE SUPPOSED TO BE COOPERATING.
I AM COOPERATING.
WEAR THE HAT.
I'M NOT WEARING THE HAT

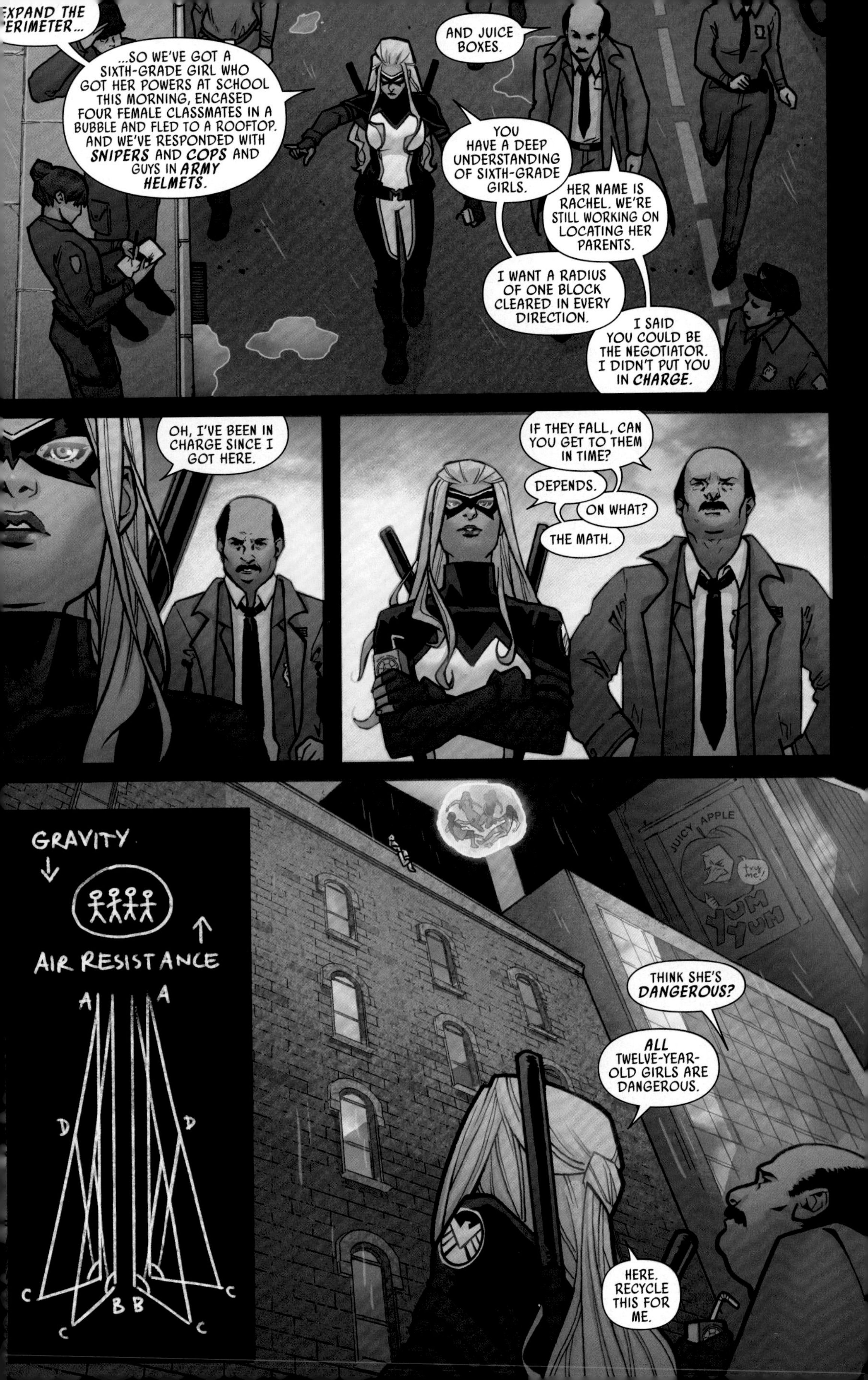
EXPAND THE PERIMETER...
...SO WE'VE GOT A SIXTH-GRADE GIRL WHO GOT HER POWERS AT SCHOOL THIS MORNING, ENCASED FOUR FEMALE CLASSMATES IN A BUBBLE AND FLED TO A ROOFTOP. AND WE'VE RESPONDED WITH SNIPERS AND COPS AND GUYS IN ARMY HELMETS.
AND JUICE BOXES.
YOU HAVE A DEEP UNDERSTANDING OF SIXTH-GRADE GIRLS.
HER NAME IS RACHEL. WE'RE STILL WORKING ON LOCATING HER PARENTS.
I WANT A RADIUS OF ONE BLOCK CLEARED IN EVERY DIRECTION.
I SAID YOU COULD BE THE NEGOTIATOR. I DIDN'T PUT YOU IN CHARGE.
OH, I'VE BEEN IN CHARGE SINCE I GOT HERE.
IF THEY FALL, CAN YOU GET TO THEM IN TIME?
DEPENDS.
ON WHAT?
THE MATH.
GRAVITY
AIR RESISTANCE
A
A
D
D
C
B B
C
C
C
JUICY APPLE
try me!
YUM YUM
THINK SHE'S DANGEROUS?
ALL TWELVE-YEAR-OLD GIRLS ARE DANGEROUS.
HERE. RECYCLE THIS FOR ME.

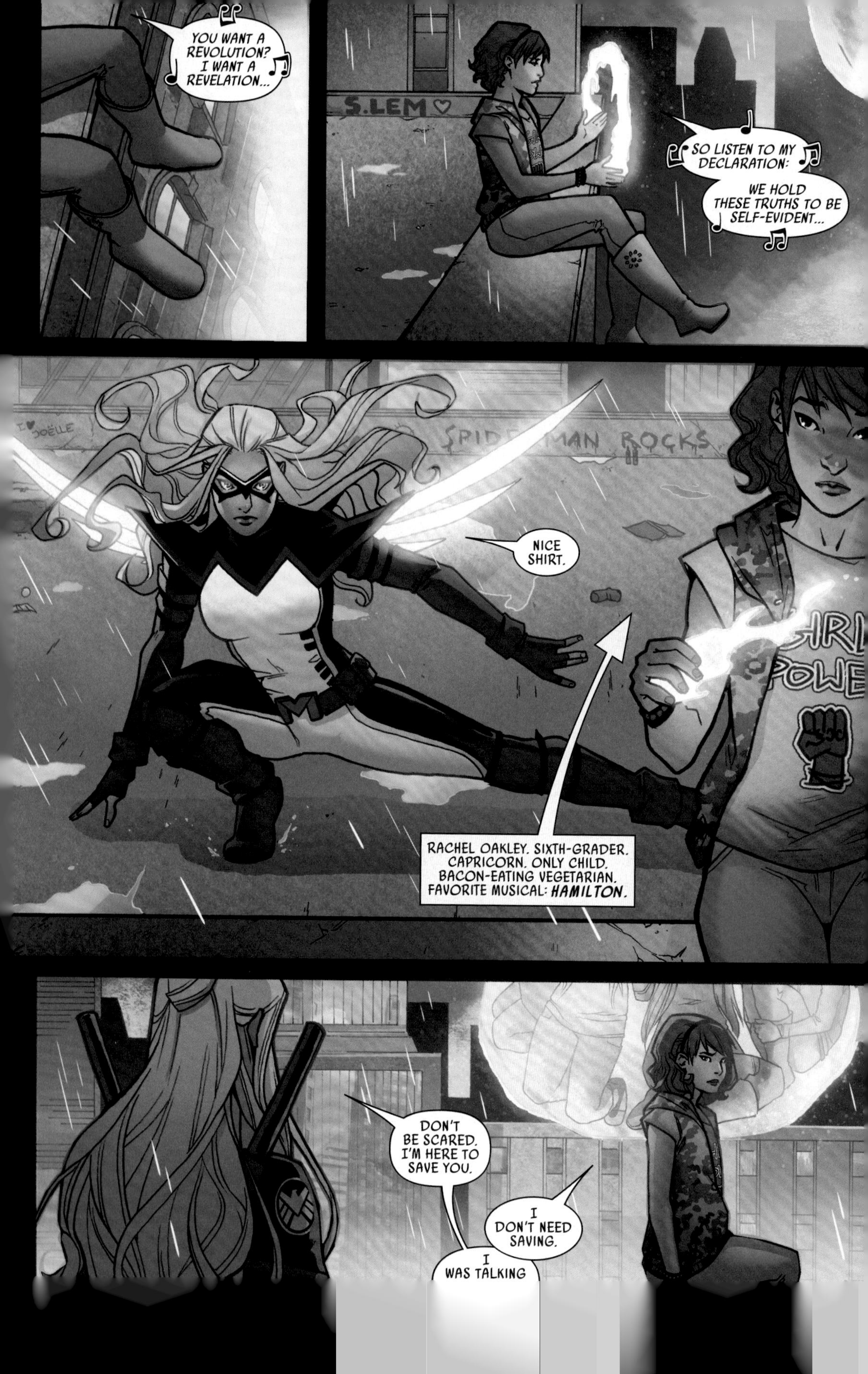

YOU WANT A REVOLUTION? I WANT A REVELATION...
S.LEM
SO LISTEN TO MY DECLARATION:
WE HOLD THESE TRUTHS TO BE SELF-EVIDENT...
I ♥ JOËLLE
SPIDER-MAN ROCKS
NICE SHIRT.
RACHEL OAKLEY. SIXTH-GRADER. CAPRICORN. ONLY CHILD. BACON-EATING VEGETARIAN. FAVORITE MUSICAL: HAMILTON.
GIRL POWE
DON'T BE SCARED. I'M HERE TO SAVE YOU.
I DON'T NEED SAVING.
I WAS TALKING

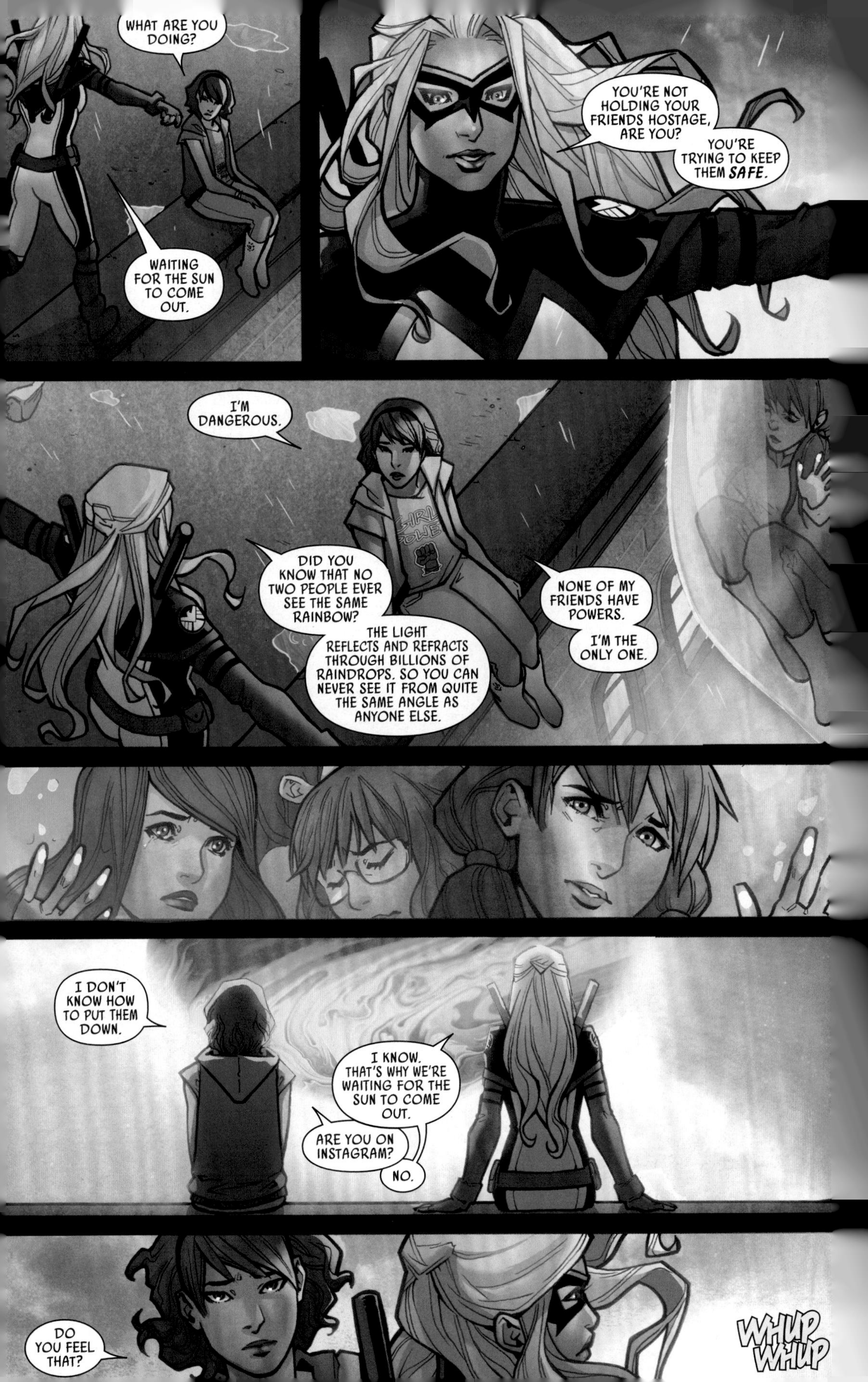
WHAT ARE YOU DOING?
WAITING FOR THE SUN TO COME OUT.
YOU'RE NOT HOLDING YOUR FRIENDS HOSTAGE, ARE YOU?
YOU'RE TRYING TO KEEP THEM SAFE.
I'M DANGEROUS.
DID YOU KNOW THAT NO TWO PEOPLE EVER SEE THE SAME RAINBOW?
THE LIGHT REFLECTS AND REFRACTS THROUGH BILLIONS OF RAINDROPS. SO YOU CAN NEVER SEE IT FROM QUITE THE SAME ANGLE AS ANYONE ELSE.
NONE OF MY FRIENDS HAVE POWERS.
I'M THE ONLY ONE.
I DON'T KNOW HOW TO PUT THEM DOWN.
I KNOW. THAT'S WHY WE'RE WAITING FOR THE SUN TO COME OUT.
ARE YOU ON INSTAGRAM?
NO.
DO YOU FEEL THAT?
WHUP WHUP

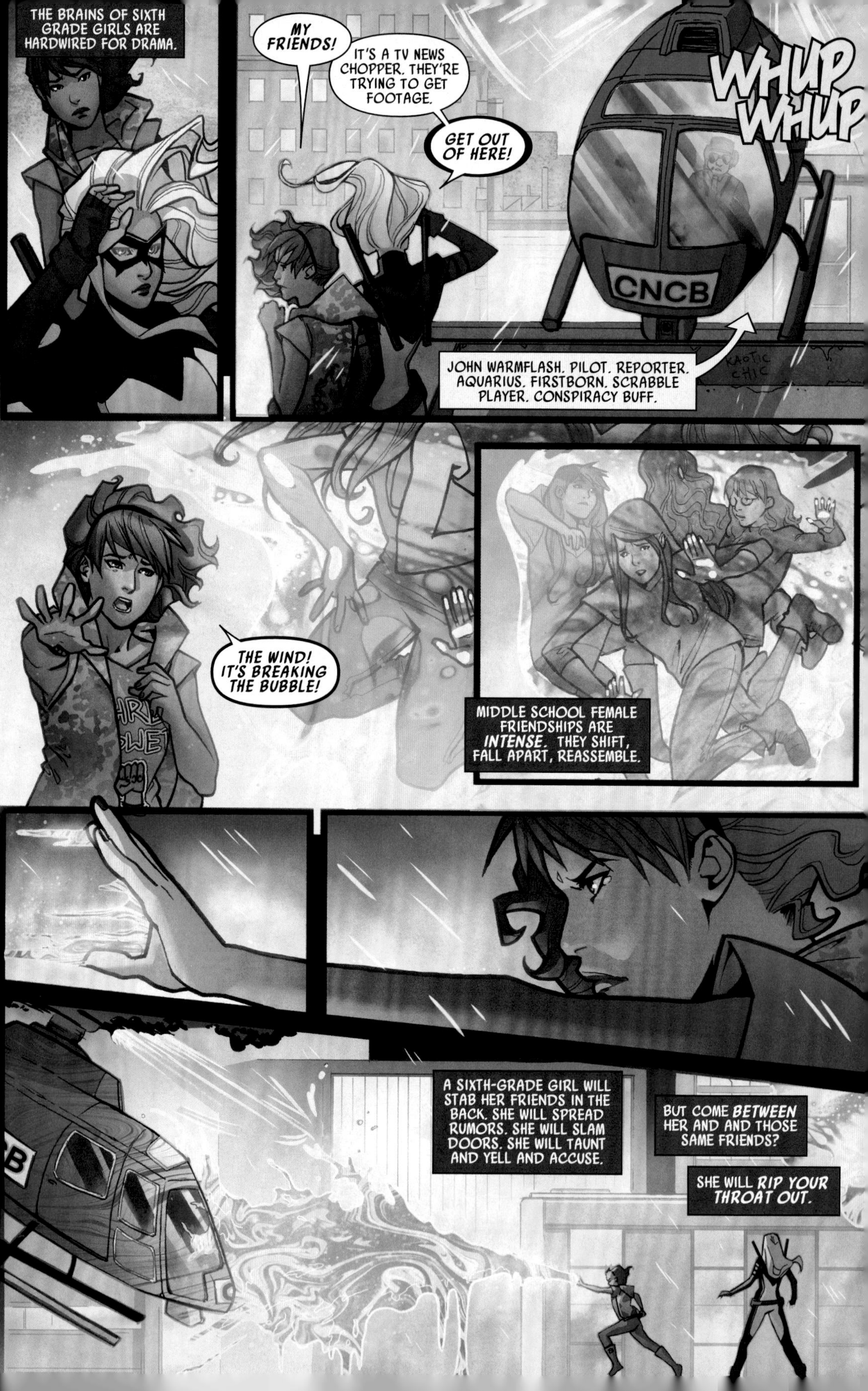
THE BRAINS OF SIXTH GRADE GIRLS ARE HARDWIRED FOR DRAMA.
MY FRIENDS!
IT'S A TV NEWS CHOPPER. THEY'RE TRYING TO GET FOOTAGE.
GET OUT OF HERE!
WHUP WHUP
CNCB
JOHN WARMFLASH. PILOT. REPORTER. AQUARIUS. FIRSTBORN. SCRABBLE PLAYER. CONSPIRACY BUFF.
KAOTIC CHIC
THE WIND! IT'S BREAKING THE BUBBLE!
MIDDLE SCHOOL FEMALE FRIENDSHIPS ARE *INTENSE.* THEY SHIFT, FALL APART, REASSEMBLE.
A SIXTH-GRADE GIRL WILL STAB HER FRIENDS IN THE BACK. SHE WILL SPREAD RUMORS. SHE WILL SLAM DOORS. SHE WILL TAUNT AND YELL AND ACCUSE.
BUT COME *BETWEEN* HER AND AND THOSE SAME FRIENDS?
SHE WILL *RIP YOUR THROAT OUT.*

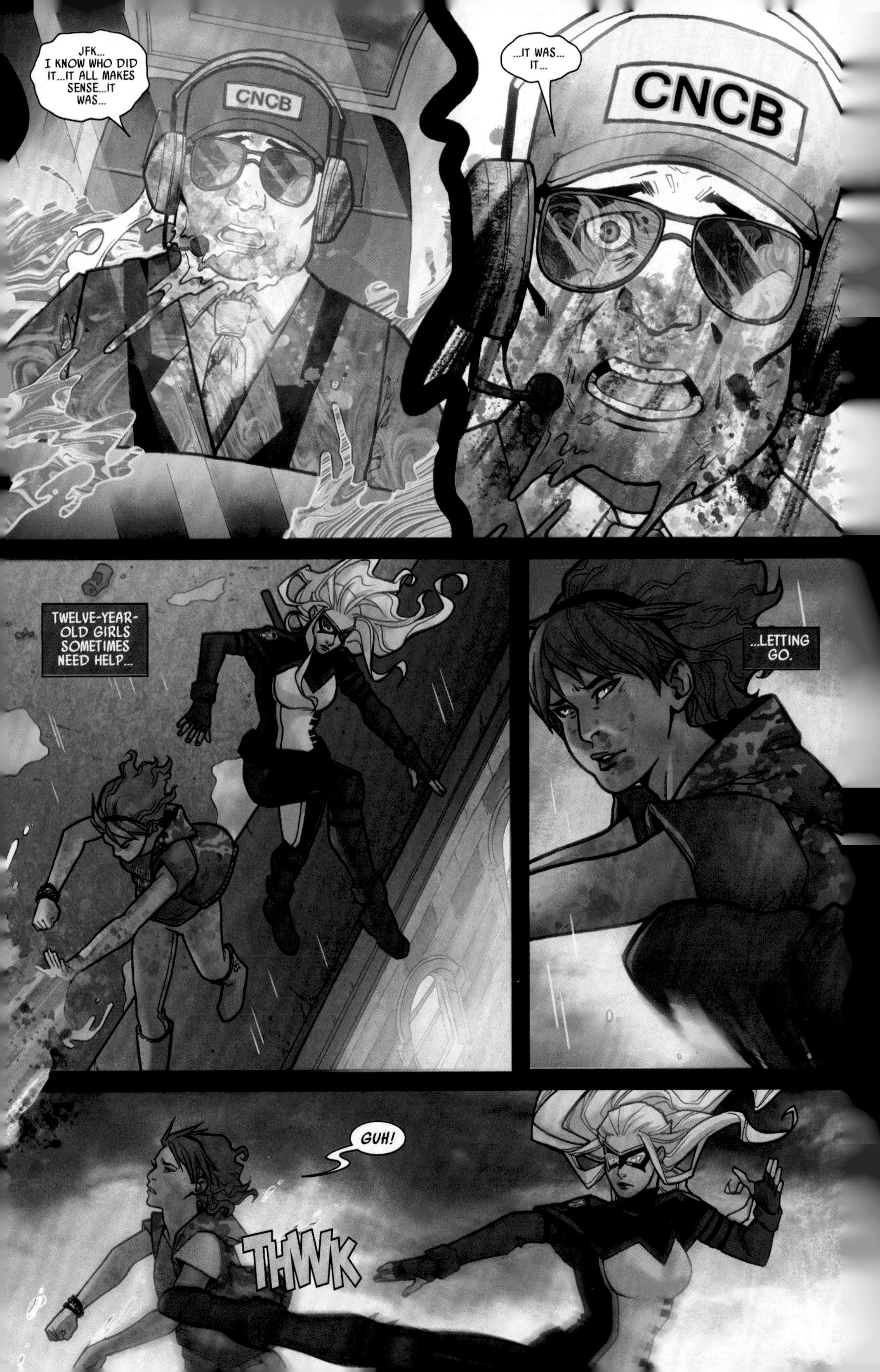
JFK... I KNOW WHO DID IT...IT ALL MAKES SENSE...IT WAS...
CNCB
...IT WAS... IT...
CNCB
TWELVE-YEAR-OLD GIRLS SOMETIMES NEED HELP...
...LETTING GO.
GUH!
THWK

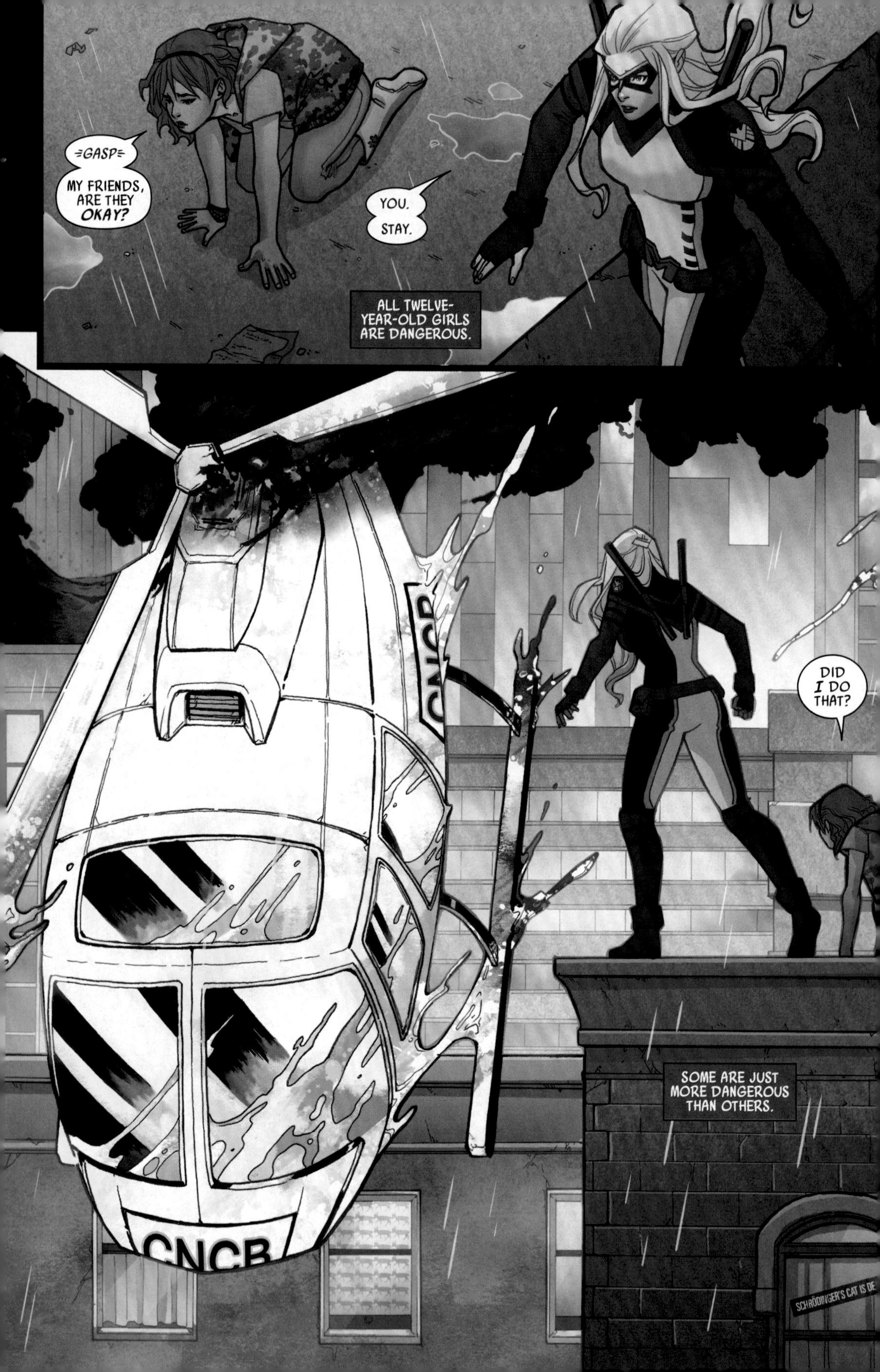

=GASP=
MY FRIENDS, ARE THEY OKAY?
YOU. STAY.
ALL TWELVE-YEAR-OLD GIRLS ARE DANGEROUS.
CNCB
DID I DO THAT?
SOME ARE JUST MORE DANGEROUS THAN OTHERS.
CNCB
SCHRÖDINGER'S CAT IS DE

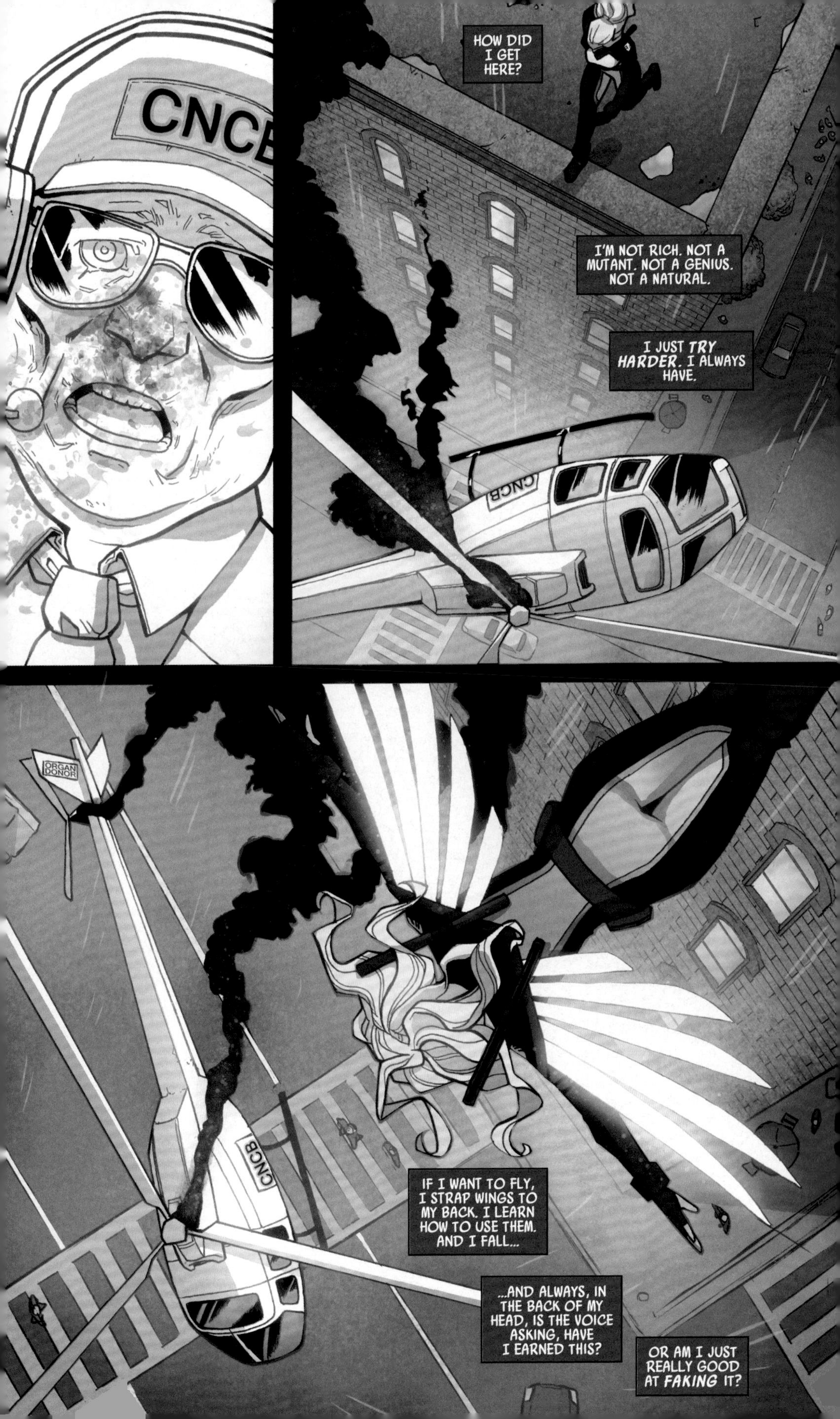
CNCB
HOW DID I GET HERE?
I'M NOT RICH. NOT A MUTANT. NOT A GENIUS. NOT A NATURAL.
I JUST TRY HARDER. I ALWAYS HAVE.
CNCB
ORGAN DONOR
CNCB
IF I WANT TO FLY, I STRAP WINGS TO MY BACK. I LEARN HOW TO USE THEM. AND I FALL...
...AND ALWAYS, IN THE BACK OF MY HEAD, IS THE VOICE ASKING, HAVE I EARNED THIS?
OR AM I JUST REALLY GOOD AT FAKING IT?

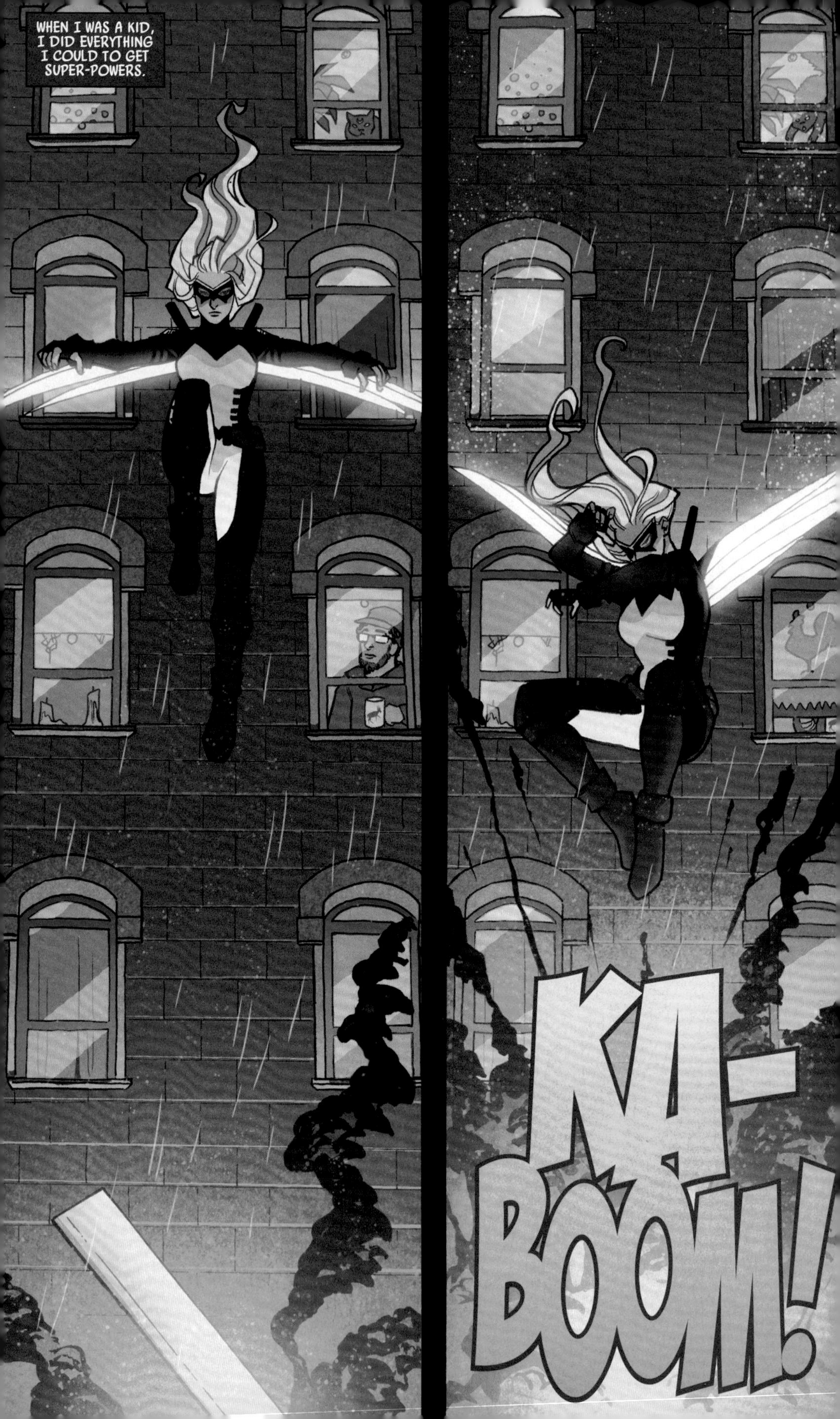
WHEN I WAS A KID, I DID EVERYTHING I COULD TO GET SUPER-POWERS.
KA-BOOM!

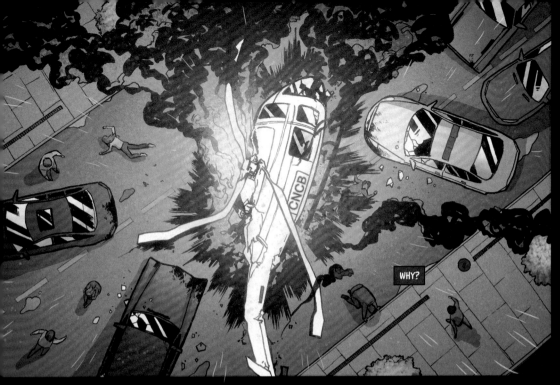

WHY?

I WANTED TO BE A HERO.

I WANTED TO BE CAPTAIN AMERICA.

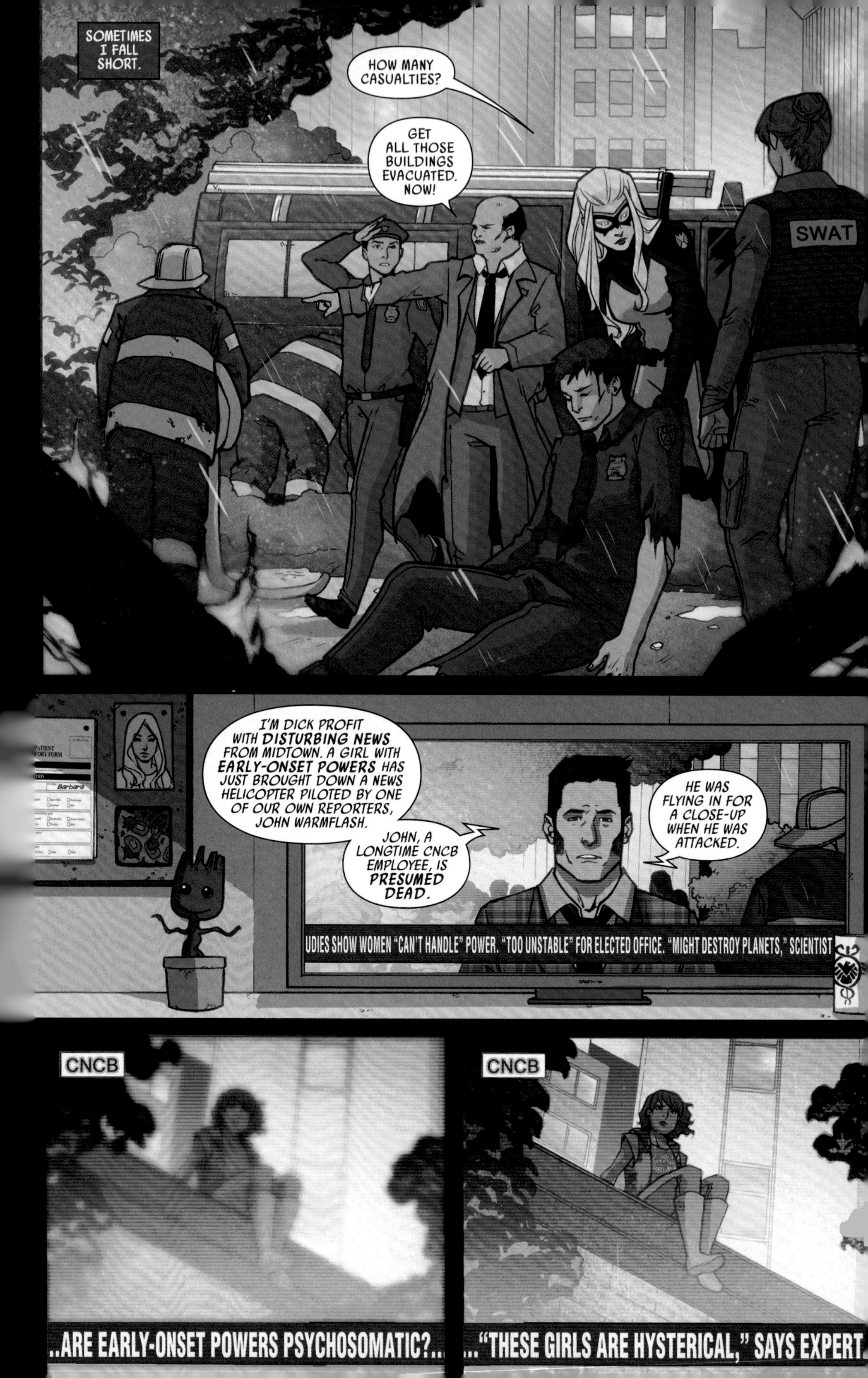
SOMETIMES I FALL SHORT.
HOW MANY CASUALTIES?
GET ALL THOSE BUILDINGS EVACUATED. NOW!
SWAT
I'M DICK PROFIT WITH DISTURBING NEWS FROM MIDTOWN. A GIRL WITH EARLY-ONSET POWERS HAS JUST BROUGHT DOWN A NEWS HELICOPTER PILOTED BY ONE OF OUR OWN REPORTERS, JOHN WARMFLASH.
JOHN, A LONGTIME CNCB EMPLOYEE, IS PRESUMED DEAD.
HE WAS FLYING IN FOR A CLOSE-UP WHEN HE WAS ATTACKED.
UDIES SHOW WOMEN "CAN'T HANDLE" POWER. "TOO UNSTABLE" FOR ELECTED OFFICE. "MIGHT DESTROY PLANETS," SCIENTIST
CNCB
..ARE EARLY-ONSET POWERS PSYCHOSOMATIC?...
CNCB
..."THESE GIRLS ARE HYSTERICAL," SAYS EXPERT.

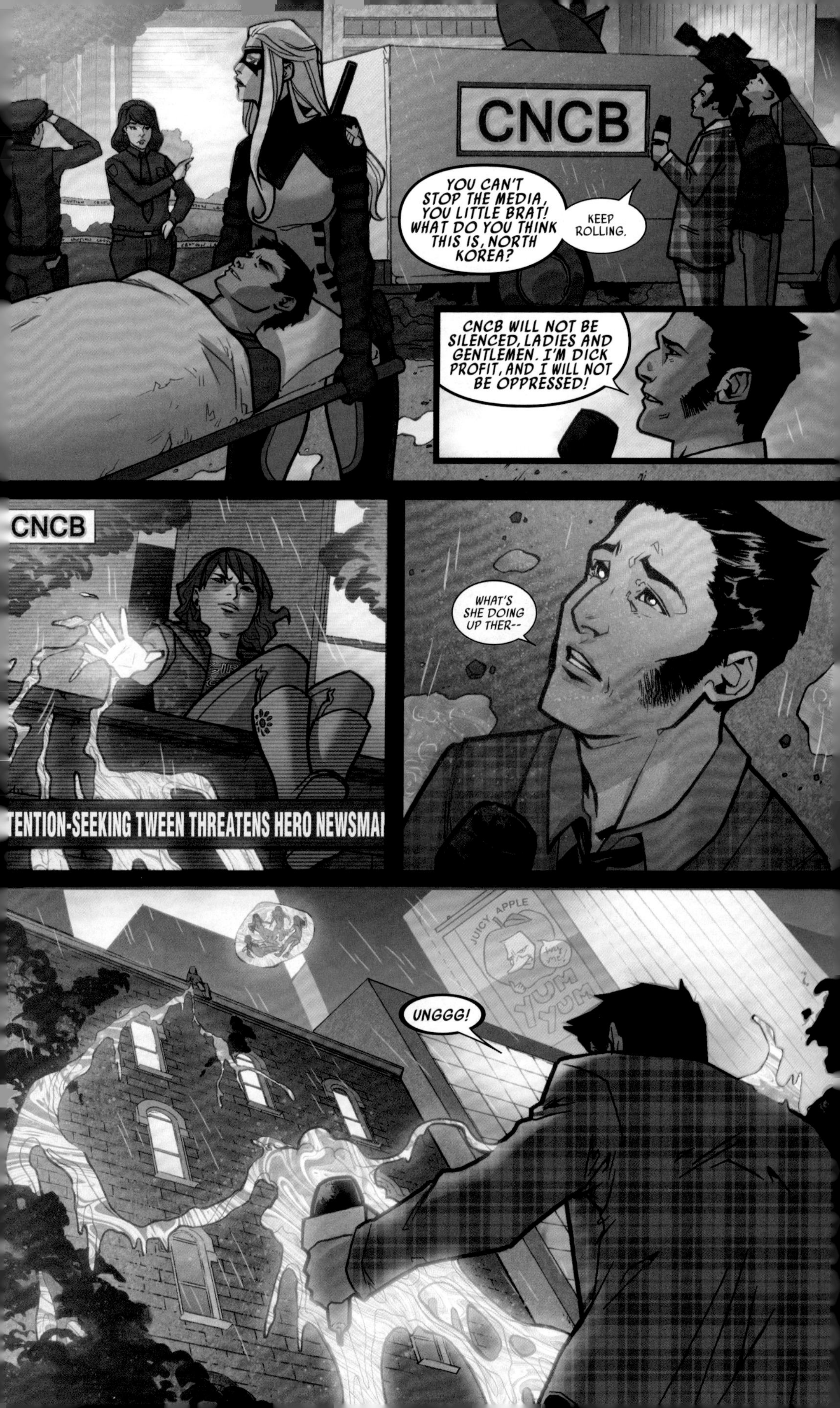
CNCB
YOU CAN'T STOP THE MEDIA, YOU LITTLE BRAT! WHAT DO YOU THINK THIS IS, NORTH KOREA?
KEEP ROLLING.
CNCB WILL NOT BE SILENCED, LADIES AND GENTLEMEN. I'M DICK PROFIT, AND I WILL NOT BE OPPRESSED!
CNCB
TENTION-SEEKING TWEEN THREATENS HERO NEWSMA
WHAT'S SHE DOING UP THER--
JUICY APPLE
YUM YUM
UNGGG!

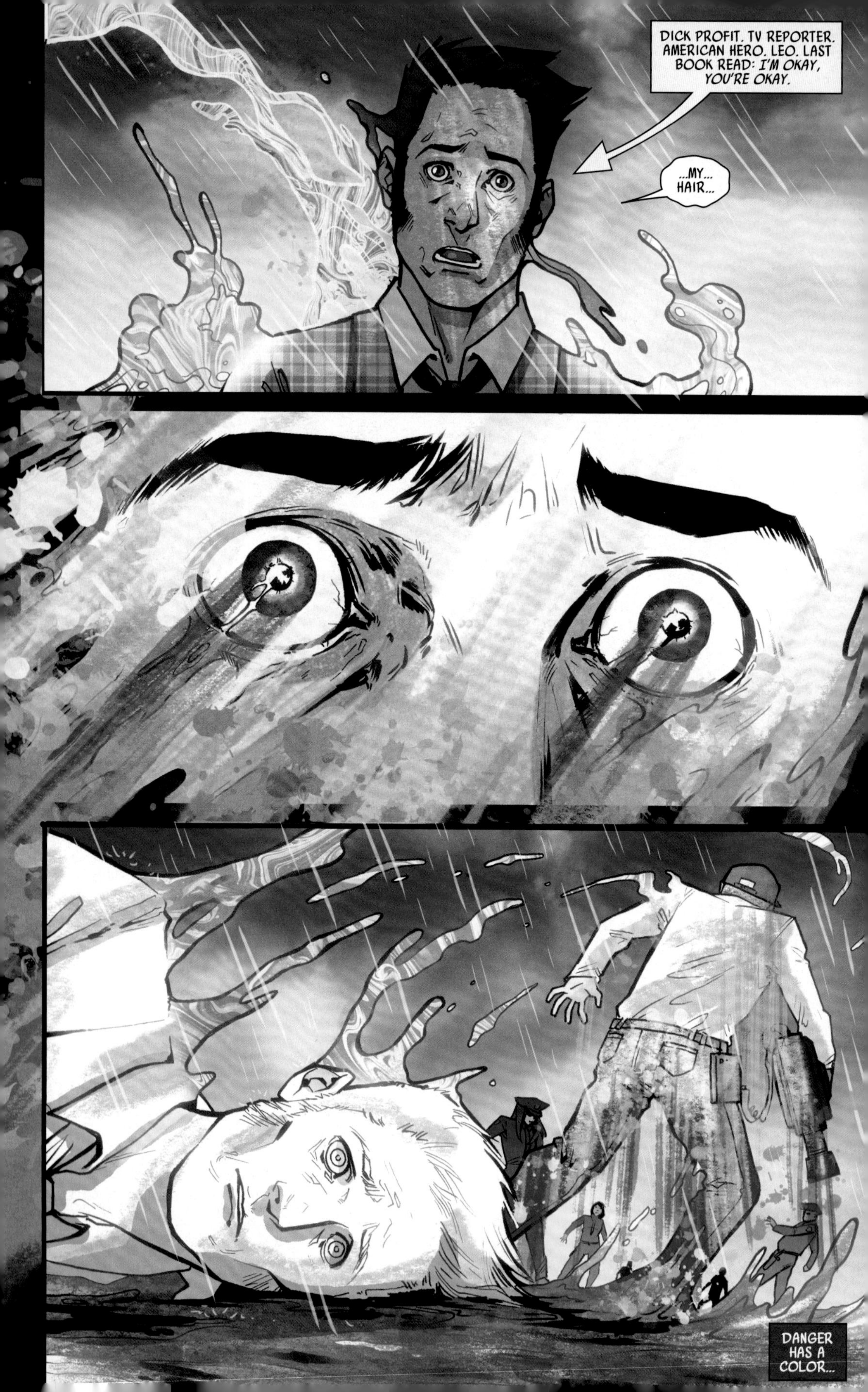
DICK PROFIT. TV REPORTER. AMERICAN HERO. LEO. LAST BOOK READ: *I'M OKAY, YOU'RE OKAY.*
...MY... HAIR...
DANGER HAS A COLOR...

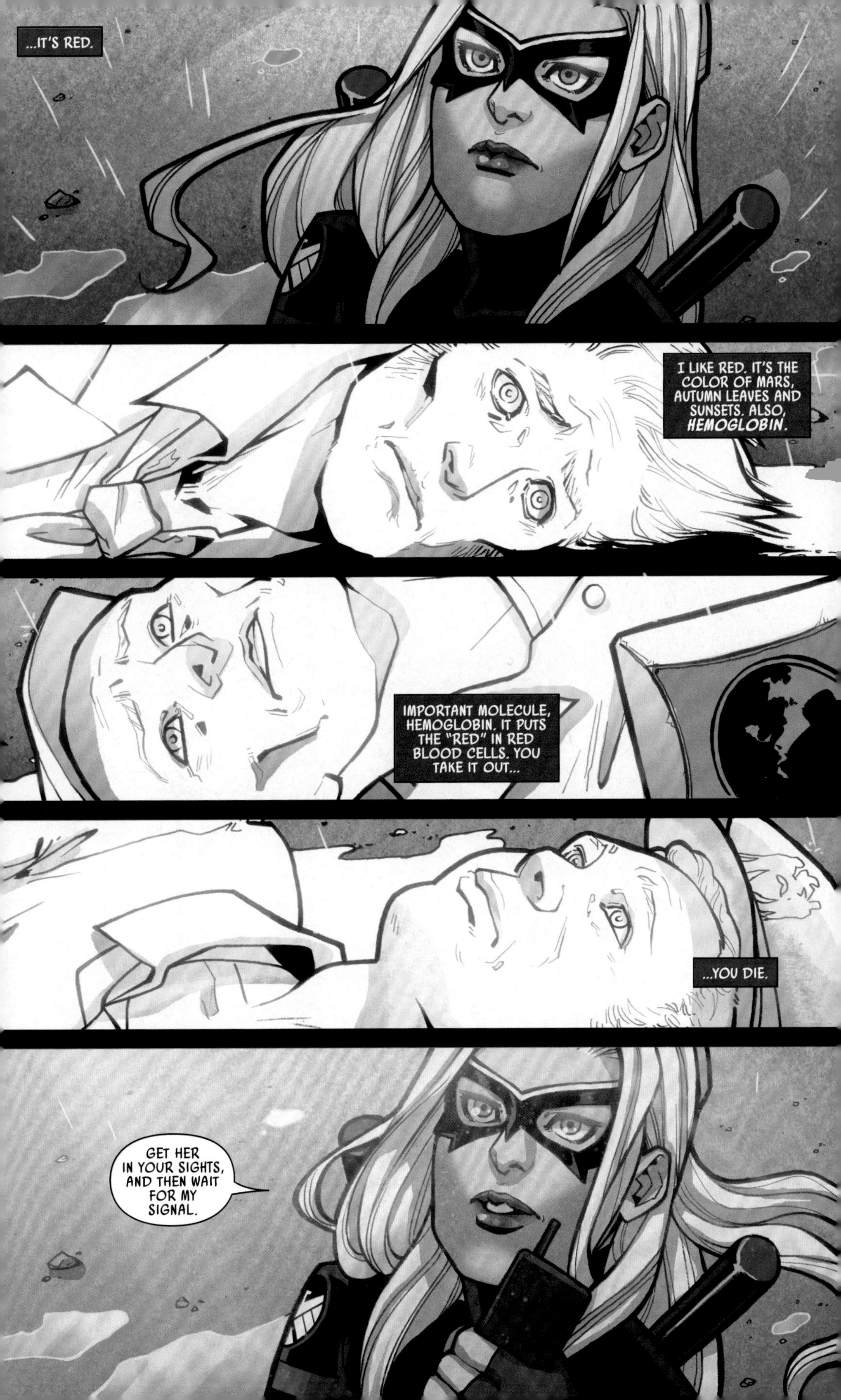
...IT'S RED.
I LIKE RED. IT'S THE COLOR OF MARS, AUTUMN LEAVES AND SUNSETS. ALSO, HEMOGLOBIN.
IMPORTANT MOLECULE, HEMOGLOBIN. IT PUTS THE "RED" IN RED BLOOD CELLS. YOU TAKE IT OUT...
...YOU DIE.
GET HER IN YOUR SIGHTS, AND THEN WAIT FOR MY SIGNAL.

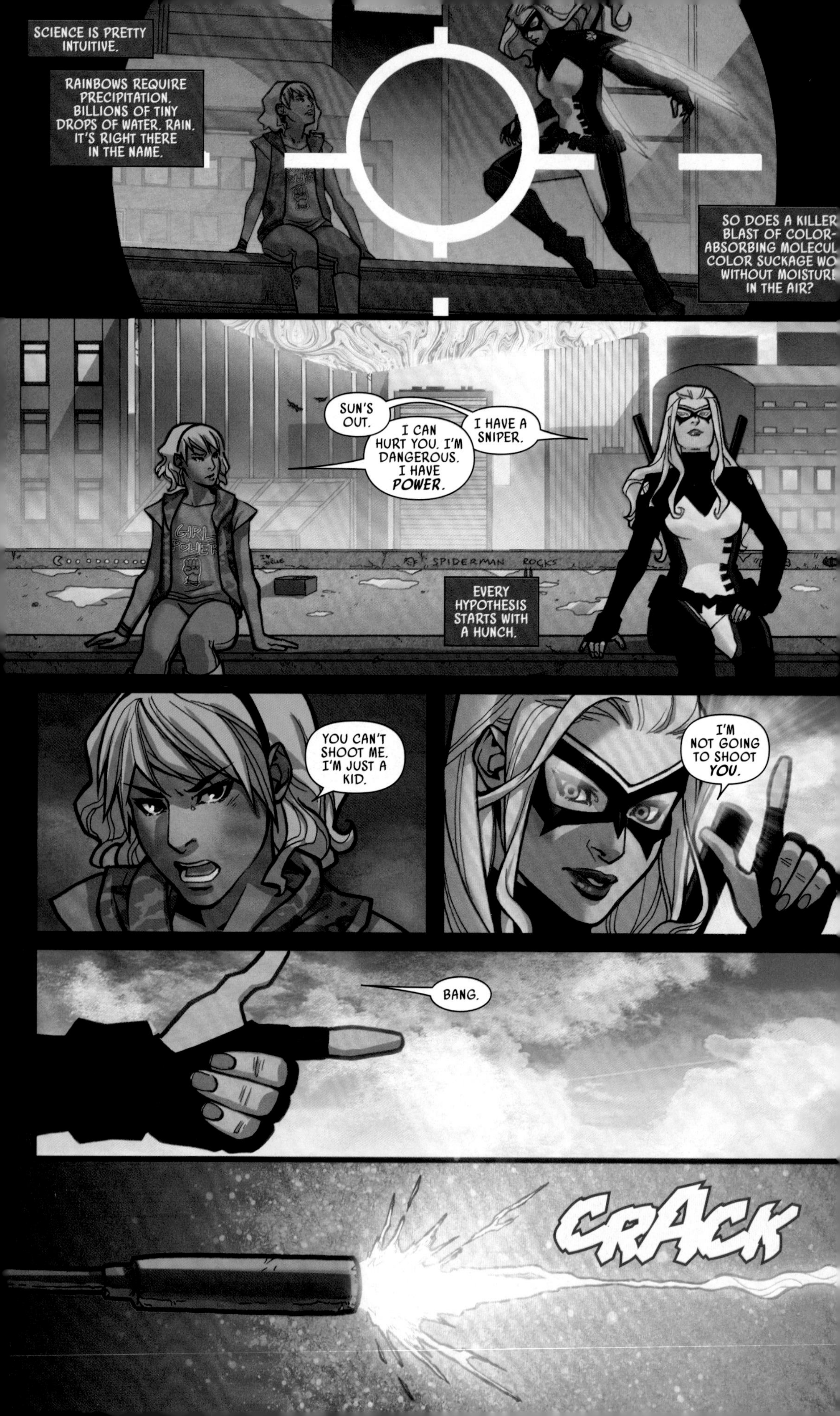
SCIENCE IS PRETTY INTUITIVE.
RAINBOWS REQUIRE PRECIPITATION. BILLIONS OF TINY DROPS OF WATER. RAIN. IT'S RIGHT THERE IN THE NAME.
SO DOES A KILLER BLAST OF COLOR-ABSORBING MOLECUL COLOR SUCKAGE WO WITHOUT MOISTUR IN THE AIR?
SUN'S OUT.
I HAVE A SNIPER.
I CAN HURT YOU. I'M DANGEROUS. I HAVE POWER.
GIRL POWER
SPIDERMAN ROCKS
EVERY HYPOTHESIS STARTS WITH A HUNCH.
YOU CAN'T SHOOT ME. I'M JUST A KID.
I'M NOT GOING TO SHOOT YOU.
BANG.
CRACK

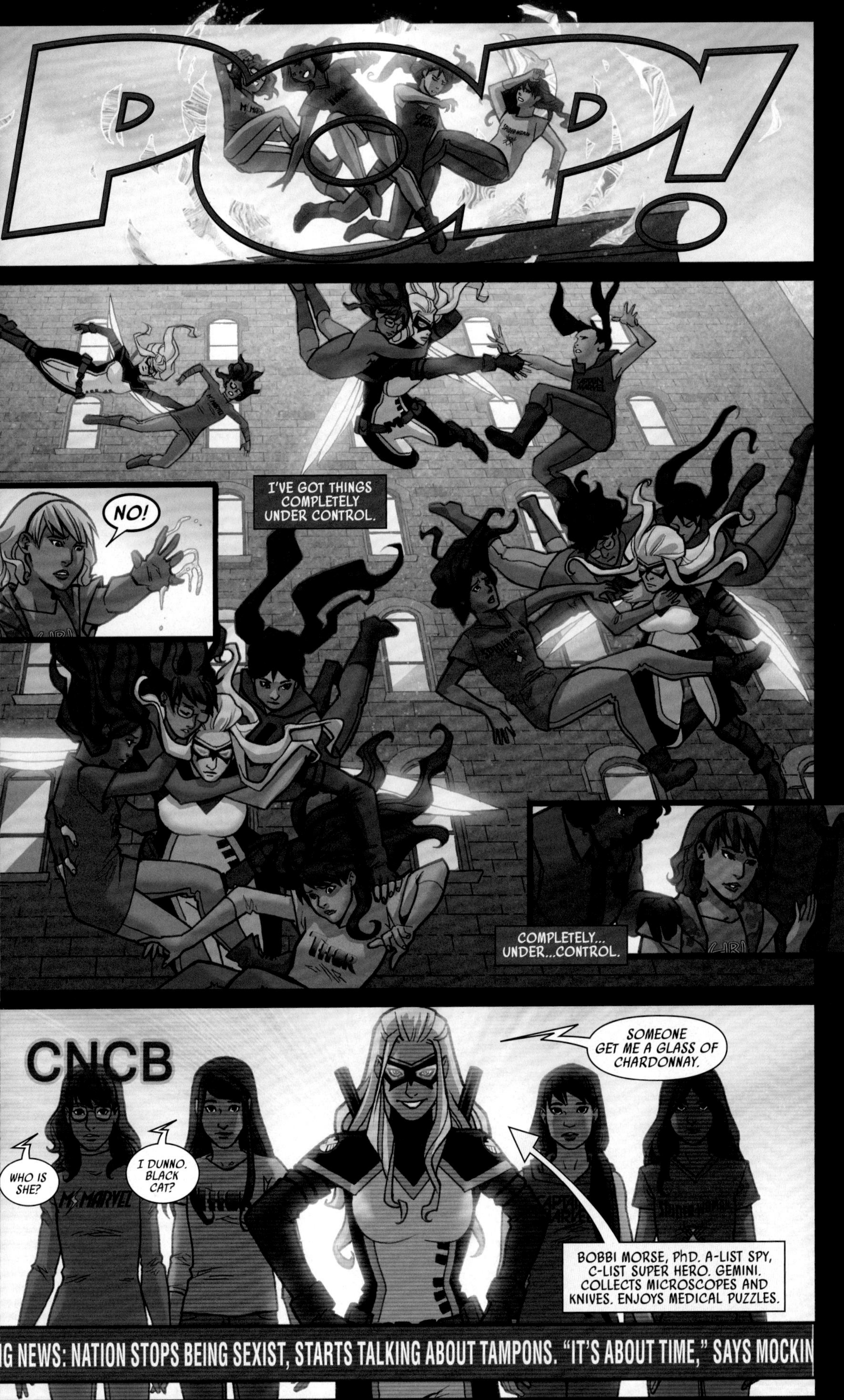
POP!
NO!
I'VE GOT THINGS COMPLETELY UNDER CONTROL.
COMPLETELY... UNDER...CONTROL.
CNCB
SOMEONE GET ME A GLASS OF CHARDONNAY.
WHO IS SHE?
I DUNNO. BLACK CAT?
BOBBI MORSE, PhD. A-LIST SPY, C-LIST SUPER HERO. GEMINI. COLLECTS MICROSCOPES AND KNIVES. ENJOYS MEDICAL PUZZLES.
G NEWS: NATION STOPS BEING SEXIST, STARTS TALKING ABOUT TAMPONS. "IT'S ABOUT TIME," SAYS MOCKIN

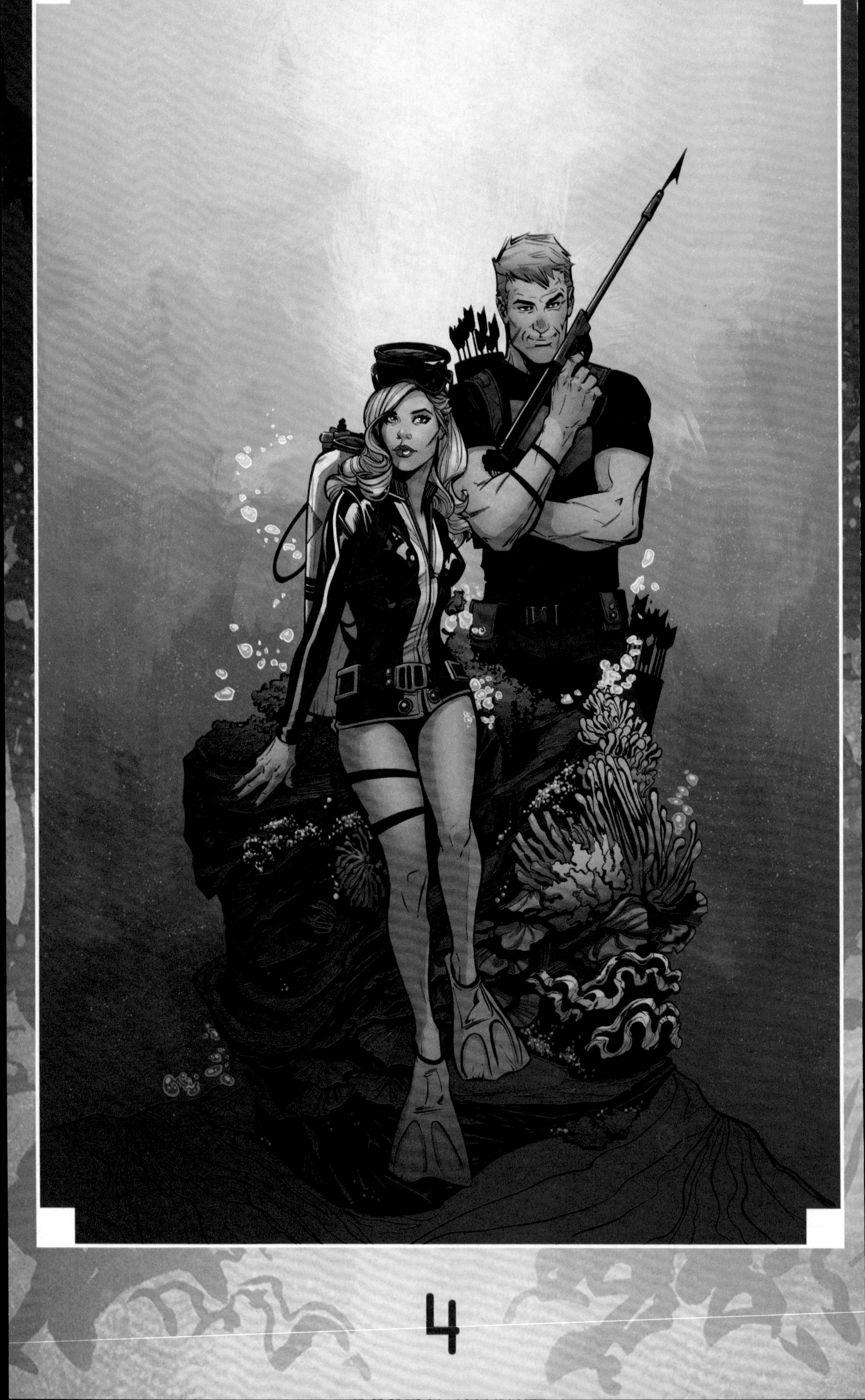

4

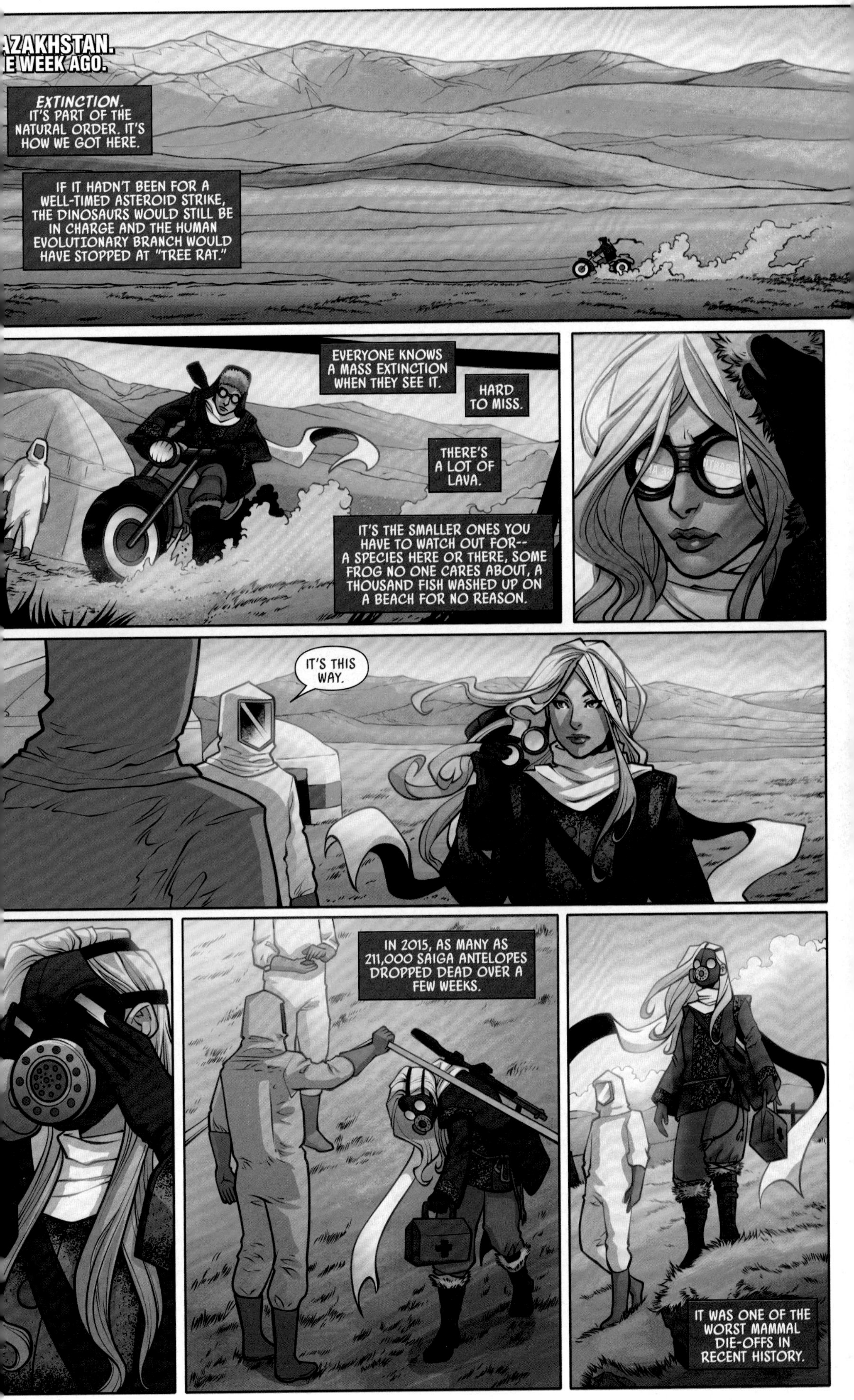

AZAKHSTAN.
E WEEK AGO.
EXTINCTION. IT'S PART OF THE NATURAL ORDER. IT'S HOW WE GOT HERE.
IF IT HADN'T BEEN FOR A WELL-TIMED ASTEROID STRIKE, THE DINOSAURS WOULD STILL BE IN CHARGE AND THE HUMAN EVOLUTIONARY BRANCH WOULD HAVE STOPPED AT "TREE RAT."
EVERYONE KNOWS A MASS EXTINCTION WHEN THEY SEE IT.
HARD TO MISS.
THERE'S A LOT OF LAVA.
IT'S THE SMALLER ONES YOU HAVE TO WATCH OUT FOR-- A SPECIES HERE OR THERE, SOME FROG NO ONE CARES ABOUT, A THOUSAND FISH WASHED UP ON A BEACH FOR NO REASON.
IT'S THIS WAY.
IN 2015, AS MANY AS 211,000 SAIGA ANTELOPES DROPPED DEAD OVER A FEW WEEKS.
IT WAS ONE OF THE WORST MAMMAL DIE-OFFS IN RECENT HISTORY.

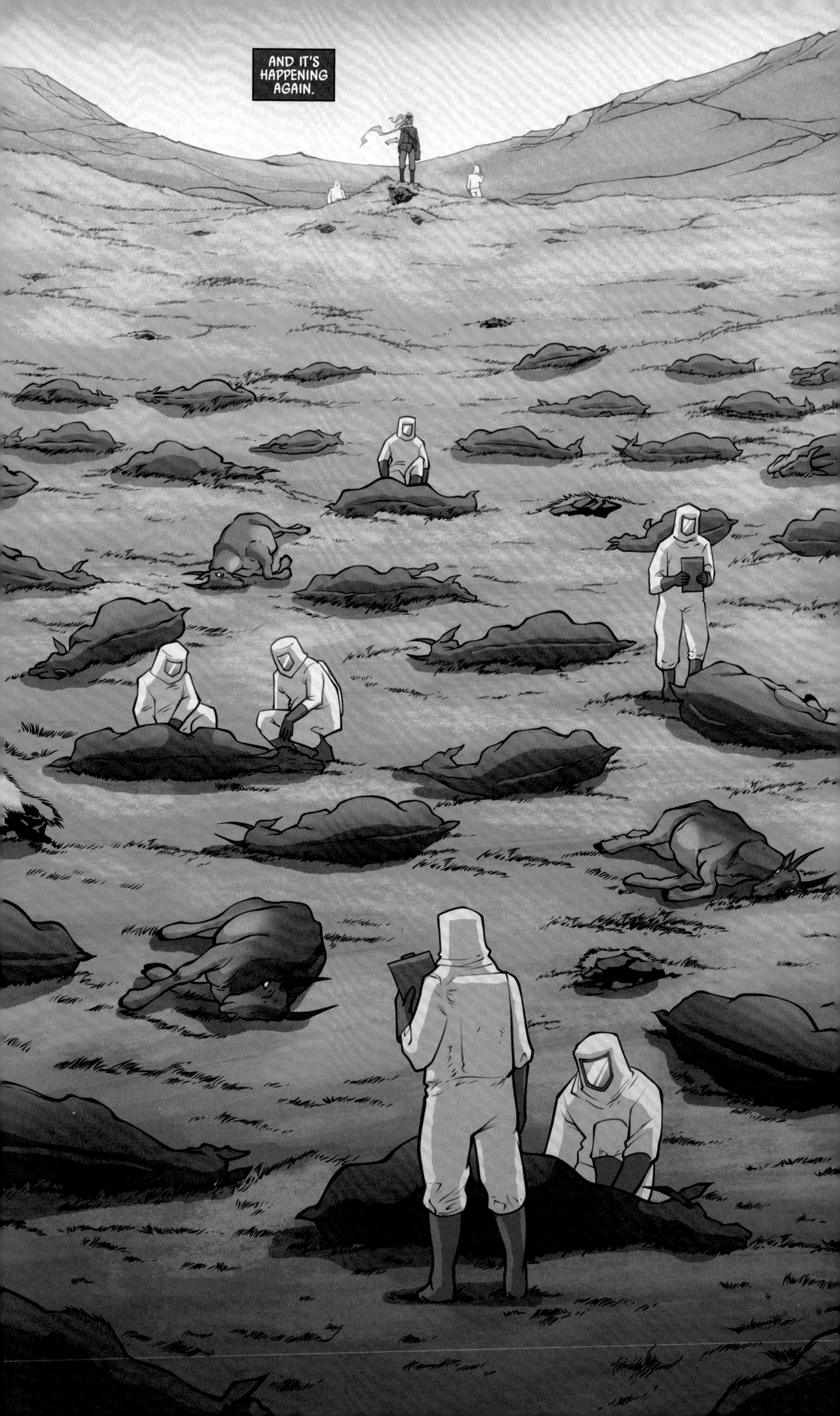
AND IT'S HAPPENING AGAIN.

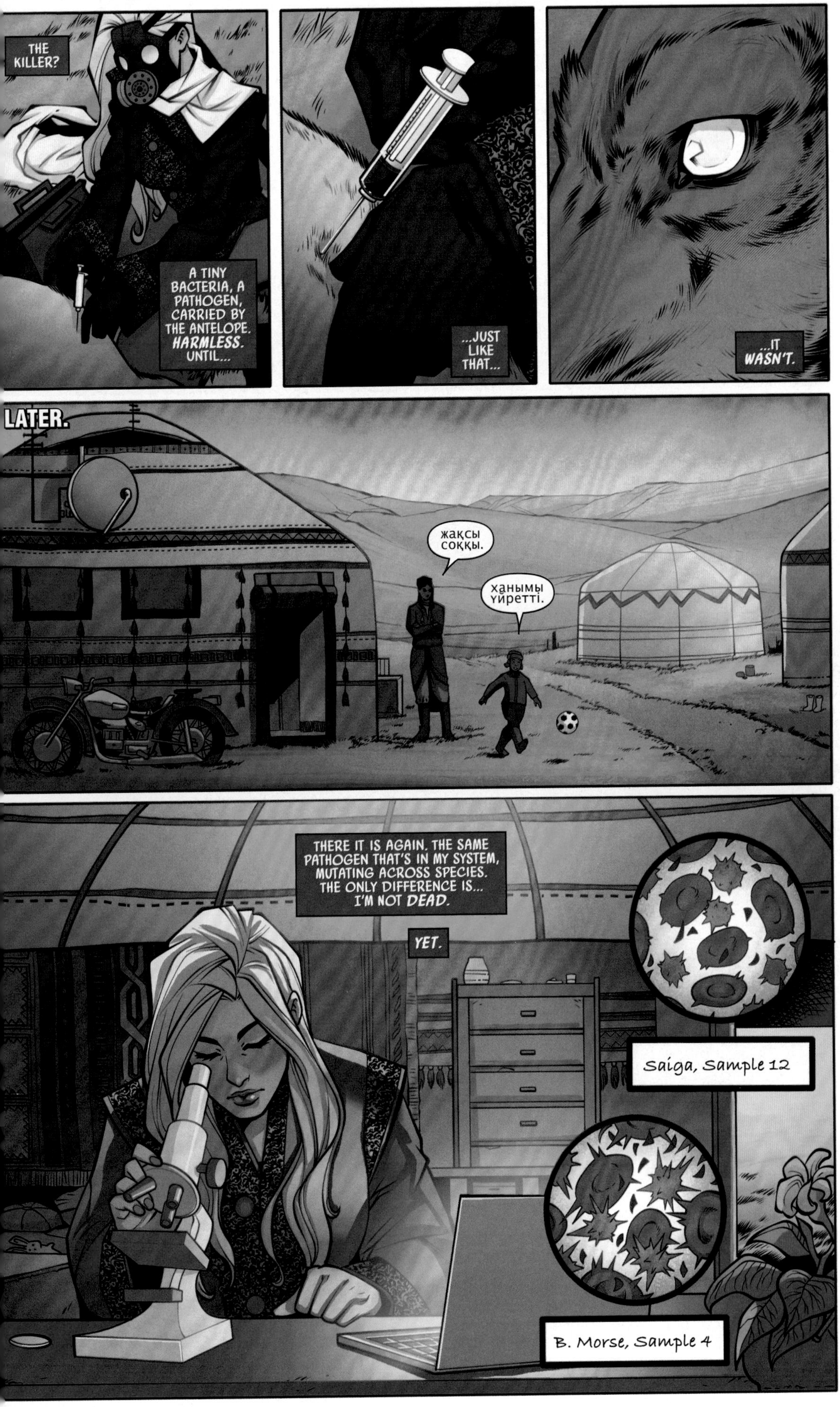
THE KILLER?
A TINY BACTERIA, A PATHOGEN, CARRIED BY THE ANTELOPE. HARMLESS. UNTIL...
...JUST LIKE THAT...
...IT WASN'T.
LATER.
жақсы соққы.
ханымы үйретті.
THERE IT IS AGAIN. THE SAME PATHOGEN THAT'S IN MY SYSTEM, MUTATING ACROSS SPECIES. THE ONLY DIFFERENCE IS... I'M NOT DEAD.
YET.
Saiga, Sample 12
B. Morse, Sample 4

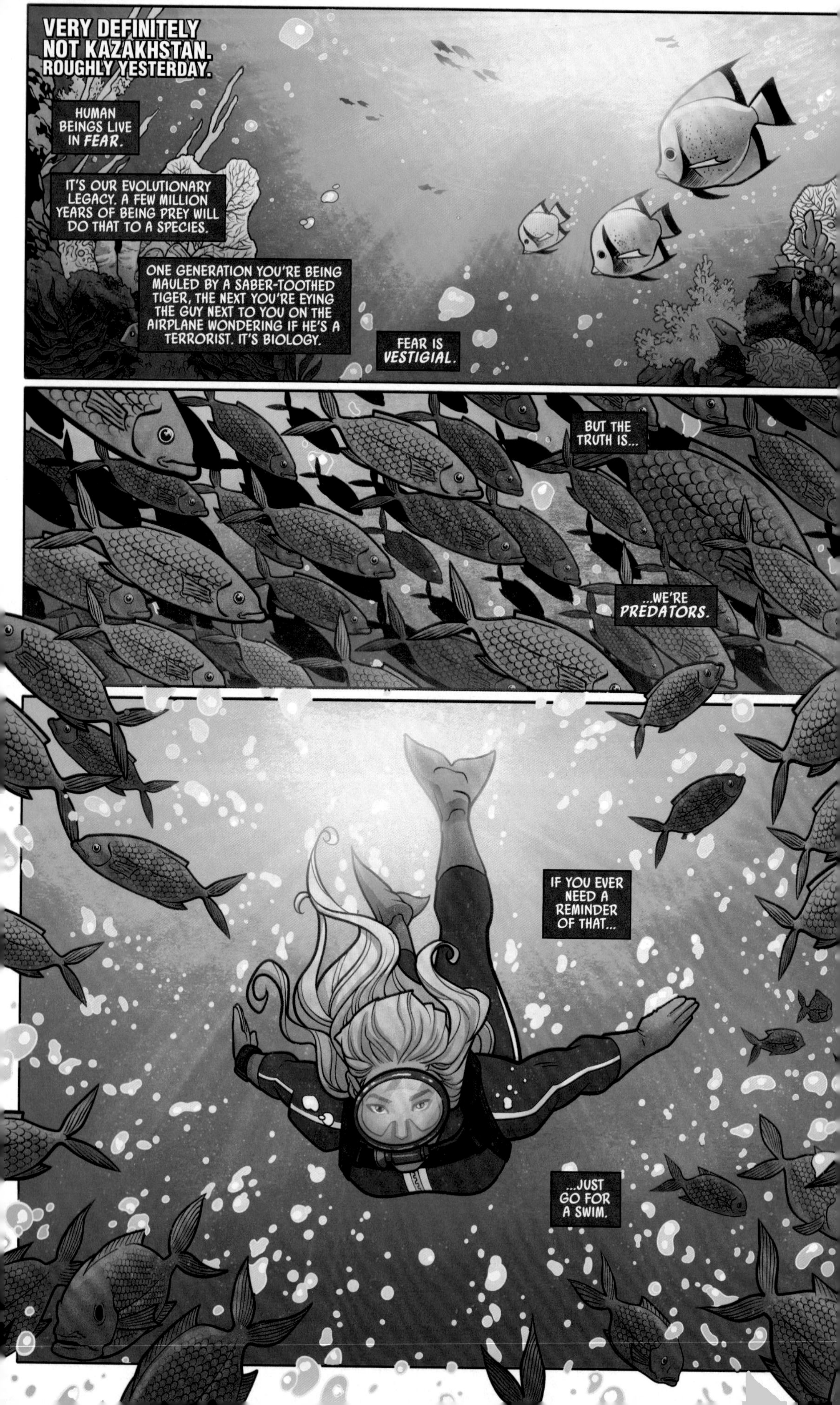
VERY DEFINITELY NOT KAZAKHSTAN. ROUGHLY YESTERDAY.
HUMAN BEINGS LIVE IN FEAR.
IT'S OUR EVOLUTIONARY LEGACY. A FEW MILLION YEARS OF BEING PREY WILL DO THAT TO A SPECIES.
ONE GENERATION YOU'RE BEING MAULED BY A SABER-TOOTHED TIGER, THE NEXT YOU'RE EYING THE GUY NEXT TO YOU ON THE AIRPLANE WONDERING IF HE'S A TERRORIST. IT'S BIOLOGY.
FEAR IS VESTIGIAL.
BUT THE TRUTH IS...
...WE'RE PREDATORS.
IF YOU EVER NEED A REMINDER OF THAT...
...JUST GO FOR A SWIM.

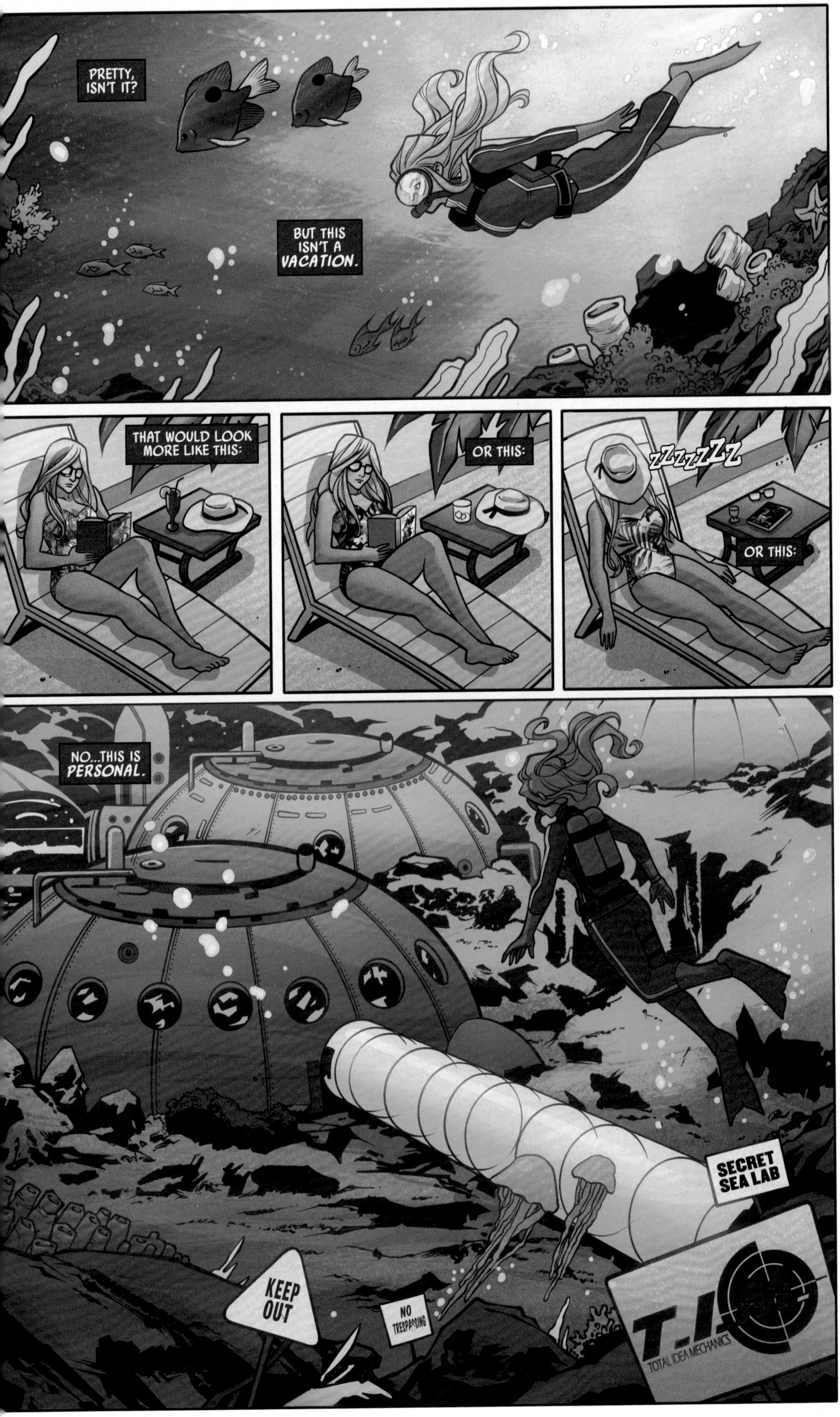
PRETTY, ISN'T IT?
BUT THIS ISN'T A *VACATION*.
THAT WOULD LOOK MORE LIKE THIS:
OR THIS:
ZZZZZZZ
OR THIS:
NO...THIS IS *PERSONAL*.
SECRET SEA LAB
KEEP OUT
NO TRESPASSING
TOTAL IDEA MECHANICS

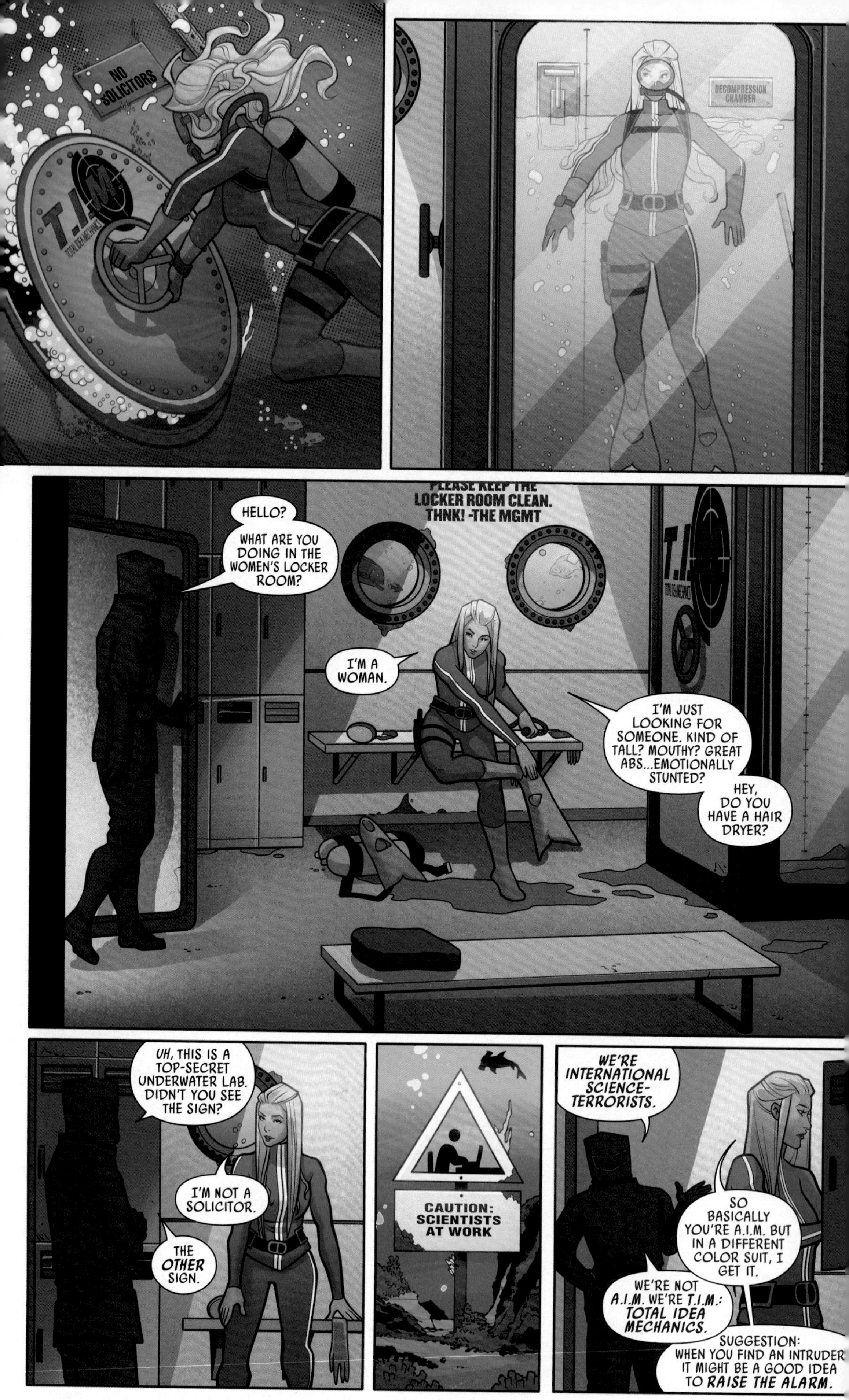
NO SOLICITORS
T.I.M. TOTAL IDEA MECHANICS
DECOMPRESSION CHAMBER
PLEASE KEEP THE LOCKER ROOM CLEAN. THNK! -THE MGMT
HELLO?
WHAT ARE YOU DOING IN THE WOMEN'S LOCKER ROOM?
I'M A WOMAN.
I'M JUST LOOKING FOR SOMEONE. KIND OF TALL? MOUTHY? GREAT ABS...EMOTIONALLY STUNTED?
HEY, DO YOU HAVE A HAIR DRYER?
UH, THIS IS A TOP-SECRET UNDERWATER LAB. DIDN'T YOU SEE THE SIGN?
I'M NOT A SOLICITOR.
THE OTHER SIGN.
CAUTION: SCIENTISTS AT WORK
WE'RE INTERNATIONAL SCIENCE-TERRORISTS.
SO BASICALLY YOU'RE A.I.M. BUT IN A DIFFERENT COLOR SUIT, I GET IT.
WE'RE NOT A.I.M. WE'RE T.I.M.: TOTAL IDEA MECHANICS.
SUGGESTION: WHEN YOU FIND AN INTRUDER IT MIGHT BE A GOOD IDEA TO RAISE THE ALARM.

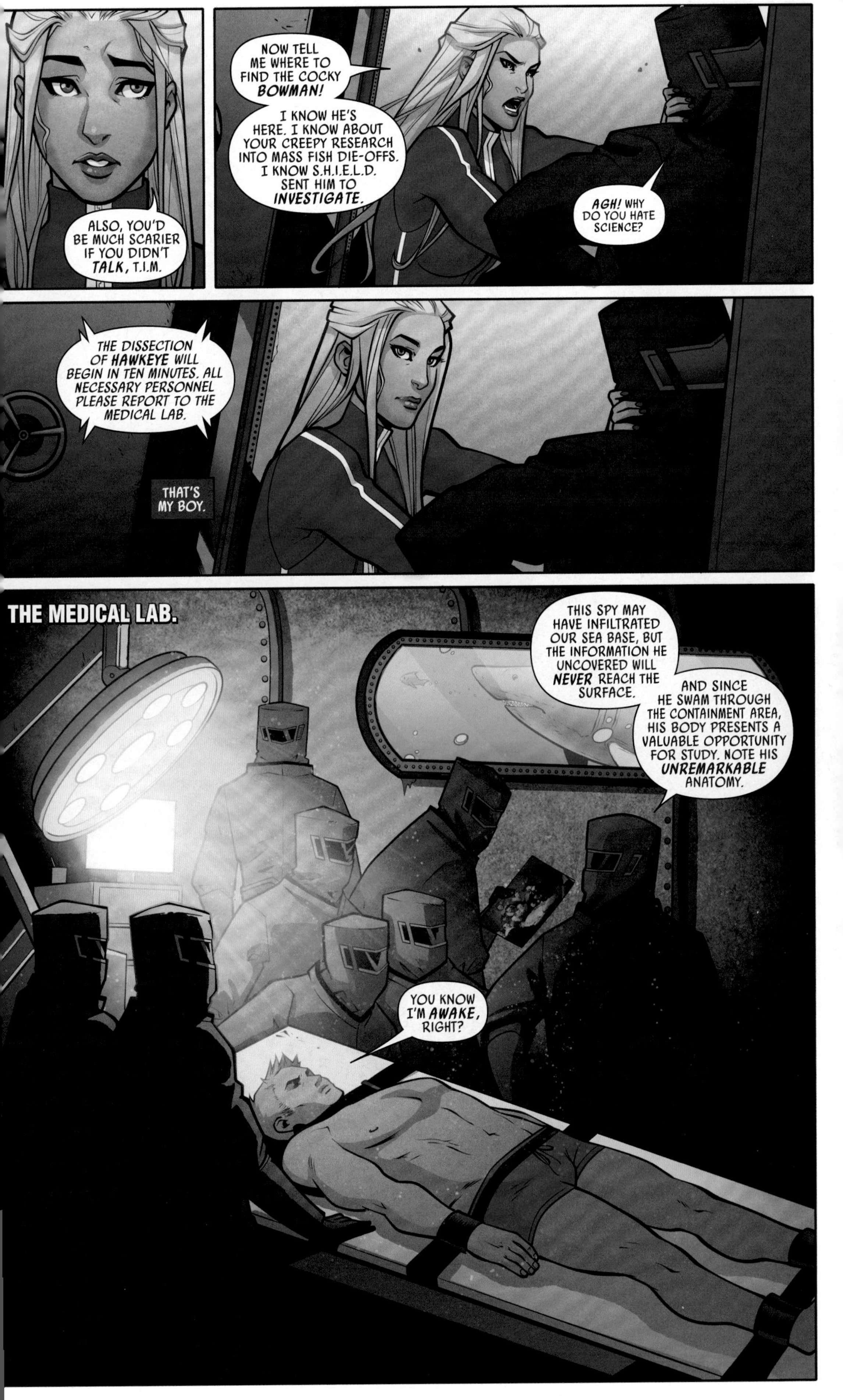
ALSO, YOU'D BE MUCH SCARIER IF YOU DIDN'T TALK, T.I.M.
NOW TELL ME WHERE TO FIND THE COCKY BOWMAN!
I KNOW HE'S HERE. I KNOW ABOUT YOUR CREEPY RESEARCH INTO MASS FISH DIE-OFFS. I KNOW S.H.I.E.L.D. SENT HIM TO INVESTIGATE.
AGH! WHY DO YOU HATE SCIENCE?
THE DISSECTION OF HAWKEYE WILL BEGIN IN TEN MINUTES. ALL NECESSARY PERSONNEL PLEASE REPORT TO THE MEDICAL LAB.
THAT'S MY BOY.
THE MEDICAL LAB.
THIS SPY MAY HAVE INFILTRATED OUR SEA BASE, BUT THE INFORMATION HE UNCOVERED WILL NEVER REACH THE SURFACE.
AND SINCE HE SWAM THROUGH THE CONTAINMENT AREA, HIS BODY PRESENTS A VALUABLE OPPORTUNITY FOR STUDY. NOTE HIS UNREMARKABLE ANATOMY.
YOU KNOW I'M AWAKE, RIGHT?

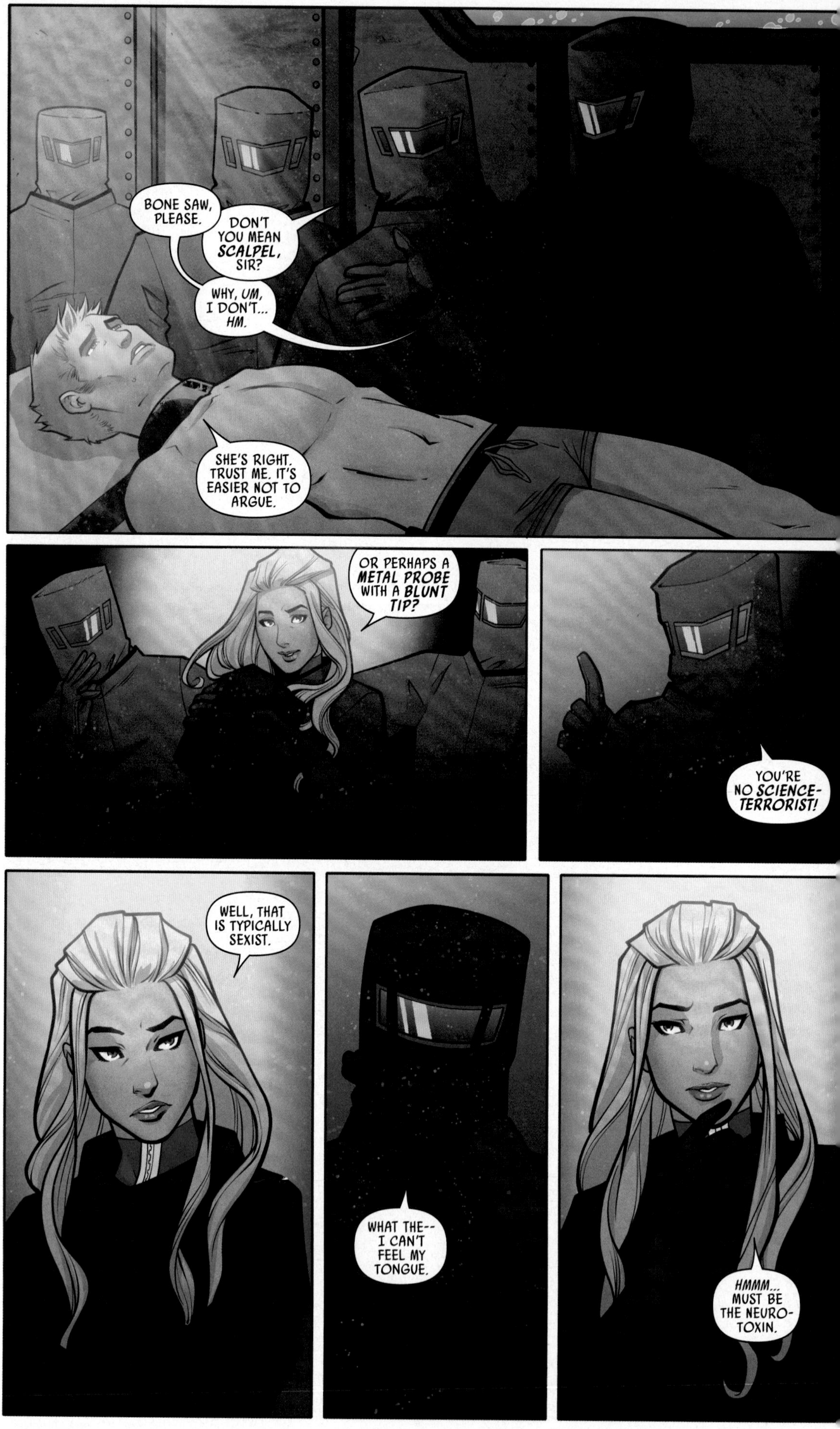
BONE SAW, PLEASE.
DON'T YOU MEAN SCALPEL, SIR?
WHY, UM, I DON'T... HM.
SHE'S RIGHT. TRUST ME. IT'S EASIER NOT TO ARGUE.
OR PERHAPS A METAL PROBE WITH A BLUNT TIP?
YOU'RE NO SCIENCE-TERRORIST!
WELL, THAT IS TYPICALLY SEXIST.
WHAT THE-- I CAN'T FEEL MY TONGUE.
HMMM... MUST BE THE NEURO-TOXIN.

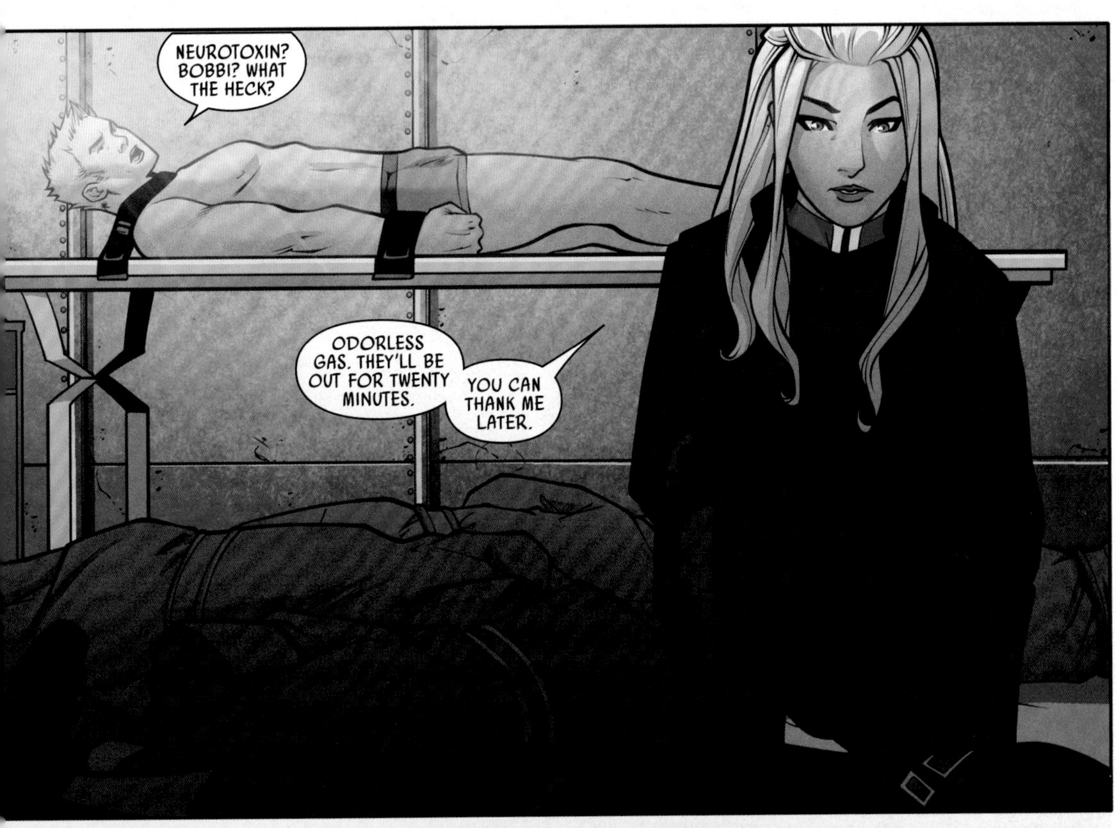
NEUROTOXIN? BOBBI? WHAT THE HECK?
ODORLESS GAS. THEY'LL BE OUT FOR TWENTY MINUTES.
YOU CAN THANK ME LATER.

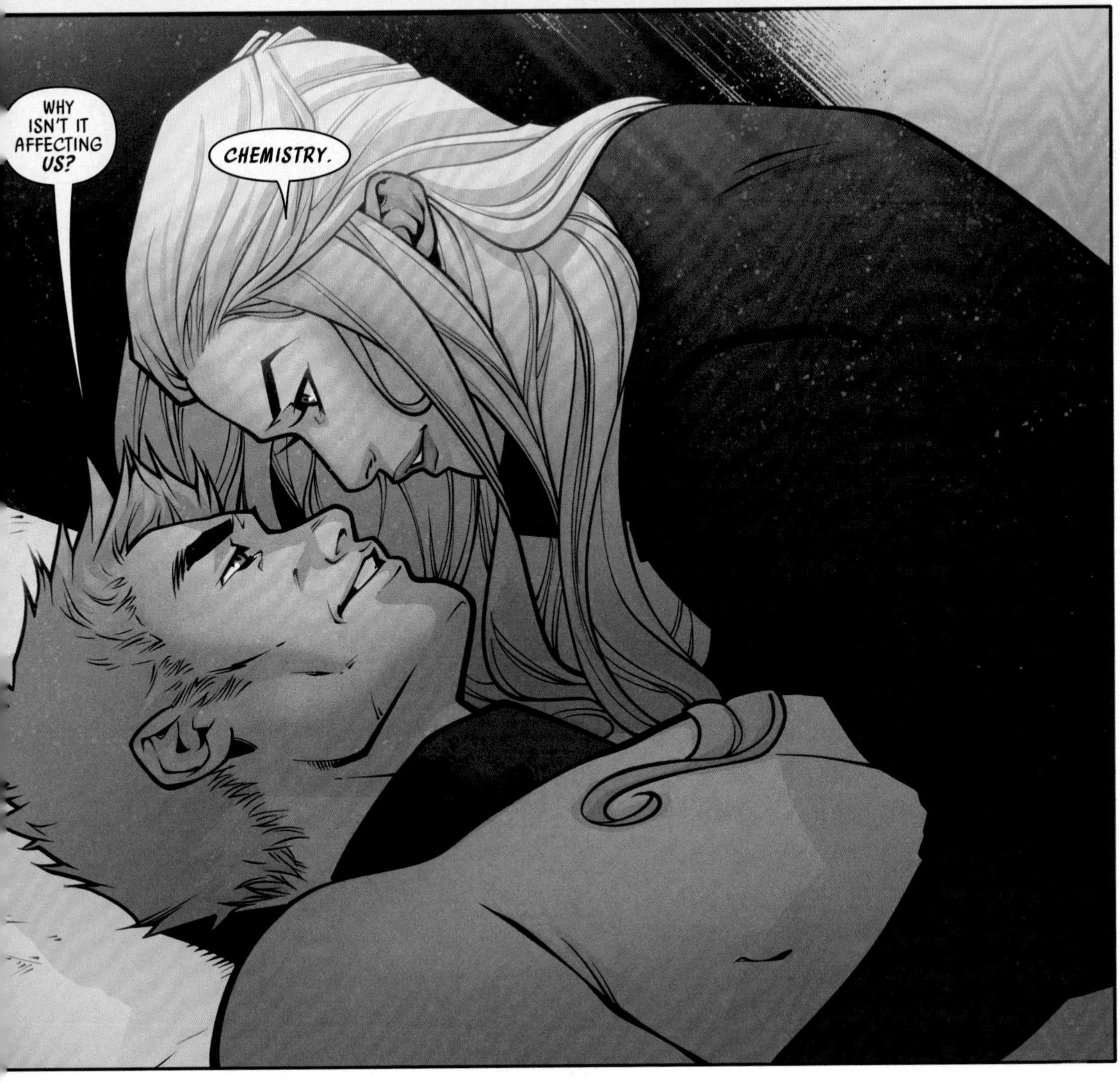
WHY ISN'T IT AFFECTING *US?*
CHEMISTRY.

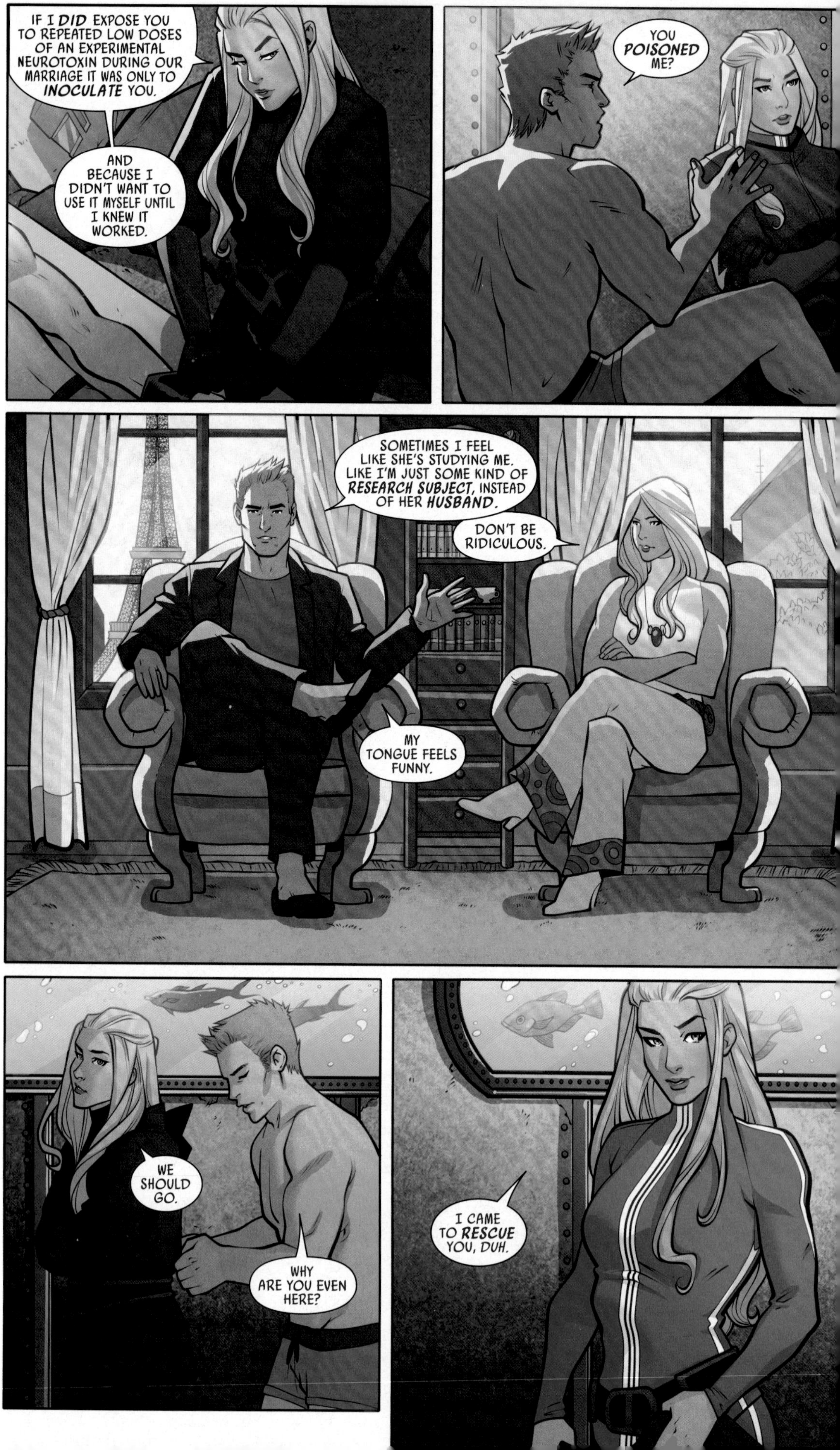
IF I DID EXPOSE YOU TO REPEATED LOW DOSES OF AN EXPERIMENTAL NEUROTOXIN DURING OUR MARRIAGE IT WAS ONLY TO INOCULATE YOU.
AND BECAUSE I DIDN'T WANT TO USE IT MYSELF UNTIL I KNEW IT WORKED.
YOU POISONED ME?
SOMETIMES I FEEL LIKE SHE'S STUDYING ME. LIKE I'M JUST SOME KIND OF RESEARCH SUBJECT, INSTEAD OF HER HUSBAND.
DON'T BE RIDICULOUS.
MY TONGUE FEELS FUNNY.
WE SHOULD GO.
WHY ARE YOU EVEN HERE?
I CAME TO RESCUE YOU, DUH.

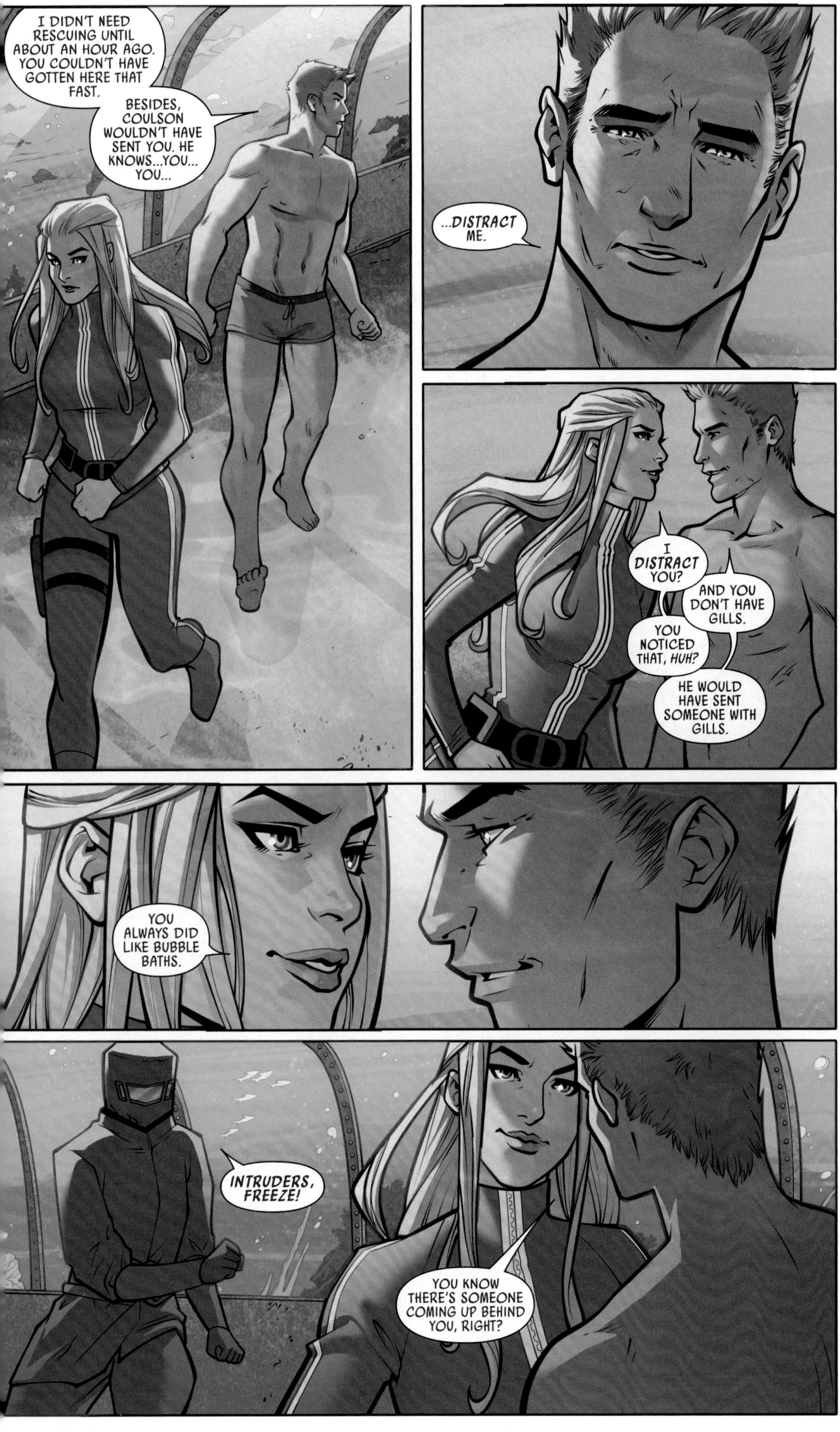
I DIDN'T NEED RESCUING UNTIL ABOUT AN HOUR AGO. YOU COULDN'T HAVE GOTTEN HERE THAT FAST.
BESIDES, COULSON WOULDN'T HAVE SENT YOU. HE KNOWS...YOU... YOU...
...DISTRACT ME.
I DISTRACT YOU?
AND YOU DON'T HAVE GILLS.
YOU NOTICED THAT, HUH?
HE WOULD HAVE SENT SOMEONE WITH GILLS.
YOU ALWAYS DID LIKE BUBBLE BATHS.
INTRUDERS, FREEZE!
YOU KNOW THERE'S SOMEONE COMING UP BEHIND YOU, RIGHT?

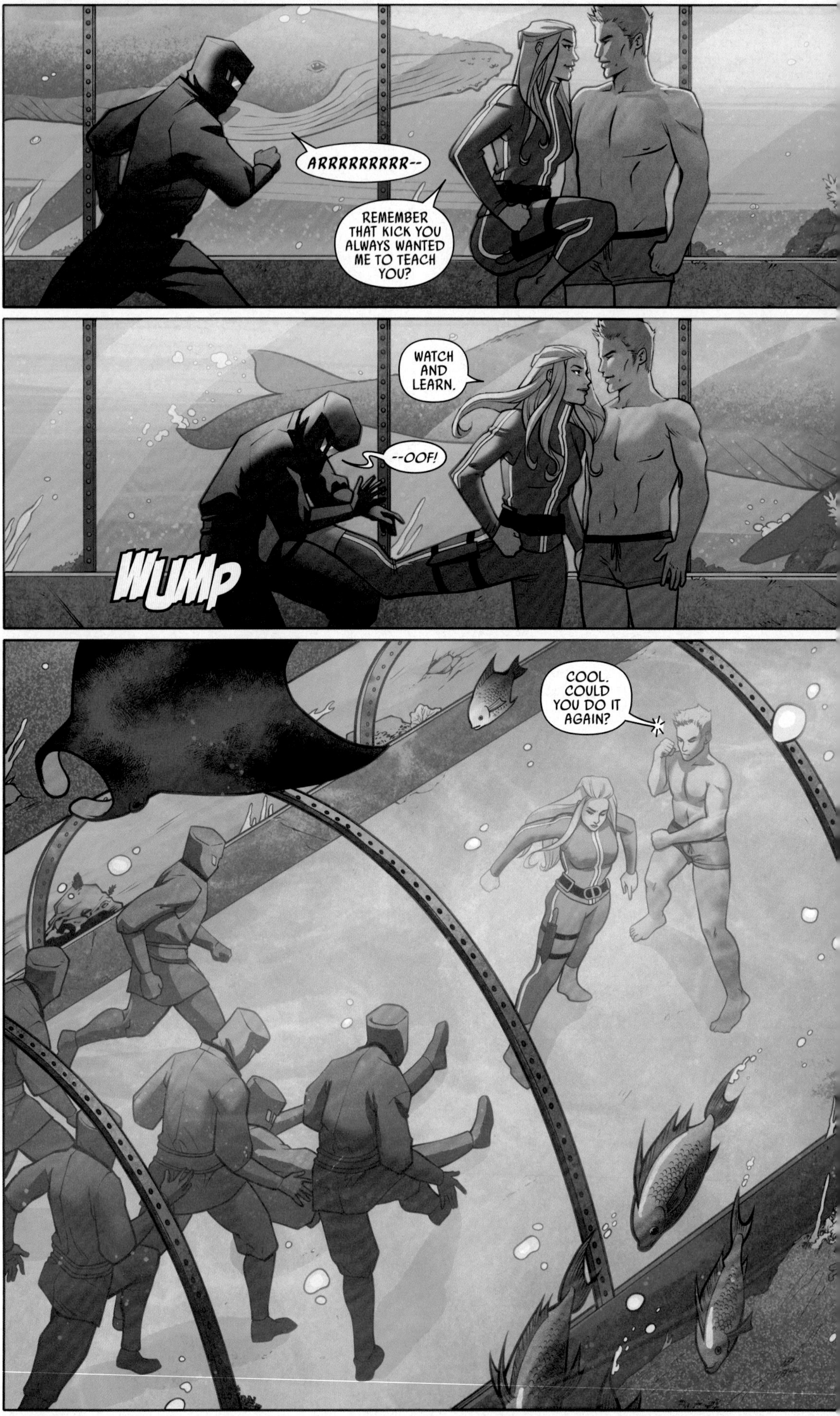
ARRRRRRRRR--
REMEMBER THAT KICK YOU ALWAYS WANTED ME TO TEACH YOU?
WATCH AND LEARN.
--OOF!
WUMP
COOL. COULD YOU DO IT AGAIN?

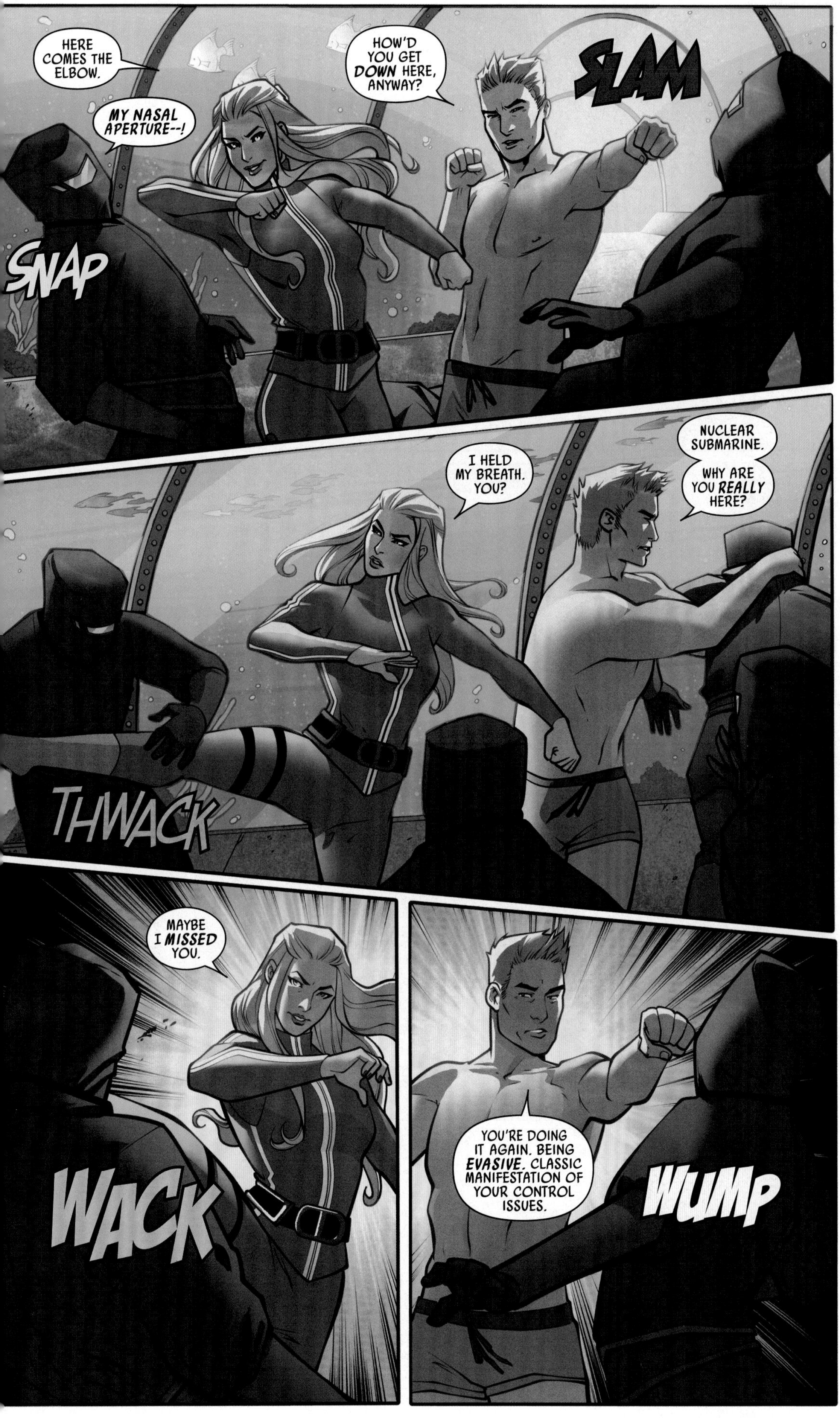
HERE COMES THE ELBOW.
MY NASAL APERTURE--!
HOW'D YOU GET DOWN HERE, ANYWAY?
SLAM
SNAP
I HELD MY BREATH. YOU?
NUCLEAR SUBMARINE.
WHY ARE YOU REALLY HERE?
THWACK
MAYBE I MISSED YOU.
WACK
YOU'RE DOING IT AGAIN. BEING EVASIVE. CLASSIC MANIFESTATION OF YOUR CONTROL ISSUES.
WUMP

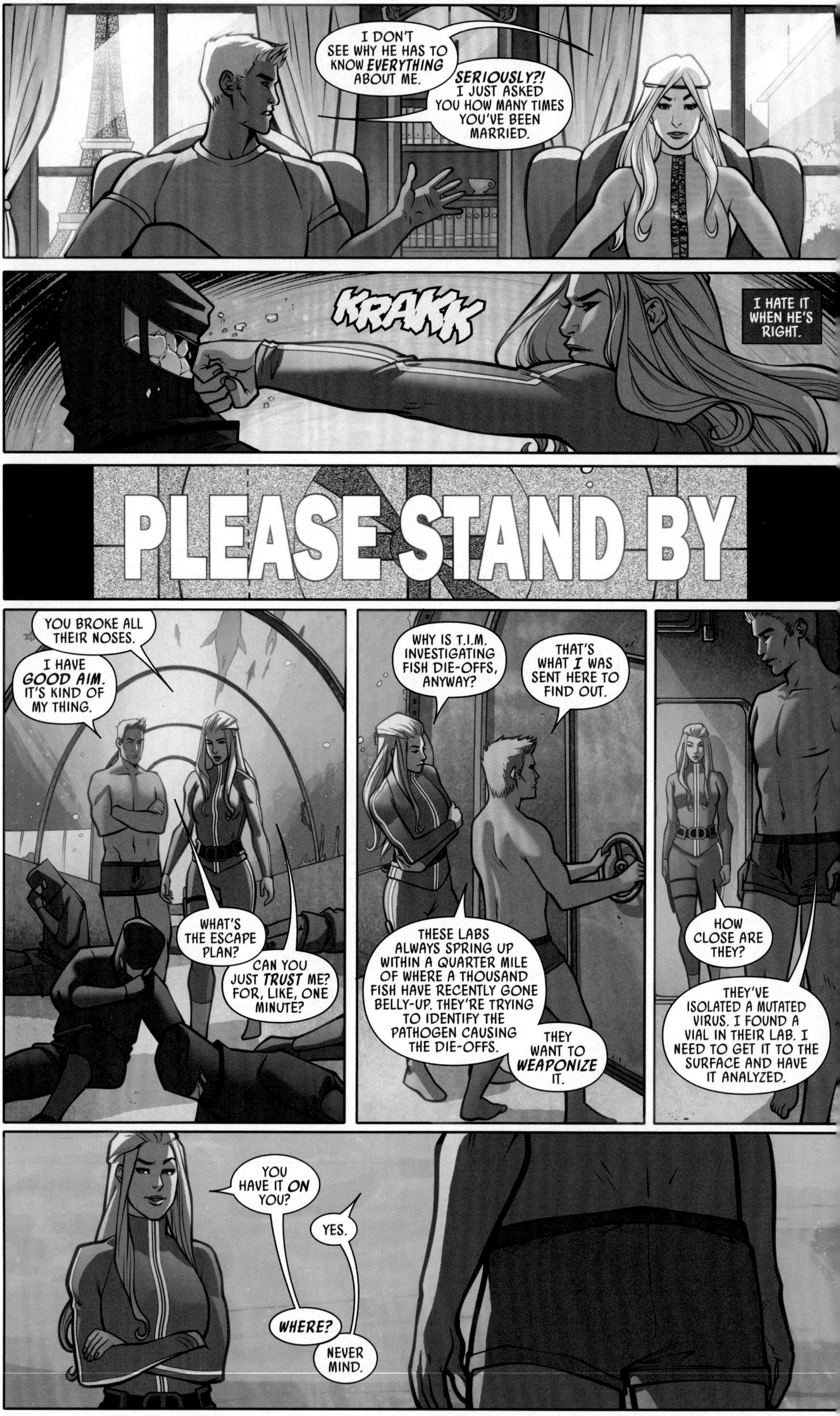
I DON'T SEE WHY HE HAS TO KNOW EVERYTHING ABOUT ME.
SERIOUSLY?! I JUST ASKED YOU HOW MANY TIMES YOU'VE BEEN MARRIED.
KRAKK
I HATE IT WHEN HE'S RIGHT.
PLEASE STAND BY
YOU BROKE ALL THEIR NOSES.
I HAVE GOOD AIM. IT'S KIND OF MY THING.
WHAT'S THE ESCAPE PLAN?
CAN YOU JUST TRUST ME? FOR, LIKE, ONE MINUTE?
WHY IS T.I.M. INVESTIGATING FISH DIE-OFFS, ANYWAY?
THAT'S WHAT I WAS SENT HERE TO FIND OUT.
THESE LABS ALWAYS SPRING UP WITHIN A QUARTER MILE OF WHERE A THOUSAND FISH HAVE RECENTLY GONE BELLY-UP. THEY'RE TRYING TO IDENTIFY THE PATHOGEN CAUSING THE DIE-OFFS.
THEY WANT TO WEAPONIZE IT.
HOW CLOSE ARE THEY?
THEY'VE ISOLATED A MUTATED VIRUS. I FOUND A VIAL IN THEIR LAB. I NEED TO GET IT TO THE SURFACE AND HAVE IT ANALYZED.
YOU HAVE IT ON YOU?
YES.
WHERE?
NEVER MIND.

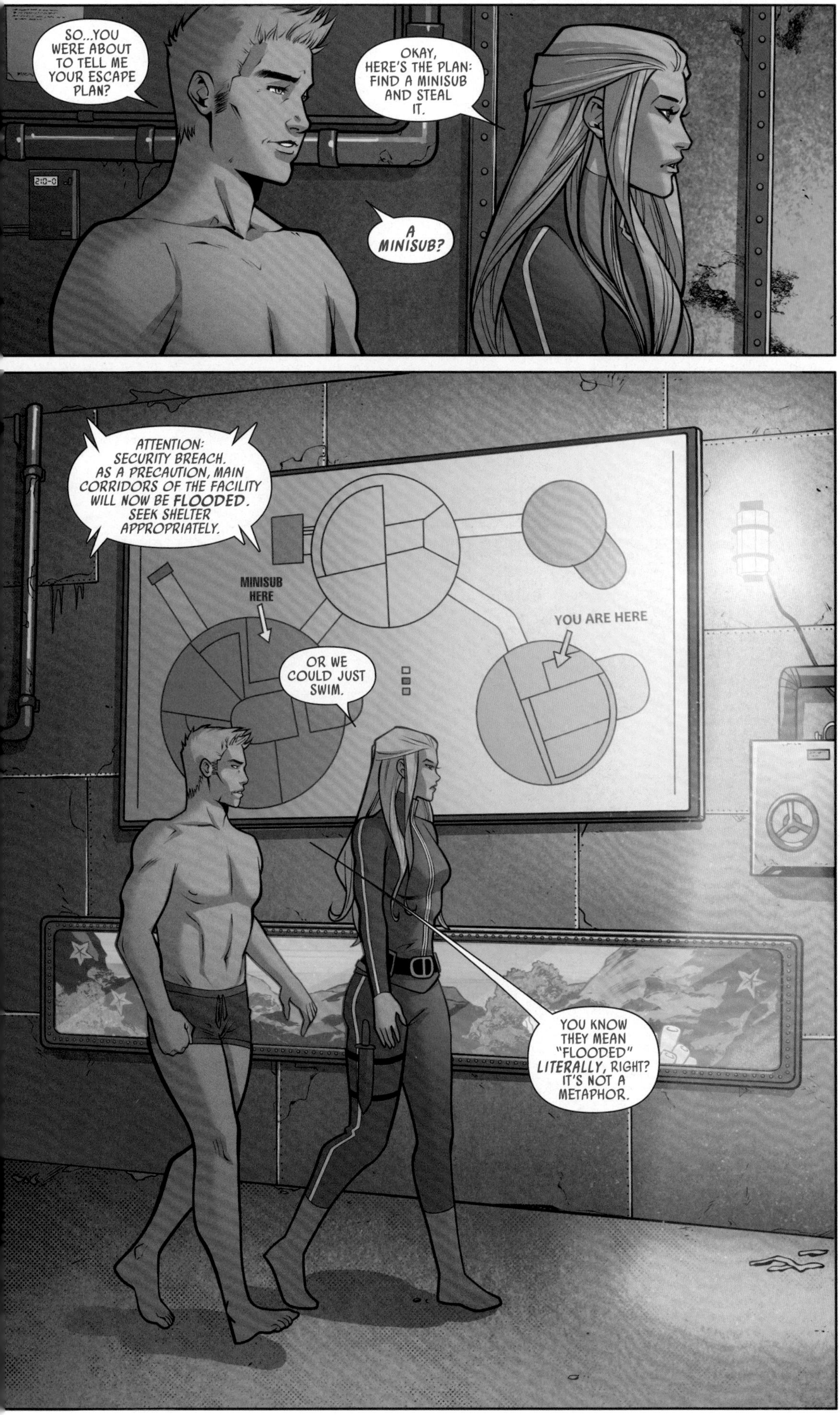

SO...YOU WERE ABOUT TO TELL ME YOUR ESCAPE PLAN?
OKAY, HERE'S THE PLAN: FIND A MINISUB AND STEAL IT.
A MINISUB?
ATTENTION: SECURITY BREACH. AS A PRECAUTION, MAIN CORRIDORS OF THE FACILITY WILL NOW BE FLOODED. SEEK SHELTER APPROPRIATELY.
MINISUB HERE
YOU ARE HERE
OR WE COULD JUST SWIM.
YOU KNOW THEY MEAN "FLOODED" LITERALLY, RIGHT? IT'S NOT A METAPHOR.

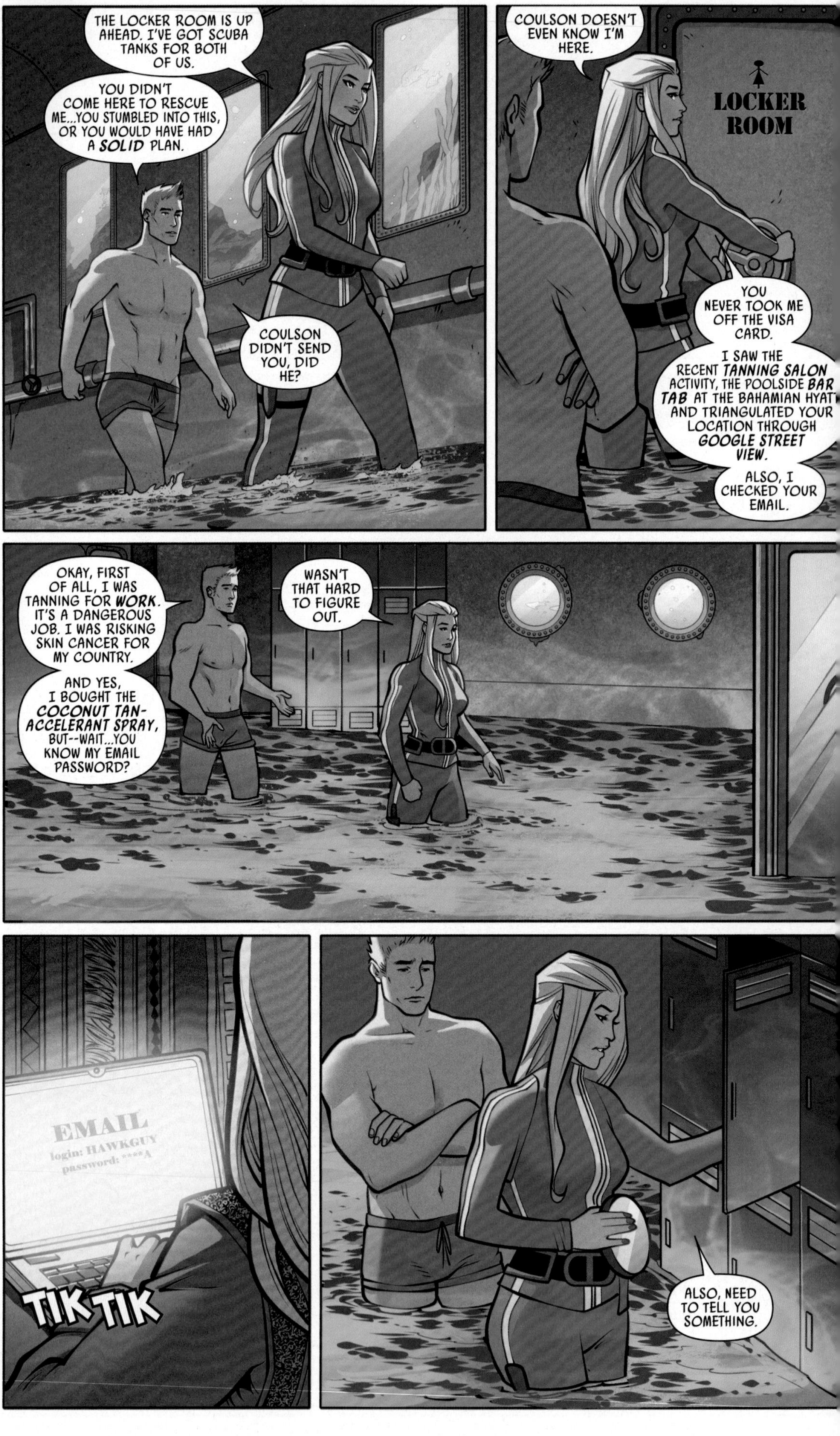
THE LOCKER ROOM IS UP AHEAD. I'VE GOT SCUBA TANKS FOR BOTH OF US.
YOU DIDN'T COME HERE TO RESCUE ME...YOU STUMBLED INTO THIS, OR YOU WOULD HAVE HAD A SOLID PLAN.
COULSON DIDN'T SEND YOU, DID HE?
COULSON DOESN'T EVEN KNOW I'M HERE.
LOCKER ROOM
YOU NEVER TOOK ME OFF THE VISA CARD.
I SAW THE RECENT TANNING SALON ACTIVITY, THE POOLSIDE BAR TAB AT THE BAHAMIAN HYAT AND TRIANGULATED YOUR LOCATION THROUGH GOOGLE STREET VIEW.
ALSO, I CHECKED YOUR EMAIL.
OKAY, FIRST OF ALL, I WAS TANNING FOR WORK. IT'S A DANGEROUS JOB. I WAS RISKING SKIN CANCER FOR MY COUNTRY.
AND YES, I BOUGHT THE COCONUT TAN-ACCELERANT SPRAY, BUT--WAIT...YOU KNOW MY EMAIL PASSWORD?
WASN'T THAT HARD TO FIGURE OUT.
EMAIL
login: HAWKGUY
password: ****A
TIK TIK
ALSO, NEED TO TELL YOU SOMETHING.

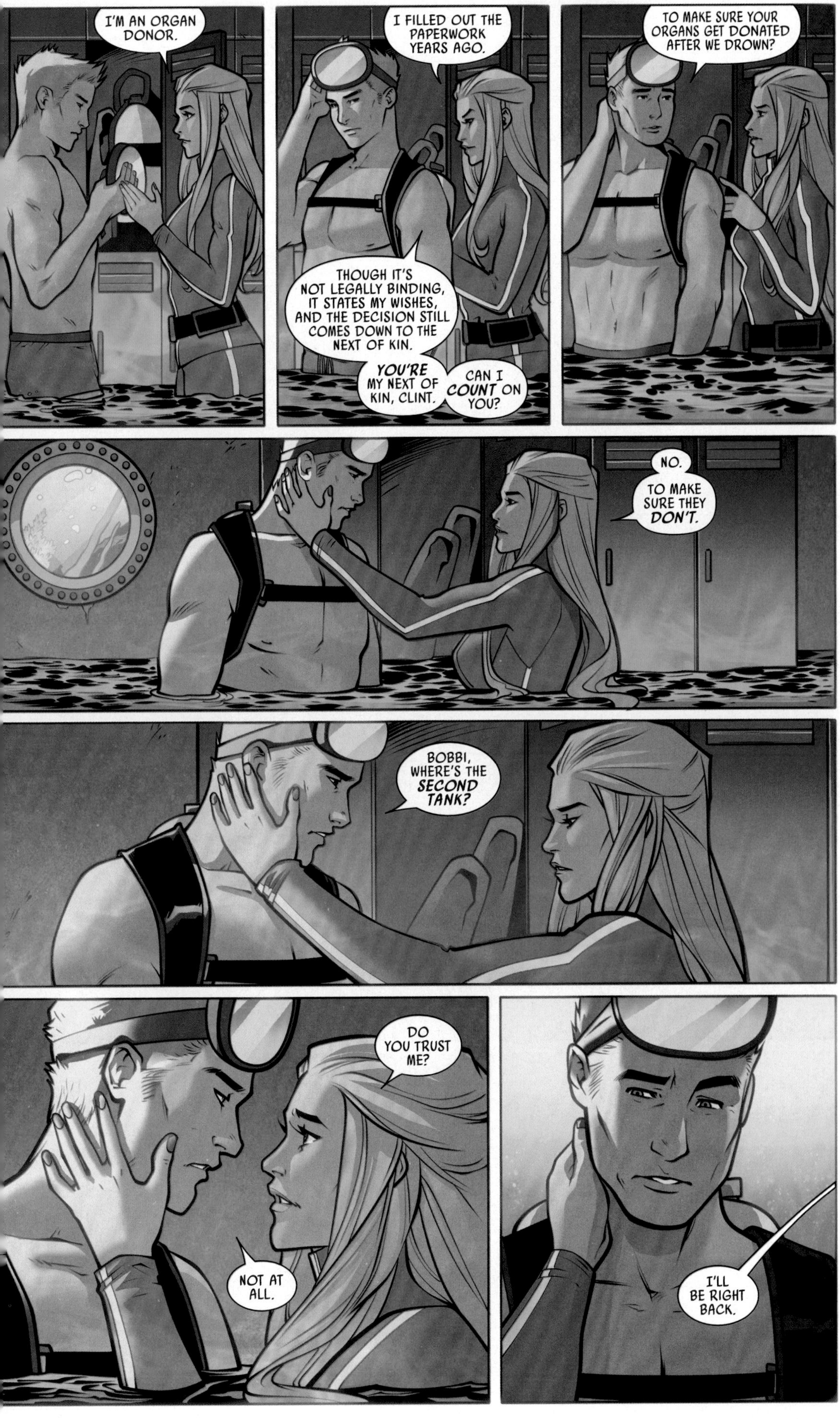
I'M AN ORGAN DONOR.
I FILLED OUT THE PAPERWORK YEARS AGO.
THOUGH IT'S NOT LEGALLY BINDING, IT STATES MY WISHES, AND THE DECISION STILL COMES DOWN TO THE NEXT OF KIN.
YOU'RE MY NEXT OF KIN, CLINT.
CAN I COUNT ON YOU?
TO MAKE SURE YOUR ORGANS GET DONATED AFTER WE DROWN?
NO.
TO MAKE SURE THEY DON'T.
BOBBI, WHERE'S THE SECOND TANK?
DO YOU TRUST ME?
NOT AT ALL.
I'LL BE RIGHT BACK.

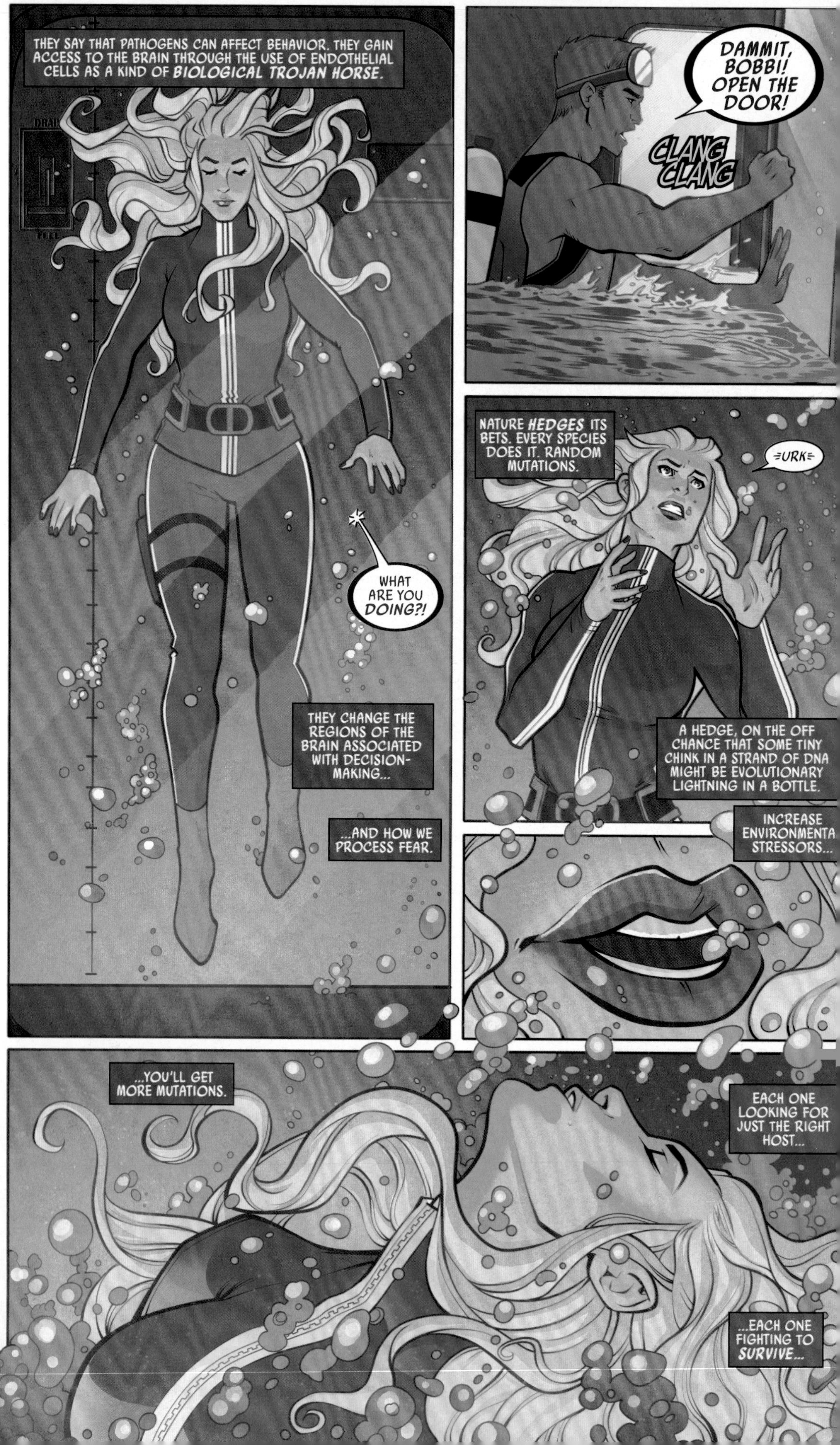
THEY SAY THAT PATHOGENS CAN AFFECT BEHAVIOR. THEY GAIN ACCESS TO THE BRAIN THROUGH THE USE OF ENDOTHELIAL CELLS AS A KIND OF BIOLOGICAL TROJAN HORSE.
WHAT ARE YOU DOING?!
THEY CHANGE THE REGIONS OF THE BRAIN ASSOCIATED WITH DECISION-MAKING...
...AND HOW WE PROCESS FEAR.
DAMMIT, BOBBI! OPEN THE DOOR!
CLANG CLANG
NATURE HEDGES ITS BETS. EVERY SPECIES DOES IT. RANDOM MUTATIONS.
URK
A HEDGE, ON THE OFF CHANCE THAT SOME TINY CHINK IN A STRAND OF DNA MIGHT BE EVOLUTIONARY LIGHTNING IN A BOTTLE.
INCREASE ENVIRONMENTA STRESSORS...
...YOU'LL GET MORE MUTATIONS.
EACH ONE LOOKING FOR JUST THE RIGHT HOST...
...EACH ONE FIGHTING TO SURVIVE...

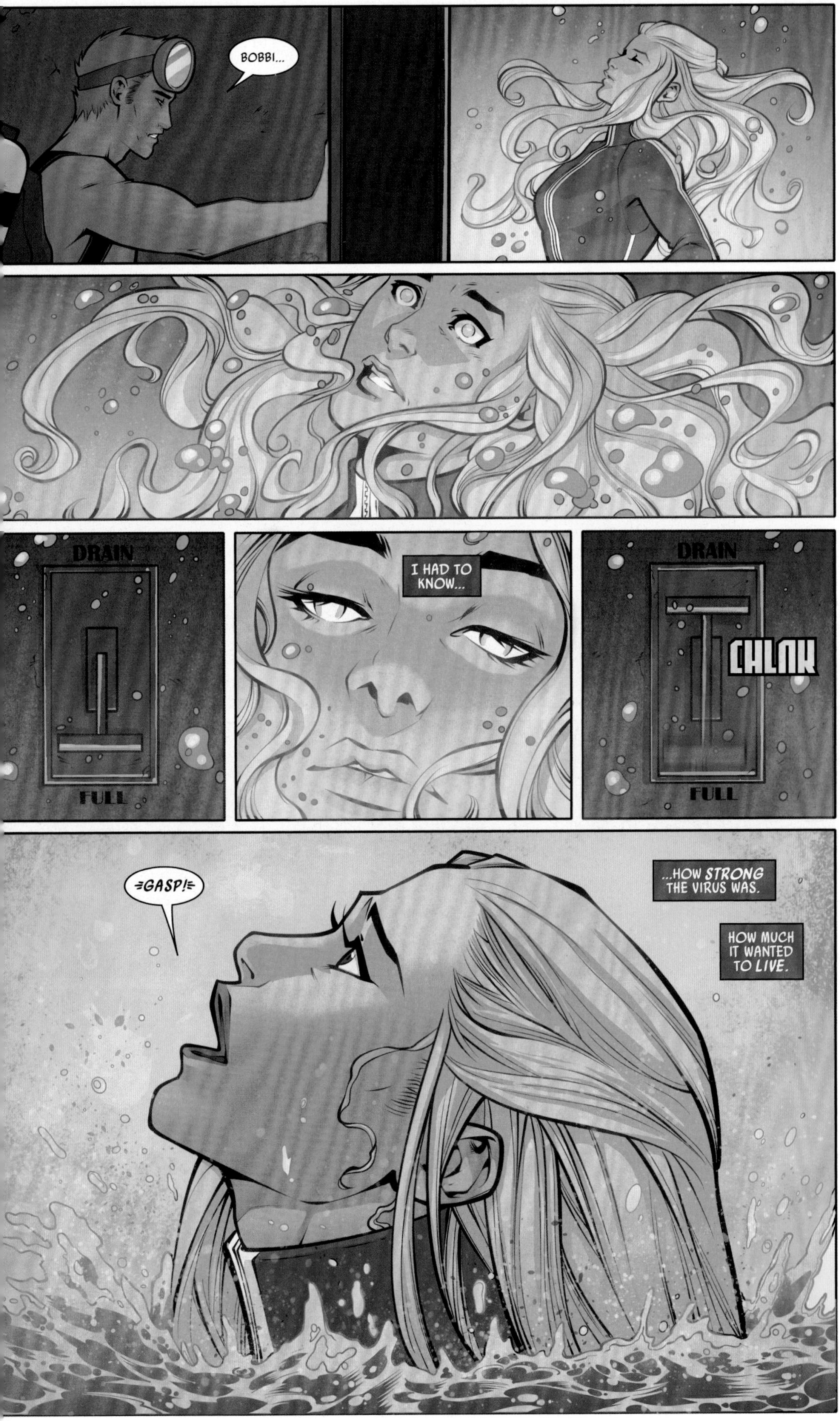
BOBBI...
DRAIN
FULL
I HAD TO KNOW...
DRAIN
CHLNK
FULL
=GASP!=
...HOW STRONG THE VIRUS WAS.
HOW MUCH IT WANTED TO LIVE.

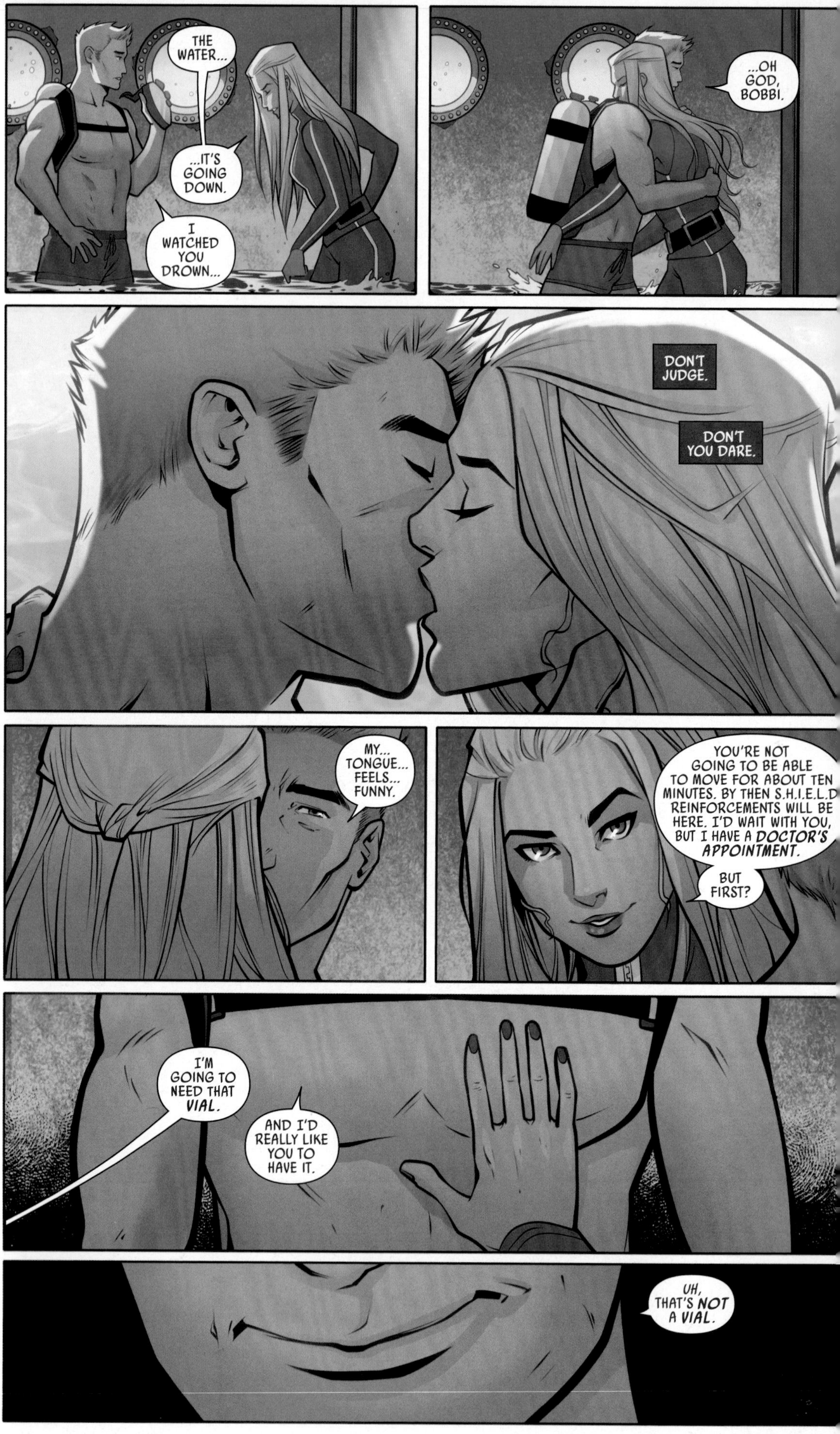
THE WATER...
...IT'S GOING DOWN.
I WATCHED YOU DROWN...
...OH GOD, BOBBI.
DON'T JUDGE.
DON'T YOU DARE.
MY... TONGUE... FEELS... FUNNY.
YOU'RE NOT GOING TO BE ABLE TO MOVE FOR ABOUT TEN MINUTES. BY THEN S.H.I.E.L.D. REINFORCEMENTS WILL BE HERE. I'D WAIT WITH YOU, BUT I HAVE A DOCTOR'S APPOINTMENT.
BUT FIRST?
I'M GOING TO NEED THAT VIAL.
AND I'D REALLY LIKE YOU TO HAVE IT.
UH, THAT'S NOT A VIAL.

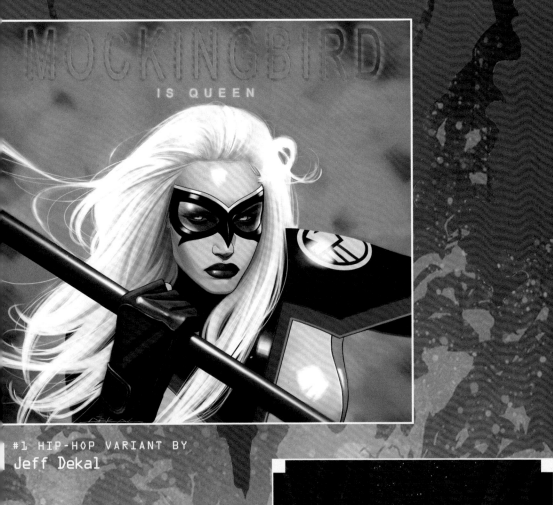

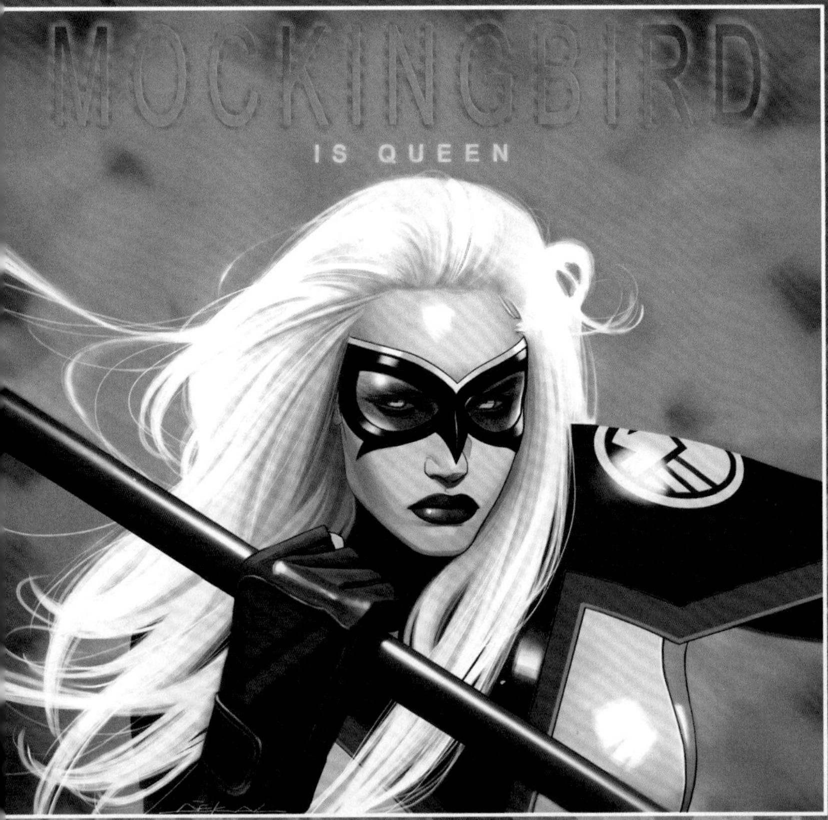
MOCKINGBIRD
IS QUEEN

#1 HIP-HOP VARIANT BY
Jeff Dekal

#1 VARIANT BY
Afu Chan

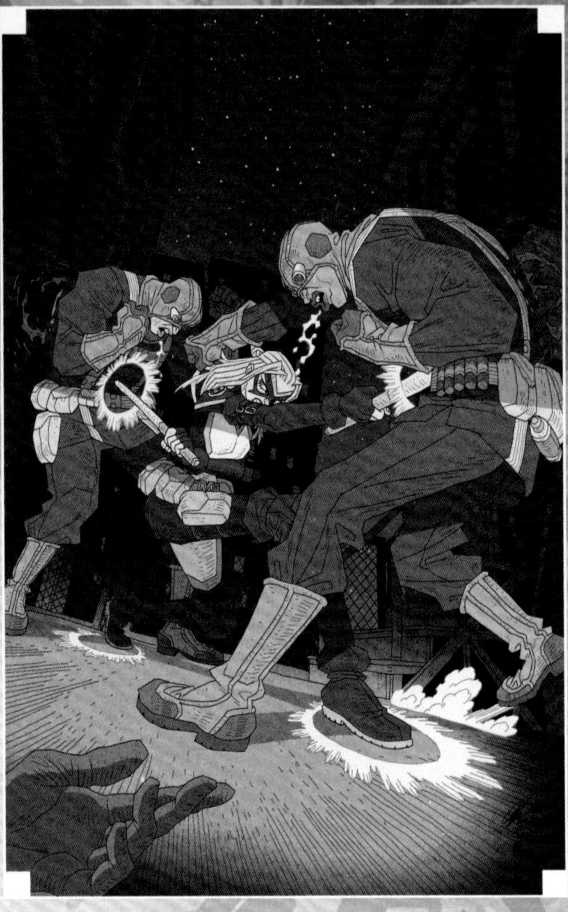

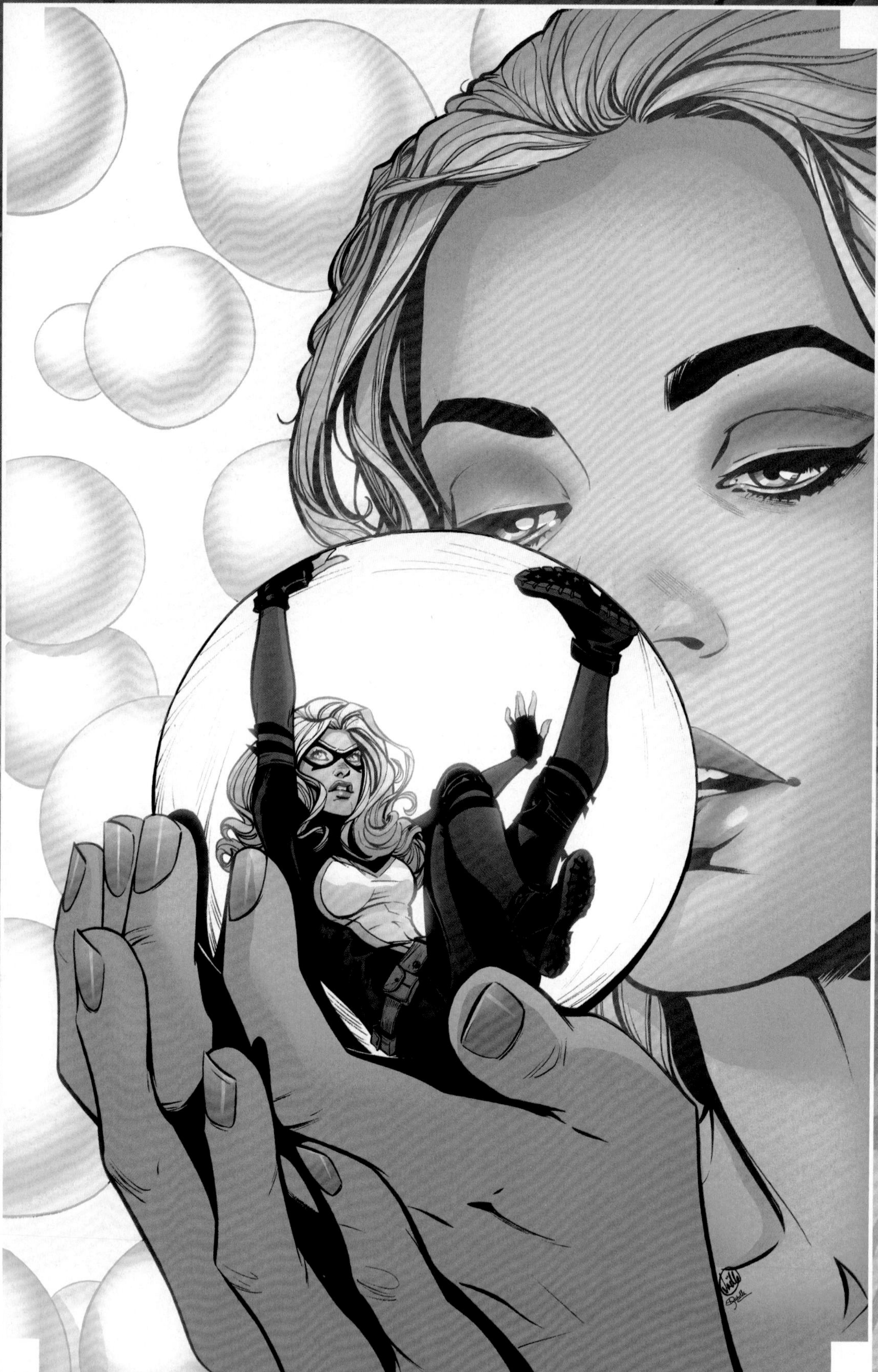

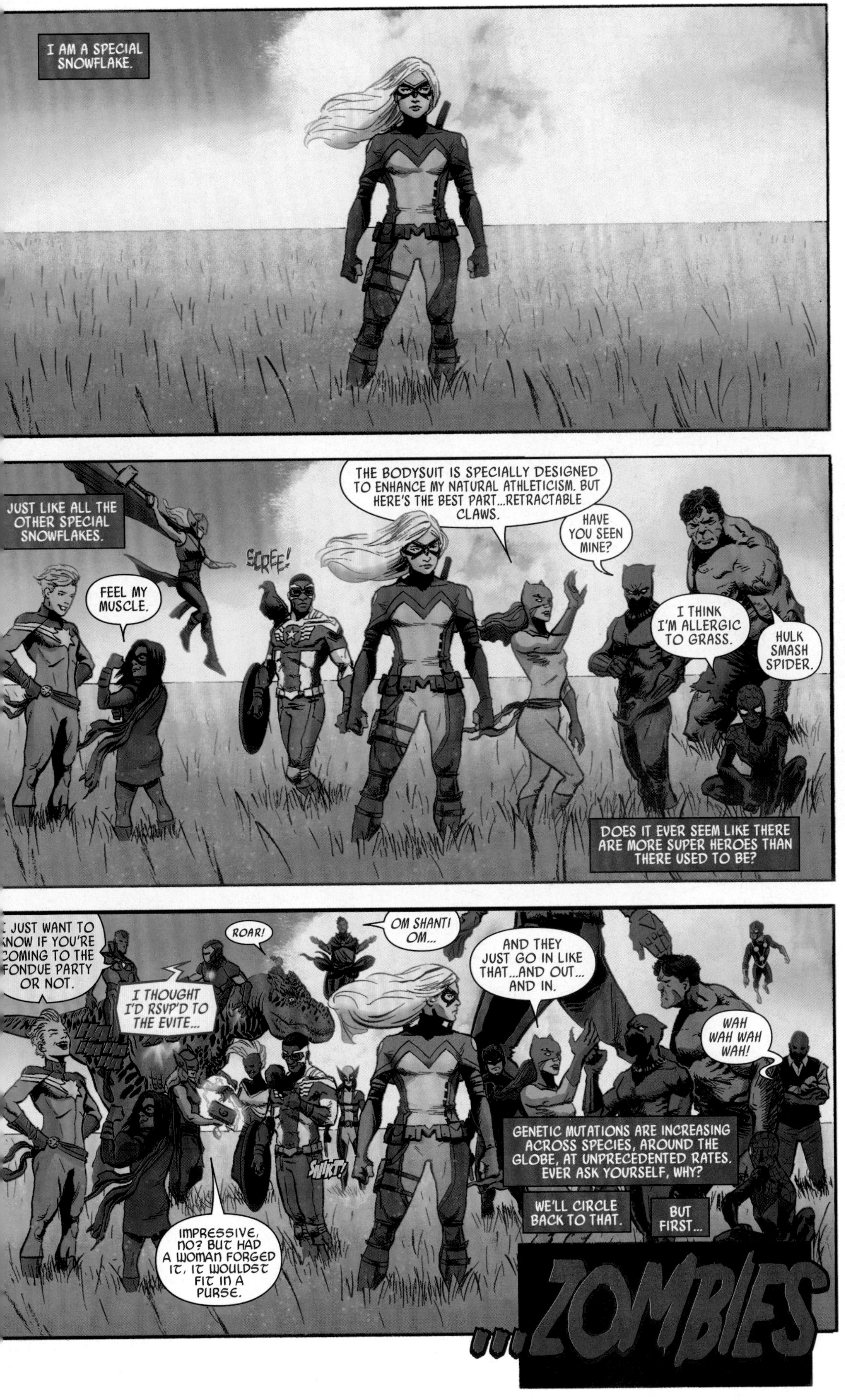
I AM A SPECIAL SNOWFLAKE.
JUST LIKE ALL THE OTHER SPECIAL SNOWFLAKES.
FEEL MY MUSCLE.
SCREE!
THE BODYSUIT IS SPECIALLY DESIGNED TO ENHANCE MY NATURAL ATHLETICISM. BUT HERE'S THE BEST PART...RETRACTABLE CLAWS.
HAVE YOU SEEN MINE?
I THINK I'M ALLERGIC TO GRASS.
HULK SMASH SPIDER.
DOES IT EVER SEEM LIKE THERE ARE MORE SUPER HEROES THAN THERE USED TO BE?
I JUST WANT TO KNOW IF YOU'RE COMING TO THE FONDUE PARTY OR NOT.
I THOUGHT I'D RSVP'D TO THE EVITE...
ROAR!
OM SHANTI OM...
AND THEY JUST GO IN LIKE THAT...AND OUT... AND IN.
WAH WAH WAH WAH!
SNIKT!
IMPRESSIVE, NO? BUT HAD A WOMAN FORGED IT, IT WOULDST FIT IN A PURSE.
GENETIC MUTATIONS ARE INCREASING ACROSS SPECIES, AROUND THE GLOBE, AT UNPRECEDENTED RATES. EVER ASK YOURSELF, WHY?
WE'LL CIRCLE BACK TO THAT.
BUT FIRST...
...ZOMBIES

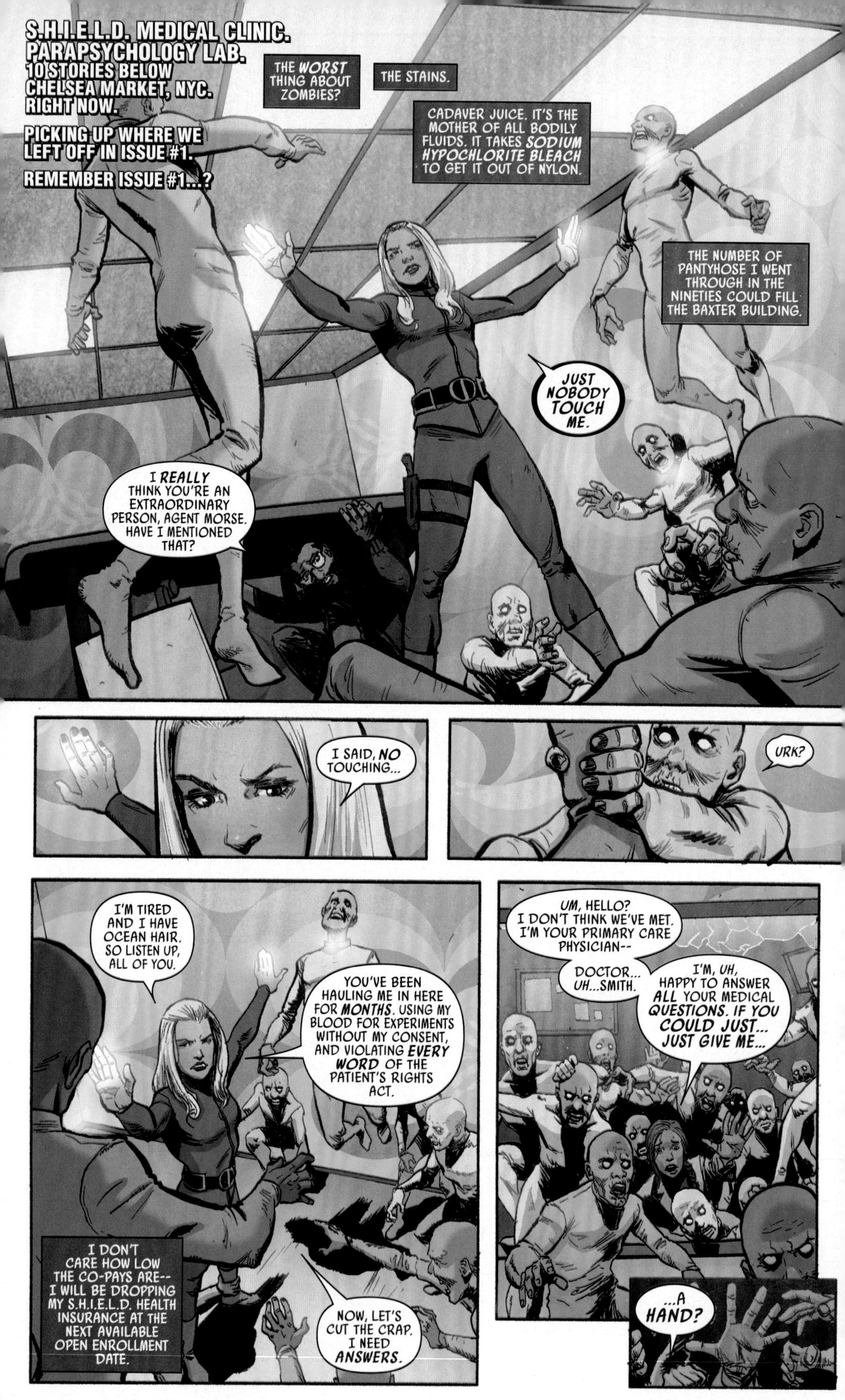
S.H.I.E.L.D. MEDICAL CLINIC. PARAPSYCHOLOGY LAB. 10 STORIES BELOW CHELSEA MARKET, NYC. RIGHT NOW.
PICKING UP WHERE WE LEFT OFF IN ISSUE #1.
REMEMBER ISSUE #1...?
THE WORST THING ABOUT ZOMBIES?
THE STAINS.
CADAVER JUICE. IT'S THE MOTHER OF ALL BODILY FLUIDS. IT TAKES SODIUM HYPOCHLORITE BLEACH TO GET IT OUT OF NYLON.
THE NUMBER OF PANTYHOSE I WENT THROUGH IN THE NINETIES COULD FILL THE BAXTER BUILDING.
JUST NOBODY TOUCH ME.
I REALLY THINK YOU'RE AN EXTRAORDINARY PERSON, AGENT MORSE. HAVE I MENTIONED THAT?
I SAID, NO TOUCHING...
URK?
I'M TIRED AND I HAVE OCEAN HAIR. SO LISTEN UP, ALL OF YOU.
YOU'VE BEEN HAULING ME IN HERE FOR MONTHS. USING MY BLOOD FOR EXPERIMENTS WITHOUT MY CONSENT, AND VIOLATING EVERY WORD OF THE PATIENT'S RIGHTS ACT.
I DON'T CARE HOW LOW THE CO-PAYS ARE-- I WILL BE DROPPING MY S.H.I.E.L.D. HEALTH INSURANCE AT THE NEXT AVAILABLE OPEN ENROLLMENT DATE.
NOW, LET'S CUT THE CRAP. I NEED ANSWERS.
UM, HELLO? I DON'T THINK WE'VE MET. I'M YOUR PRIMARY CARE PHYSICIAN--
DOCTOR... UH...SMITH.
I'M, UH, HAPPY TO ANSWER ALL YOUR MEDICAL QUESTIONS. IF YOU COULD JUST... JUST GIVE ME...
...A HAND?

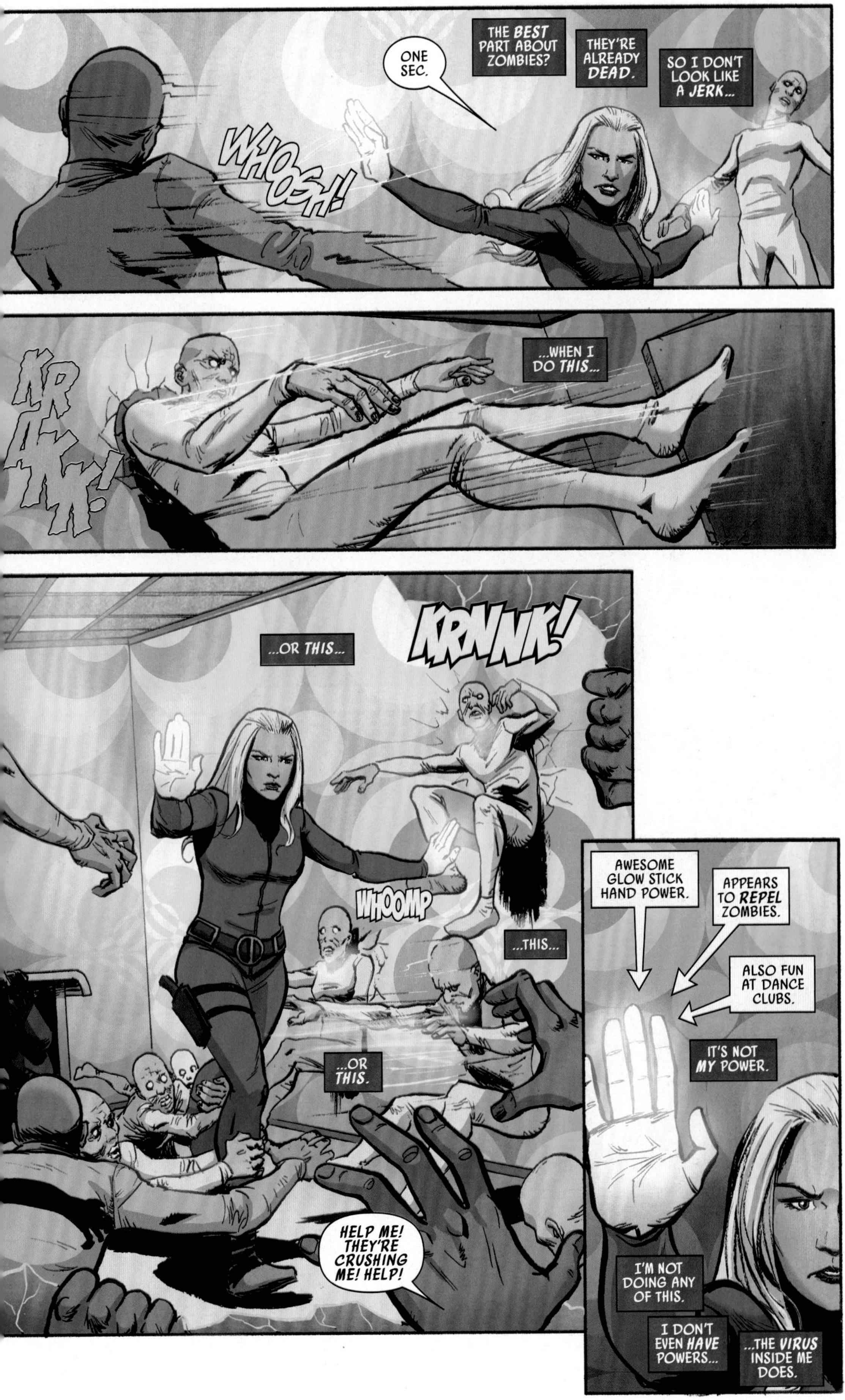

ONE SEC.
THE BEST PART ABOUT ZOMBIES?
THEY'RE ALREADY DEAD.
SO I DON'T LOOK LIKE A JERK...
WHOOSH!
KRAKK!
...WHEN I DO THIS...
...OR THIS...
KRNNK!
WHOOMP
...THIS...
...OR THIS.
HELP ME! THEY'RE CRUSHING ME! HELP!
AWESOME GLOW STICK HAND POWER.
APPEARS TO REPEL ZOMBIES.
ALSO FUN AT DANCE CLUBS.
IT'S NOT MY POWER.
I'M NOT DOING ANY OF THIS.
I DON'T EVEN HAVE POWERS...
...THE VIRUS INSIDE ME DOES.

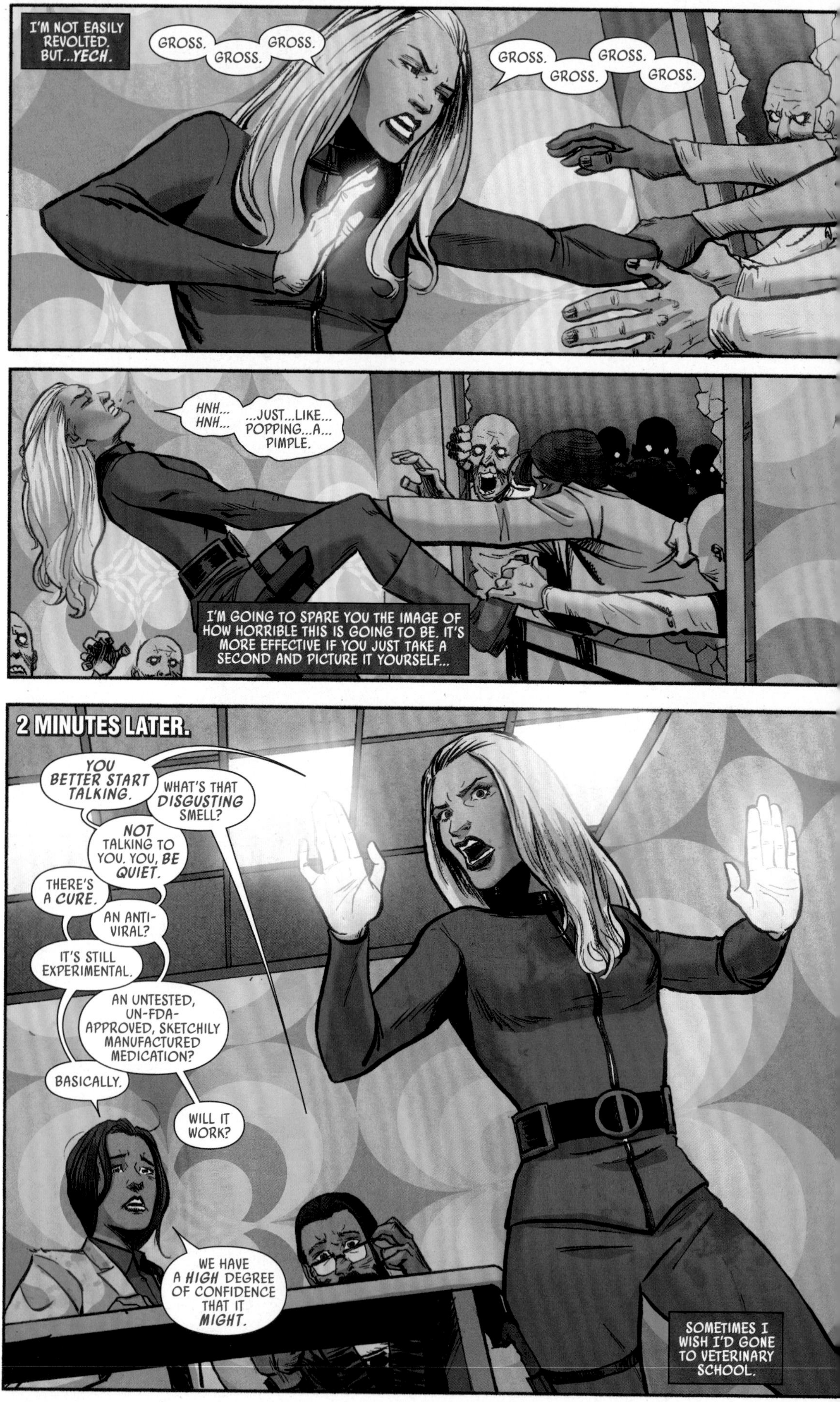

I'M NOT EASILY REVOLTED. BUT...YECH.
GROSS. GROSS. GROSS.
GROSS. GROSS. GROSS. GROSS.
HNH... HNH...
...JUST...LIKE... POPPING...A... PIMPLE.
I'M GOING TO SPARE YOU THE IMAGE OF HOW HORRIBLE THIS IS GOING TO BE. IT'S MORE EFFECTIVE IF YOU JUST TAKE A SECOND AND PICTURE IT YOURSELF...
2 MINUTES LATER.
YOU BETTER START TALKING.
WHAT'S THAT DISGUSTING SMELL?
NOT TALKING TO YOU. YOU, BE QUIET.
THERE'S A CURE.
AN ANTI-VIRAL?
IT'S STILL EXPERIMENTAL.
AN UNTESTED, UN-FDA-APPROVED, SKETCHILY MANUFACTURED MEDICATION?
BASICALLY.
WILL IT WORK?
WE HAVE A HIGH DEGREE OF CONFIDENCE THAT IT MIGHT.
SOMETIMES I WISH I'D GONE TO VETERINARY SCHOOL.

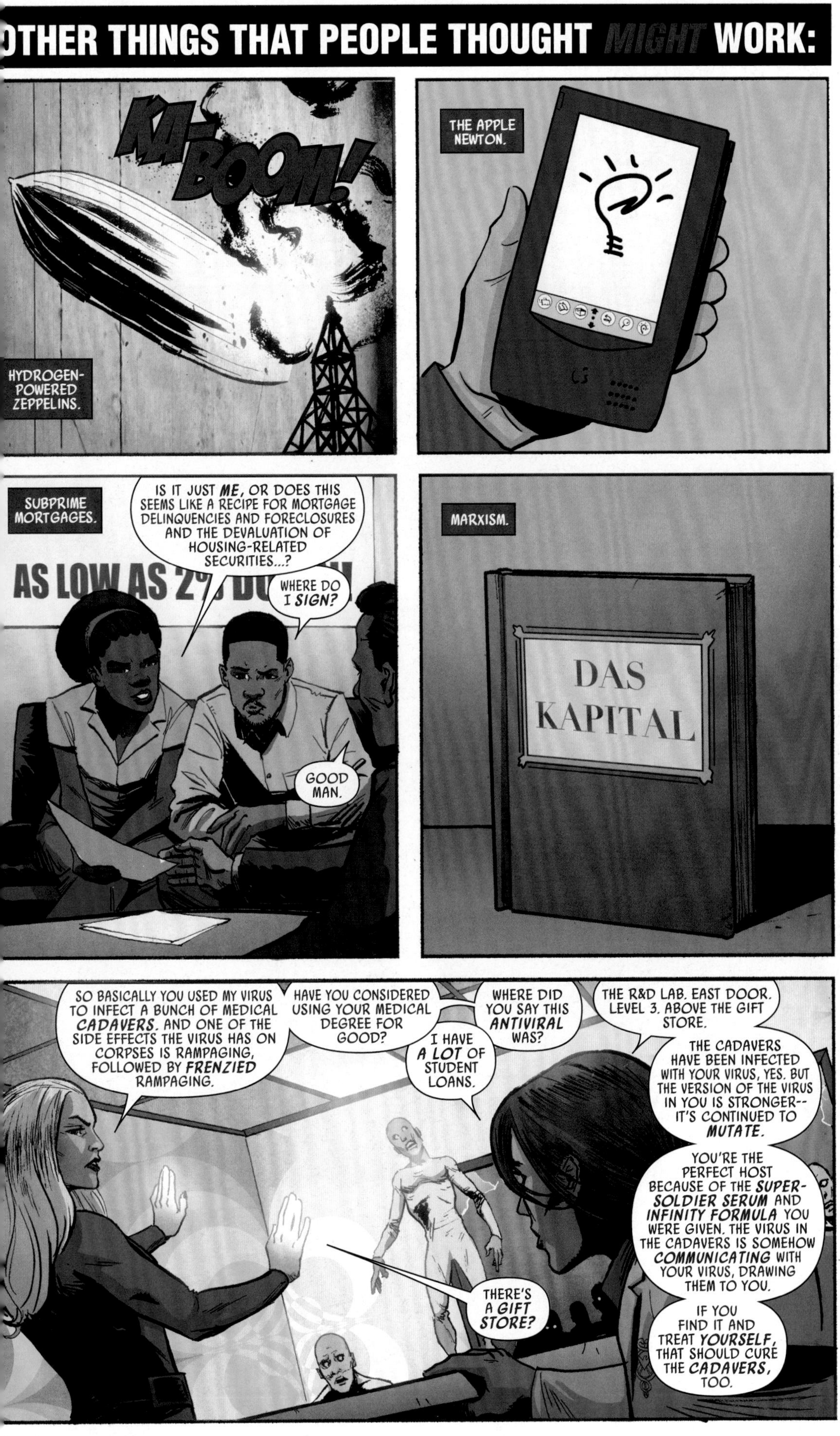
OTHER THINGS THAT PEOPLE THOUGHT MIGHT WORK:
KA-BOOM!
HYDROGEN-POWERED ZEPPELINS.
THE APPLE NEWTON.
SUBPRIME MORTGAGES.
IS IT JUST ME, OR DOES THIS SEEMS LIKE A RECIPE FOR MORTGAGE DELINQUENCIES AND FORECLOSURES AND THE DEVALUATION OF HOUSING-RELATED SECURITIES...?
WHERE DO I SIGN?
GOOD MAN.
MARXISM.
DAS KAPITAL
SO BASICALLY YOU USED MY VIRUS TO INFECT A BUNCH OF MEDICAL CADAVERS. AND ONE OF THE SIDE EFFECTS THE VIRUS HAS ON CORPSES IS RAMPAGING, FOLLOWED BY FRENZIED RAMPAGING.
HAVE YOU CONSIDERED USING YOUR MEDICAL DEGREE FOR GOOD?
I HAVE A LOT OF STUDENT LOANS.
WHERE DID YOU SAY THIS ANTIVIRAL WAS?
THE R&D LAB. EAST DOOR. LEVEL 3. ABOVE THE GIFT STORE.
THE CADAVERS HAVE BEEN INFECTED WITH YOUR VIRUS, YES. BUT THE VERSION OF THE VIRUS IN YOU IS STRONGER-- IT'S CONTINUED TO MUTATE.
YOU'RE THE PERFECT HOST BECAUSE OF THE SUPER-SOLDIER SERUM AND INFINITY FORMULA YOU WERE GIVEN. THE VIRUS IN THE CADAVERS IS SOMEHOW COMMUNICATING WITH YOUR VIRUS, DRAWING THEM TO YOU.
THERE'S A GIFT STORE?
IF YOU FIND IT AND TREAT YOURSELF, THAT SHOULD CURE THE CADAVERS, TOO.

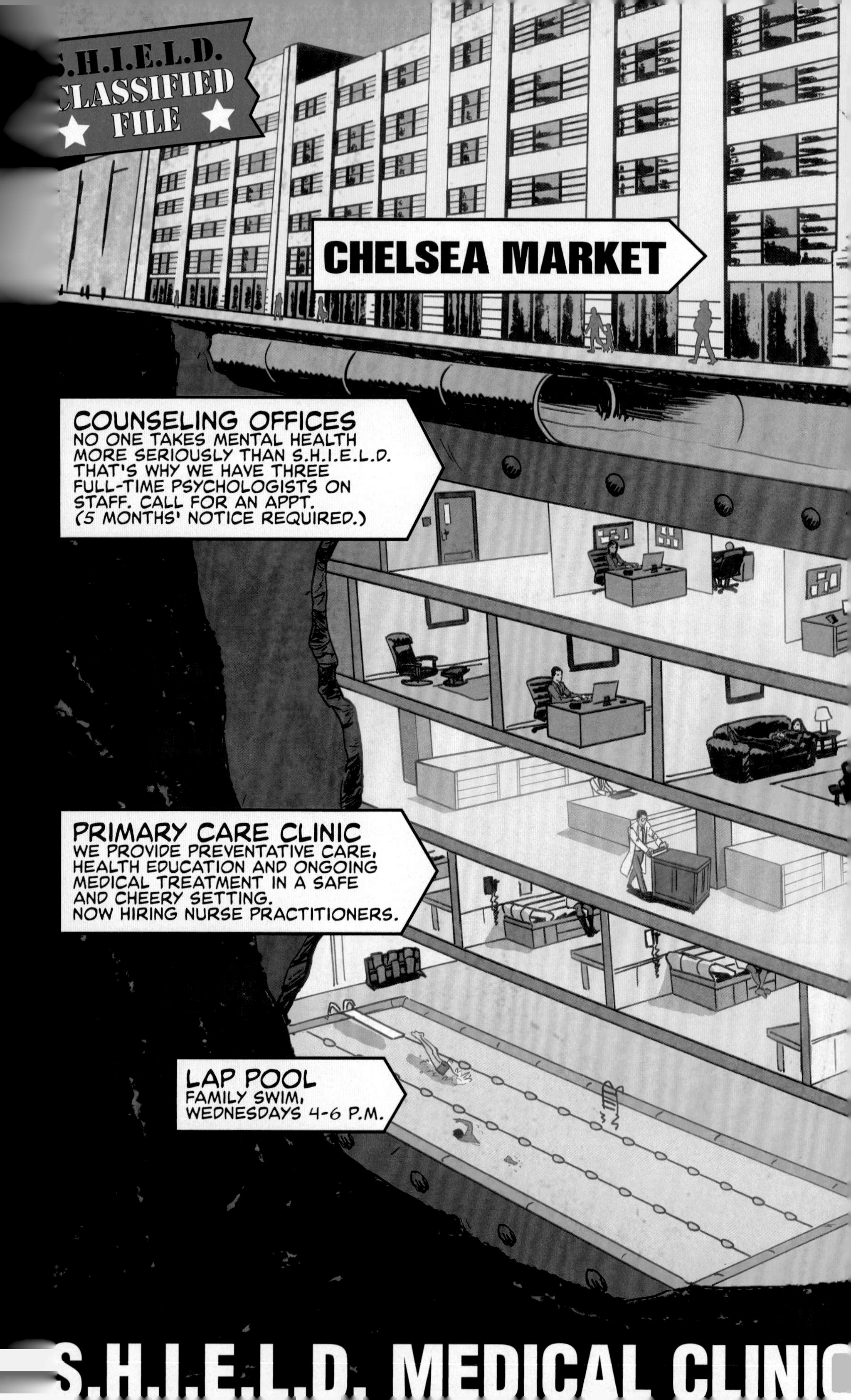

S.H.I.E.L.D. CLASSIFIED FILE
CHELSEA MARKET
COUNSELING OFFICES
NO ONE TAKES MENTAL HEALTH MORE SERIOUSLY THAN S.H.I.E.L.D. THAT'S WHY WE HAVE THREE FULL-TIME PSYCHOLOGISTS ON STAFF. CALL FOR AN APPT. (5 MONTHS' NOTICE REQUIRED.)
PRIMARY CARE CLINIC
WE PROVIDE PREVENTATIVE CARE, HEALTH EDUCATION AND ONGOING MEDICAL TREATMENT IN A SAFE AND CHEERY SETTING. NOW HIRING NURSE PRACTITIONERS.
LAP POOL
FAMILY SWIM, WEDNESDAYS 4-6 P.M.
S.H.I.E.L.D. MEDICAL CLINIC

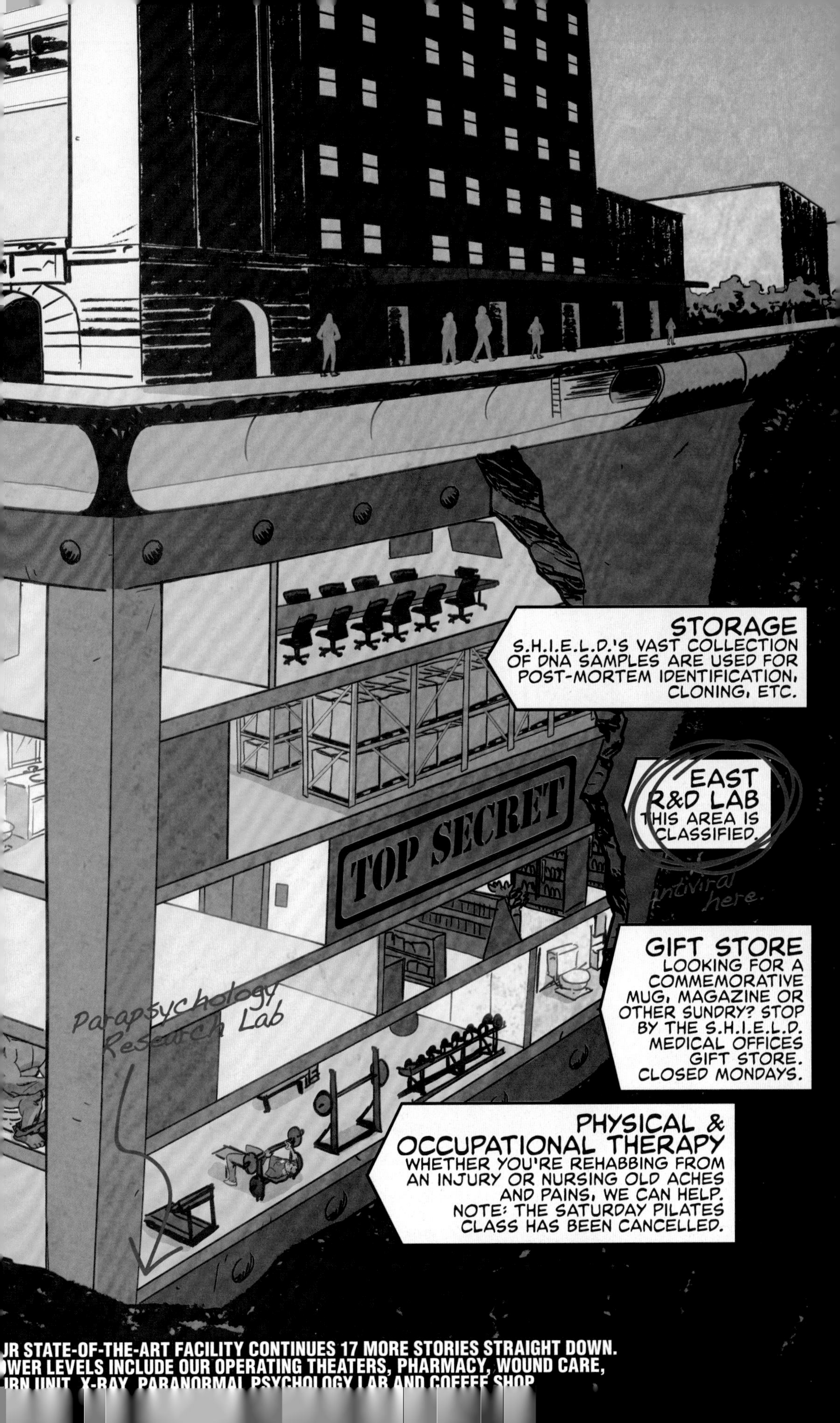

STORAGE
S.H.I.E.L.D.'S VAST COLLECTION OF DNA SAMPLES ARE USED FOR POST-MORTEM IDENTIFICATION, CLONING, ETC.
TOP SECRET
EAST R&D LAB
THIS AREA IS CLASSIFIED.
ntiviral here.
GIFT STORE
LOOKING FOR A COMMEMORATIVE MUG, MAGAZINE OR OTHER SUNDRY? STOP BY THE S.H.I.E.L.D. MEDICAL OFFICES GIFT STORE. CLOSED MONDAYS.
Parapsychology Research Lab
PHYSICAL & OCCUPATIONAL THERAPY
WHETHER YOU'RE REHABBING FROM AN INJURY OR NURSING OLD ACHES AND PAINS, WE CAN HELP. NOTE: THE SATURDAY PILATES CLASS HAS BEEN CANCELLED.
JR STATE-OF-THE-ART FACILITY CONTINUES 17 MORE STORIES STRAIGHT DOWN.
OWER LEVELS INCLUDE OUR OPERATING THEATERS, PHARMACY, WOUND CARE,

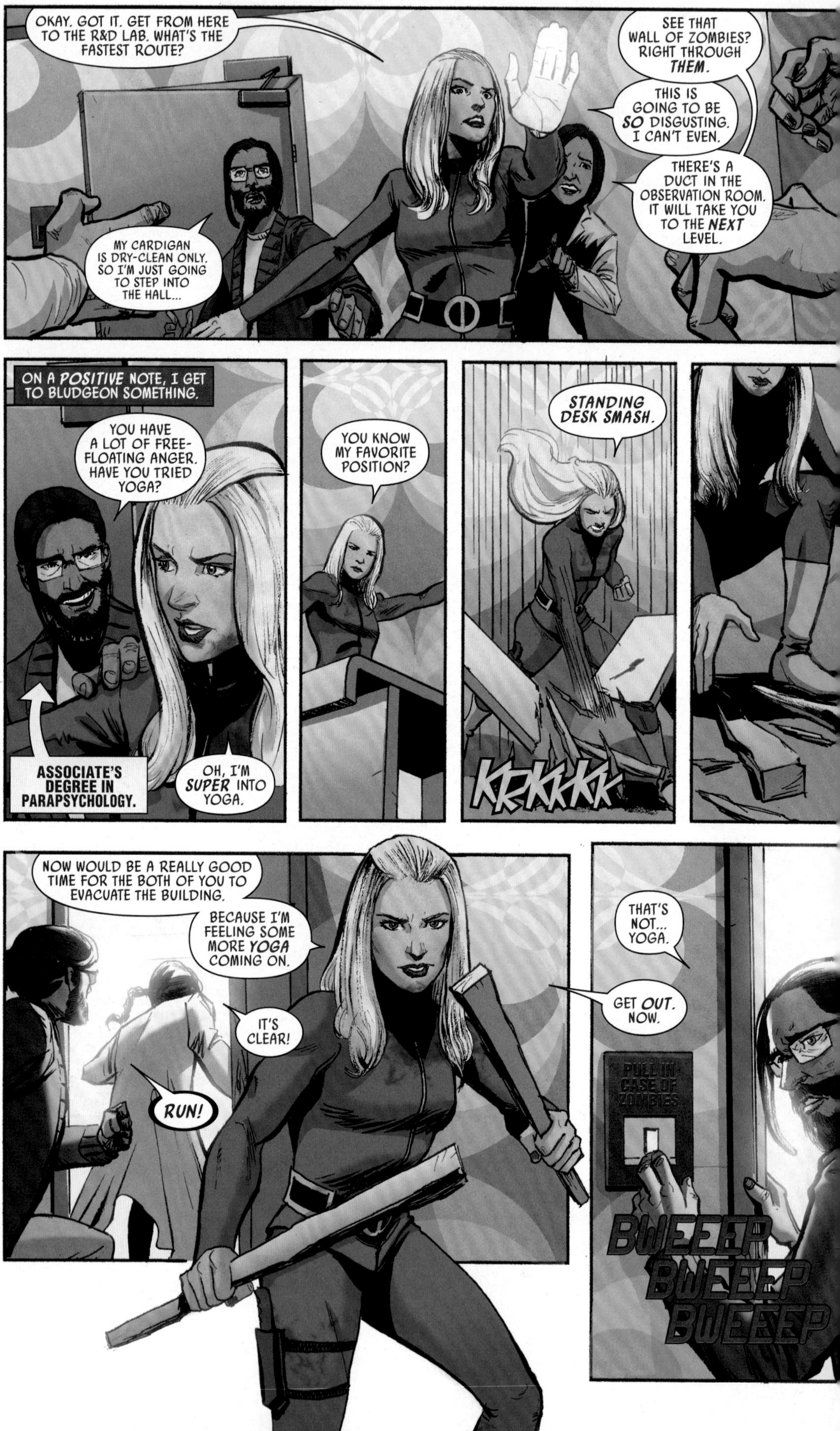
OKAY. GOT IT. GET FROM HERE TO THE R&D LAB. WHAT'S THE FASTEST ROUTE?
SEE THAT WALL OF ZOMBIES? RIGHT THROUGH THEM.
THIS IS GOING TO BE SO DISGUSTING. I CAN'T EVEN.
THERE'S A DUCT IN THE OBSERVATION ROOM. IT WILL TAKE YOU TO THE NEXT LEVEL.
MY CARDIGAN IS DRY-CLEAN ONLY. SO I'M JUST GOING TO STEP INTO THE HALL...
ON A POSITIVE NOTE, I GET TO BLUDGEON SOMETHING.
YOU HAVE A LOT OF FREE-FLOATING ANGER. HAVE YOU TRIED YOGA?
ASSOCIATE'S DEGREE IN PARAPSYCHOLOGY.
OH, I'M SUPER INTO YOGA.
YOU KNOW MY FAVORITE POSITION?
STANDING DESK SMASH.
KRKKKK
NOW WOULD BE A REALLY GOOD TIME FOR THE BOTH OF YOU TO EVACUATE THE BUILDING.
BECAUSE I'M FEELING SOME MORE YOGA COMING ON.
IT'S CLEAR!
RUN!
THAT'S NOT... YOGA.
GET OUT. NOW.
PULL IN CASE OF ZOMBIES
BWEEEP BWEEEP BWEEEP

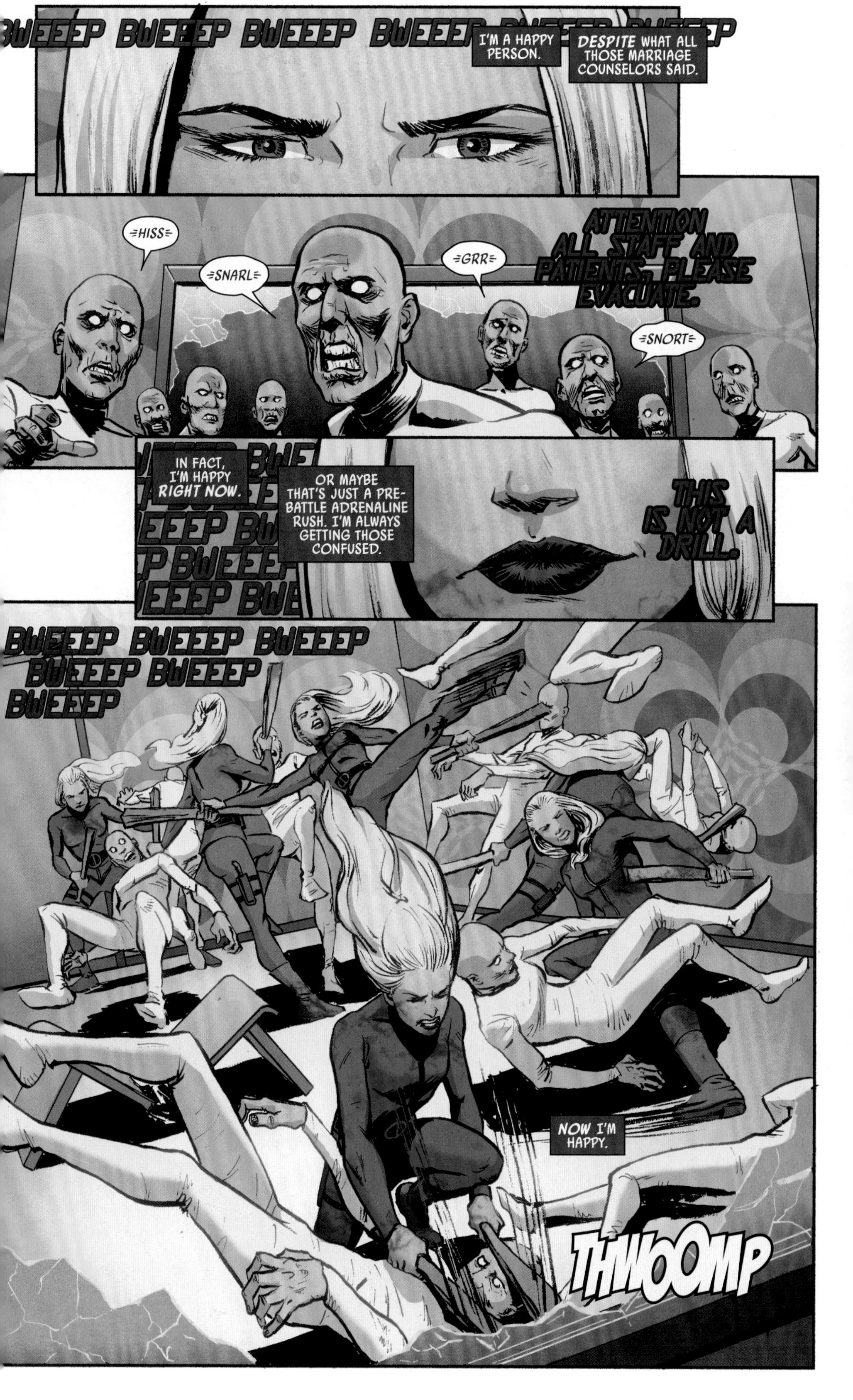
BWEEEP BWEEEP BWEEEP BWEEEP BWEEEP BWEEEP BWEEEP
I'M A HAPPY PERSON.
DESPITE WHAT ALL THOSE MARRIAGE COUNSELORS SAID.
HISS
SNARL
GRR
ATTENTION ALL STAFF AND PATIENTS, PLEASE EVACUATE.
SNORT
IN FACT, I'M HAPPY RIGHT NOW.
OR MAYBE THAT'S JUST A PRE-BATTLE ADRENALINE RUSH. I'M ALWAYS GETTING THOSE CONFUSED.
THIS IS NOT A DRILL.
BWEEEP BWEEEP BWEEEP BWEEEP BWEEEP BWEEEP
NOW I'M HAPPY.
THWOOMP

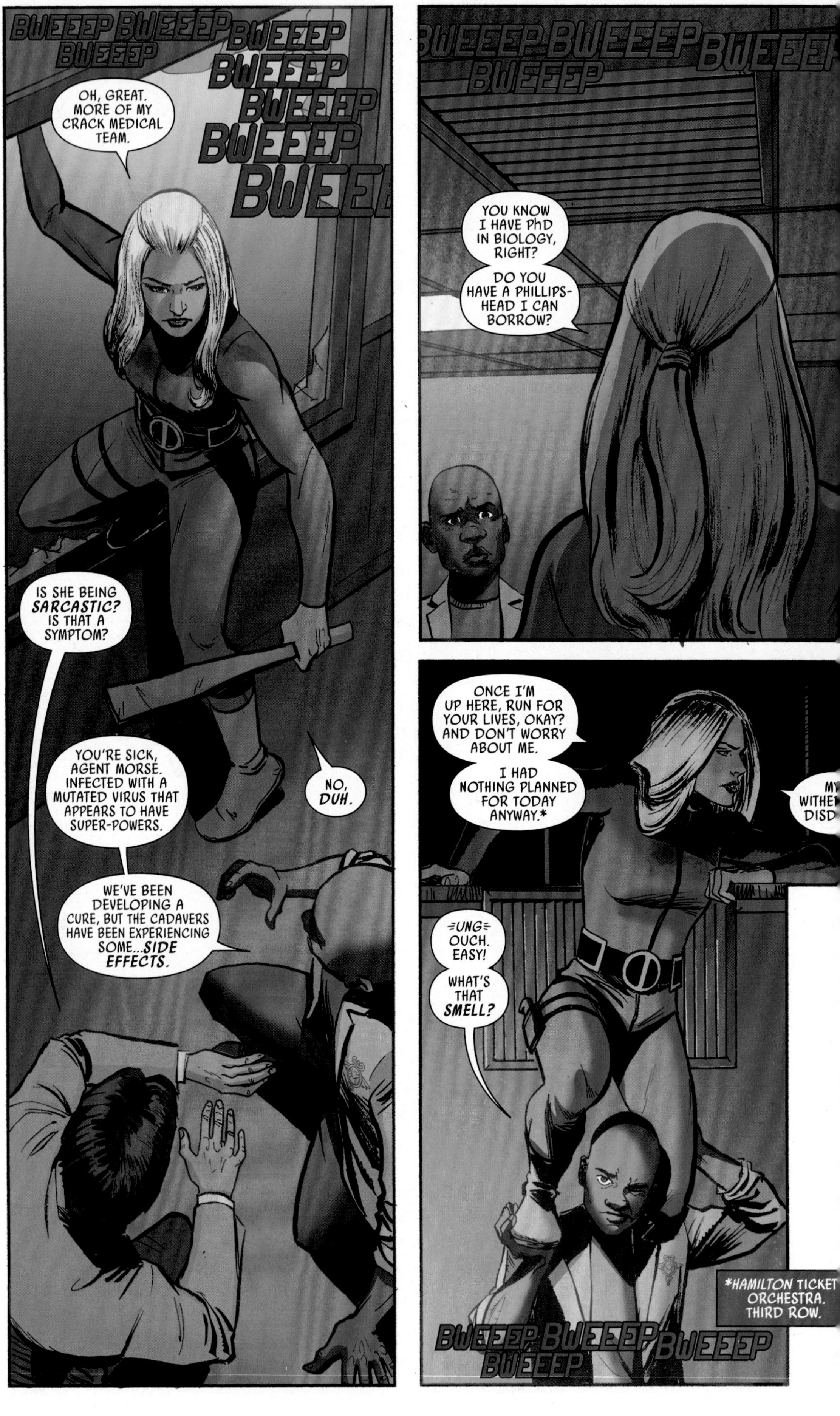
BWEEEP BWEEEP
BWEEEP
BWEEEP
BWEEEP
BWEEEP
BWEEEP
OH, GREAT. MORE OF MY CRACK MEDICAL TEAM.
IS SHE BEING SARCASTIC? IS THAT A SYMPTOM?
YOU'RE SICK, AGENT MORSE. INFECTED WITH A MUTATED VIRUS THAT APPEARS TO HAVE SUPER-POWERS.
NO, DUH.
WE'VE BEEN DEVELOPING A CURE, BUT THE CADAVERS HAVE BEEN EXPERIENCING SOME...SIDE EFFECTS.
BWEEEP BWEEEP
BWEEEP
YOU KNOW I HAVE PhD IN BIOLOGY, RIGHT?
DO YOU HAVE A PHILLIPS-HEAD I CAN BORROW?
ONCE I'M UP HERE, RUN FOR YOUR LIVES, OKAY? AND DON'T WORRY ABOUT ME.
I HAD NOTHING PLANNED FOR TODAY ANYWAY.*
=UNG= OUCH. EASY!
WHAT'S THAT SMELL?
*HAMILTON TICKET ORCHESTRA. THIRD ROW.
BWEEEP BWEEEP BWEEEP
BWEEEP

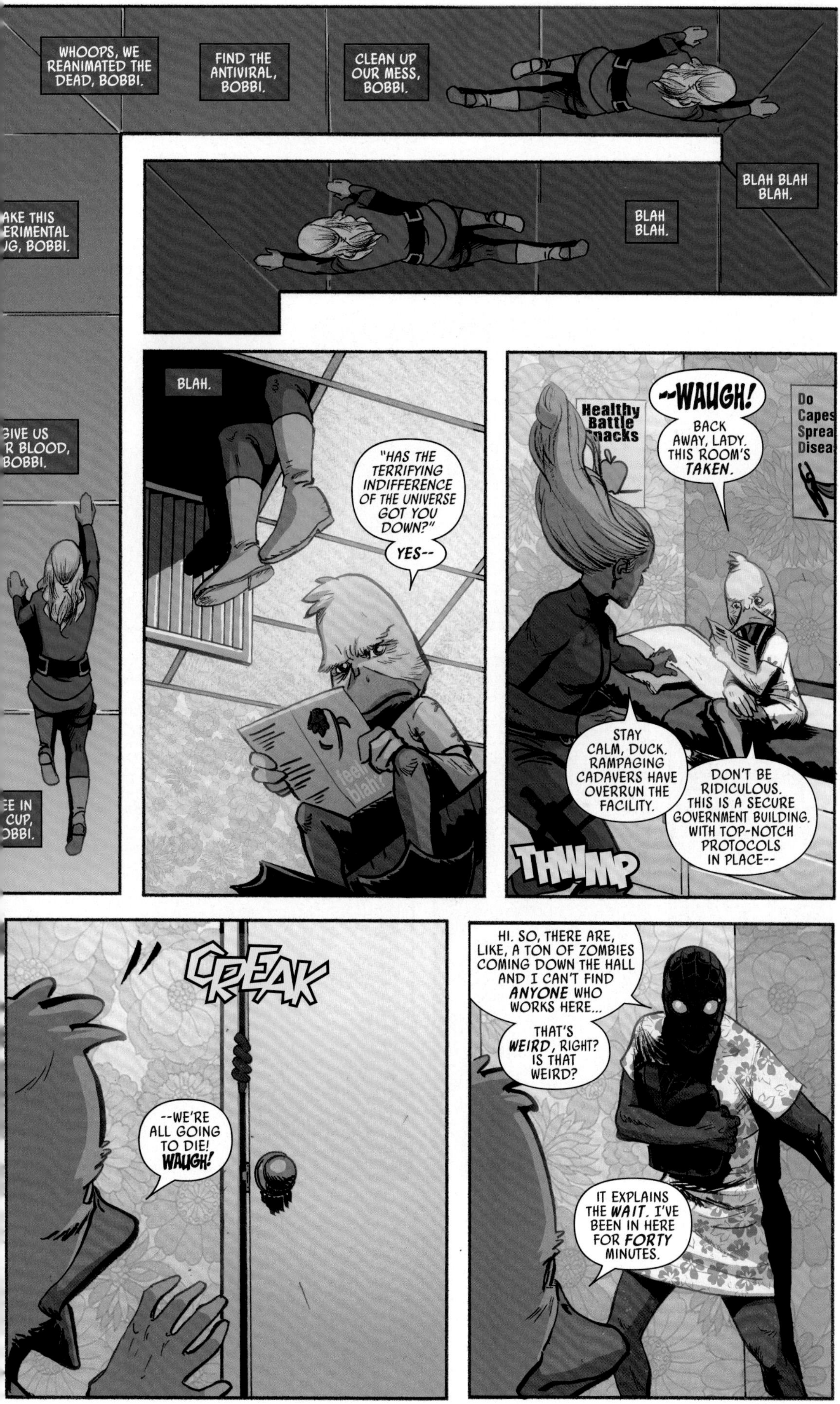

WHOOPS, WE REANIMATED THE DEAD, BOBBI.
FIND THE ANTIVIRAL, BOBBI.
CLEAN UP OUR MESS, BOBBI.
BLAH BLAH BLAH.
BLAH BLAH.
AKE THIS ERIMENTAL UG, BOBBI.
GIVE US R BLOOD, BOBBI.
EE IN CUP, OBBI.
BLAH.
"HAS THE TERRIFYING INDIFFERENCE OF THE UNIVERSE GOT YOU DOWN?"
YES--
feel blah?
--WAUGH!
BACK AWAY, LADY. THIS ROOM'S TAKEN.
Healthy Battle Snacks
STAY CALM, DUCK. RAMPAGING CADAVERS HAVE OVERRUN THE FACILITY.
DON'T BE RIDICULOUS. THIS IS A SECURE GOVERNMENT BUILDING. WITH TOP-NOTCH PROTOCOLS IN PLACE--
THWMP
CREAK
--WE'RE ALL GOING TO DIE! WAUGH!
HI. SO, THERE ARE, LIKE, A TON OF ZOMBIES COMING DOWN THE HALL AND I CAN'T FIND ANYONE WHO WORKS HERE...
THAT'S WEIRD, RIGHT? IS THAT WEIRD?
IT EXPLAINS THE WAIT. I'VE BEEN IN HERE FOR FORTY MINUTES.

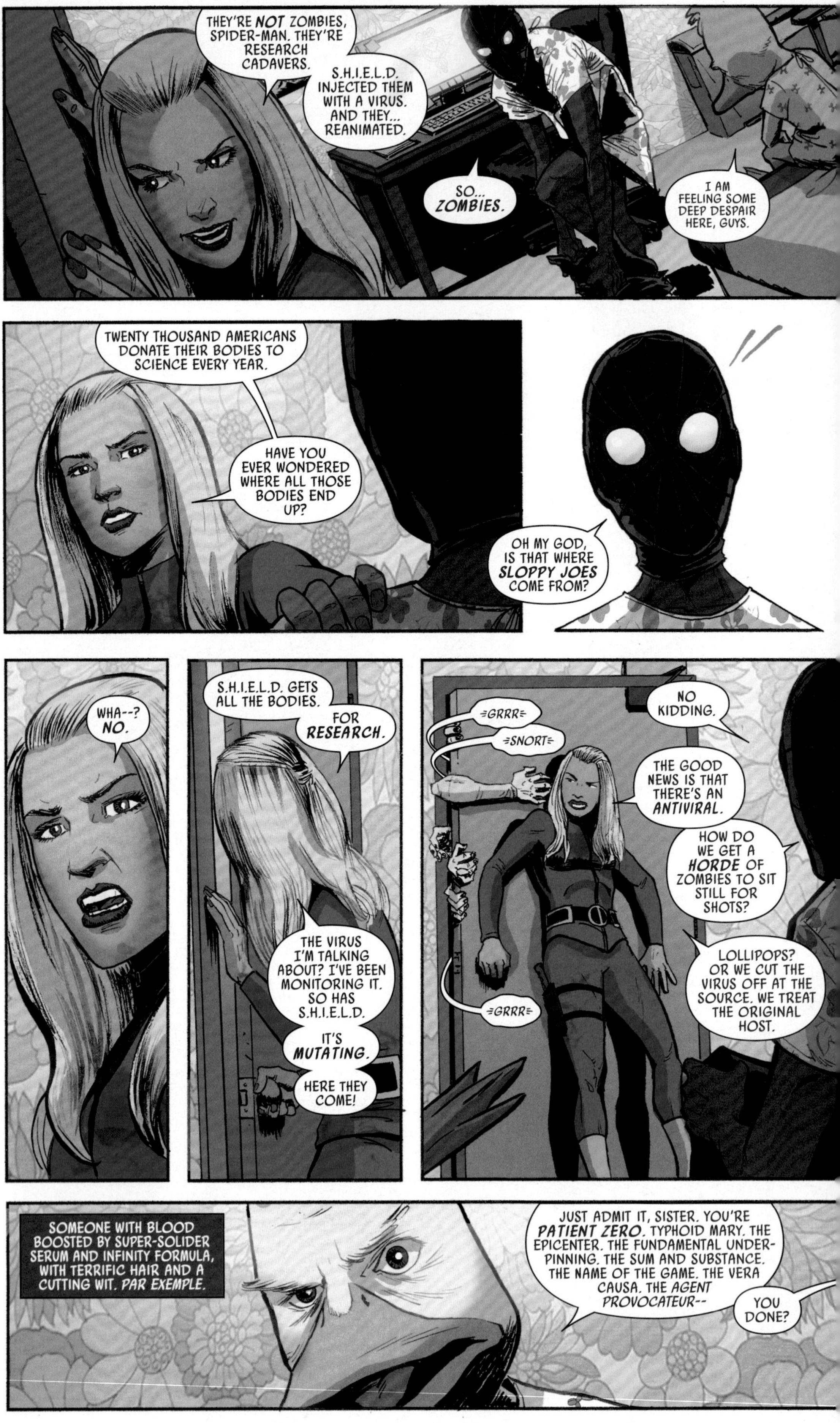

THEY'RE NOT ZOMBIES, SPIDER-MAN. THEY'RE RESEARCH CADAVERS.
S.H.I.E.L.D. INJECTED THEM WITH A VIRUS. AND THEY... REANIMATED.
SO... ZOMBIES.
I AM FEELING SOME DEEP DESPAIR HERE, GUYS.
TWENTY THOUSAND AMERICANS DONATE THEIR BODIES TO SCIENCE EVERY YEAR.
HAVE YOU EVER WONDERED WHERE ALL THOSE BODIES END UP?
OH MY GOD, IS THAT WHERE SLOPPY JOES COME FROM?
WHA--? NO.
S.H.I.E.L.D. GETS ALL THE BODIES.
FOR RESEARCH.
THE VIRUS I'M TALKING ABOUT? I'VE BEEN MONITORING IT. SO HAS S.H.I.E.L.D.
IT'S MUTATING.
HERE THEY COME!
GRRR
SNORT
GRRR
NO KIDDING.
THE GOOD NEWS IS THAT THERE'S AN ANTIVIRAL.
HOW DO WE GET A HORDE OF ZOMBIES TO SIT STILL FOR SHOTS?
LOLLIPOPS? OR WE CUT THE VIRUS OFF AT THE SOURCE. WE TREAT THE ORIGINAL HOST.
SOMEONE WITH BLOOD BOOSTED BY SUPER-SOLIDER SERUM AND INFINITY FORMULA, WITH TERRIFIC HAIR AND A CUTTING WIT. PAR EXEMPLE.
JUST ADMIT IT, SISTER. YOU'RE PATIENT ZERO. TYPHOID MARY. THE EPICENTER. THE FUNDAMENTAL UNDER-PINNING. THE SUM AND SUBSTANCE. THE NAME OF THE GAME. THE VERA CAUSA. THE AGENT PROVOCATEUR--
YOU DONE?

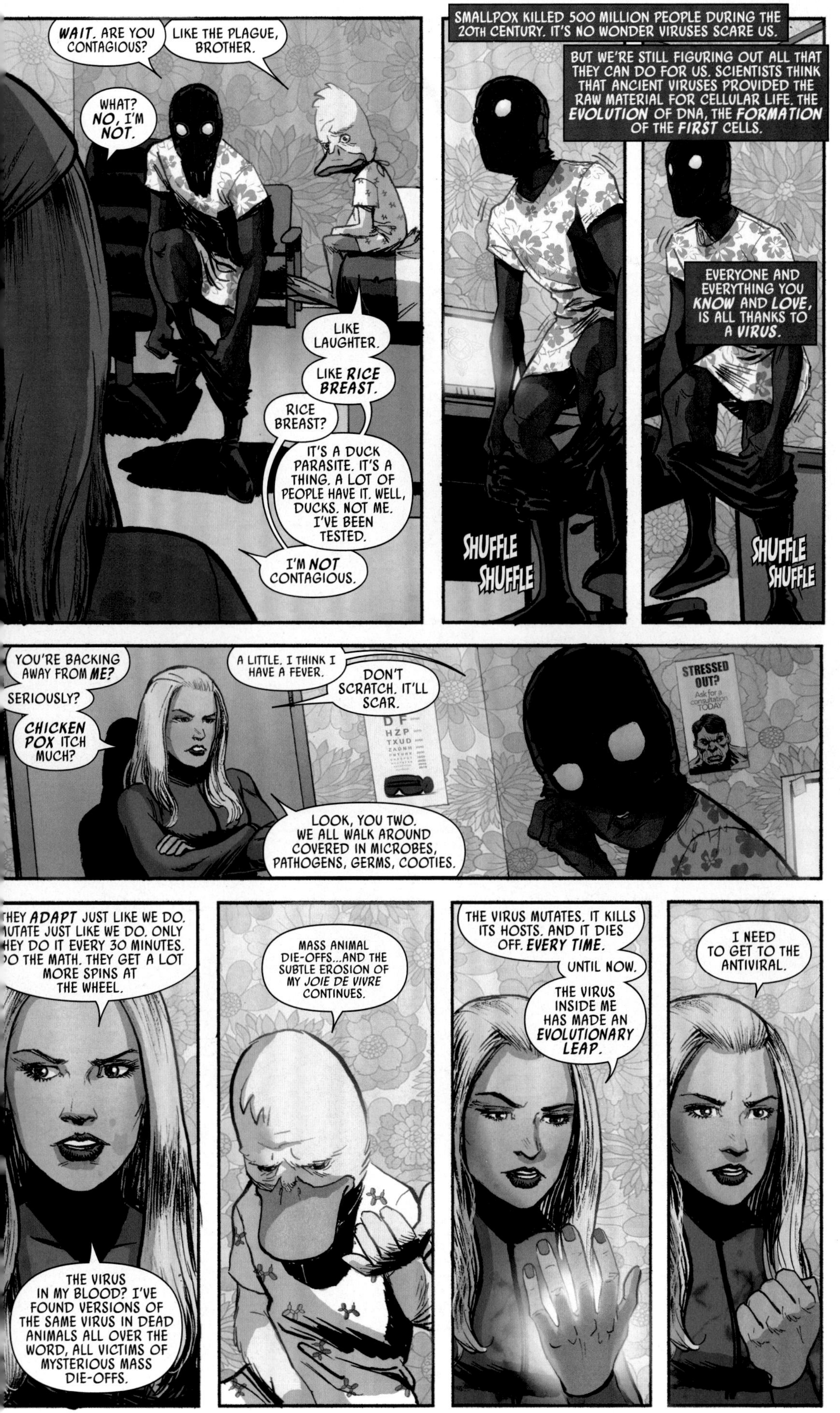
WAIT. ARE YOU CONTAGIOUS?
LIKE THE PLAGUE, BROTHER.
WHAT? NO, I'M NOT.
LIKE LAUGHTER.
LIKE RICE BREAST.
RICE BREAST?
IT'S A DUCK PARASITE. IT'S A THING. A LOT OF PEOPLE HAVE IT. WELL, DUCKS. NOT ME. I'VE BEEN TESTED.
I'M NOT CONTAGIOUS.
SMALLPOX KILLED 500 MILLION PEOPLE DURING THE 20TH CENTURY. IT'S NO WONDER VIRUSES SCARE US.
BUT WE'RE STILL FIGURING OUT ALL THAT THEY CAN DO FOR US. SCIENTISTS THINK THAT ANCIENT VIRUSES PROVIDED THE RAW MATERIAL FOR CELLULAR LIFE. THE EVOLUTION OF DNA, THE FORMATION OF THE FIRST CELLS.
SHUFFLE SHUFFLE
EVERYONE AND EVERYTHING YOU KNOW AND LOVE, IS ALL THANKS TO A VIRUS.
SHUFFLE SHUFFLE
YOU'RE BACKING AWAY FROM ME?
SERIOUSLY?
CHICKEN POX ITCH MUCH?
A LITTLE. I THINK I HAVE A FEVER.
DON'T SCRATCH. IT'LL SCAR.
STRESSED OUT?
Ask for a consultation TODAY
LOOK, YOU TWO. WE ALL WALK AROUND COVERED IN MICROBES, PATHOGENS, GERMS, COOTIES.
THEY ADAPT JUST LIKE WE DO. MUTATE JUST LIKE WE DO. ONLY THEY DO IT EVERY 30 MINUTES. DO THE MATH. THEY GET A LOT MORE SPINS AT THE WHEEL.
THE VIRUS IN MY BLOOD? I'VE FOUND VERSIONS OF THE SAME VIRUS IN DEAD ANIMALS ALL OVER THE WORD, ALL VICTIMS OF MYSTERIOUS MASS DIE-OFFS.
MASS ANIMAL DIE-OFFS...AND THE SUBTLE EROSION OF MY JOIE DE VIVRE CONTINUES.
THE VIRUS MUTATES. IT KILLS ITS HOSTS. AND IT DIES OFF. EVERY TIME.
UNTIL NOW.
THE VIRUS INSIDE ME HAS MADE AN EVOLUTIONARY LEAP.
I NEED TO GET TO THE ANTIVIRAL.

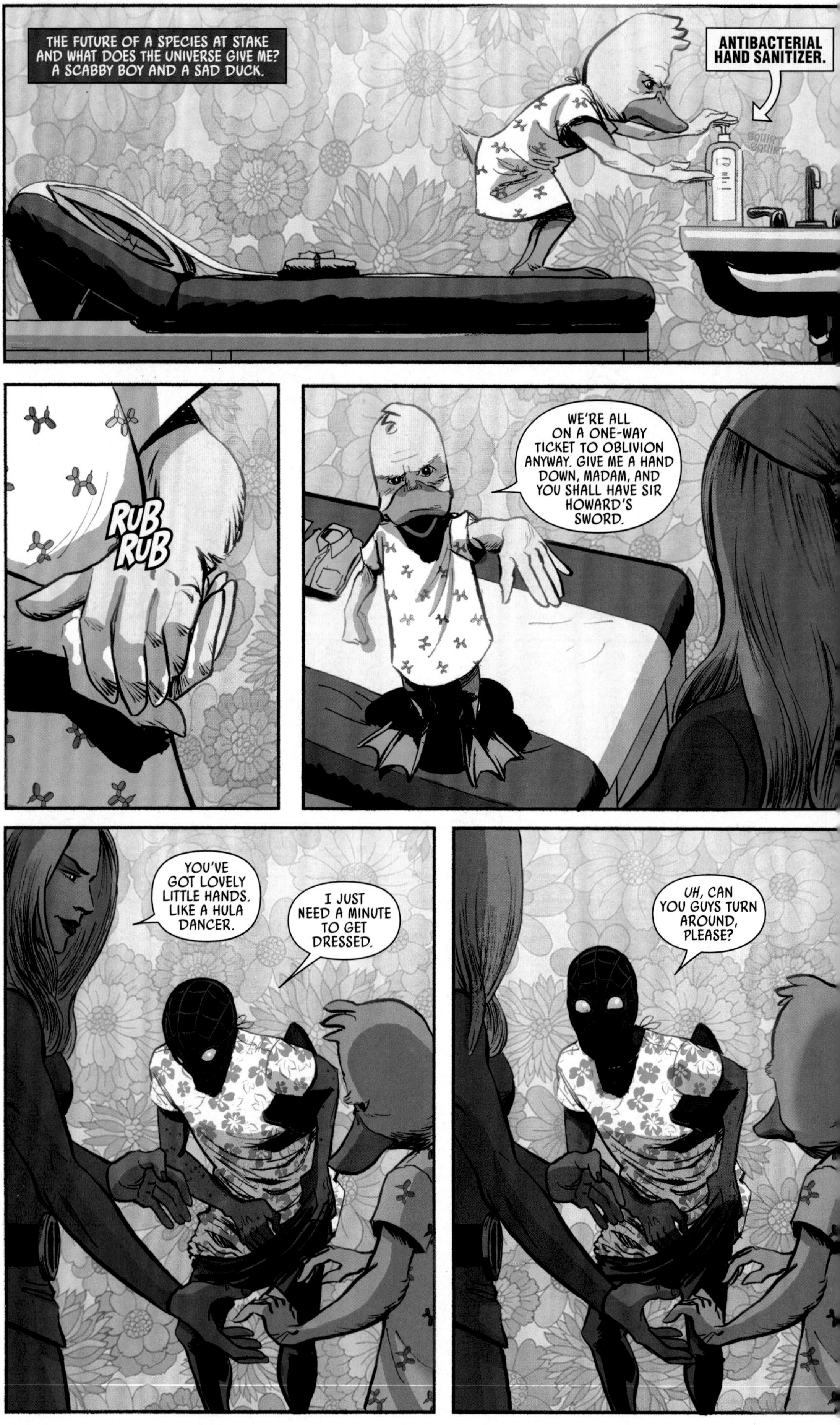
THE FUTURE OF A SPECIES AT STAKE AND WHAT DOES THE UNIVERSE GIVE ME? A SCABBY BOY AND A SAD DUCK.
ANTIBACTERIAL HAND SANITIZER.
SQUIRT SQUIRT
RUB RUB
WE'RE ALL ON A ONE-WAY TICKET TO OBLIVION ANYWAY. GIVE ME A HAND DOWN, MADAM, AND YOU SHALL HAVE SIR HOWARD'S SWORD.
YOU'VE GOT LOVELY LITTLE HANDS. LIKE A HULA DANCER.
I JUST NEED A MINUTE TO GET DRESSED.
UH, CAN YOU GUYS TURN AROUND, PLEASE?

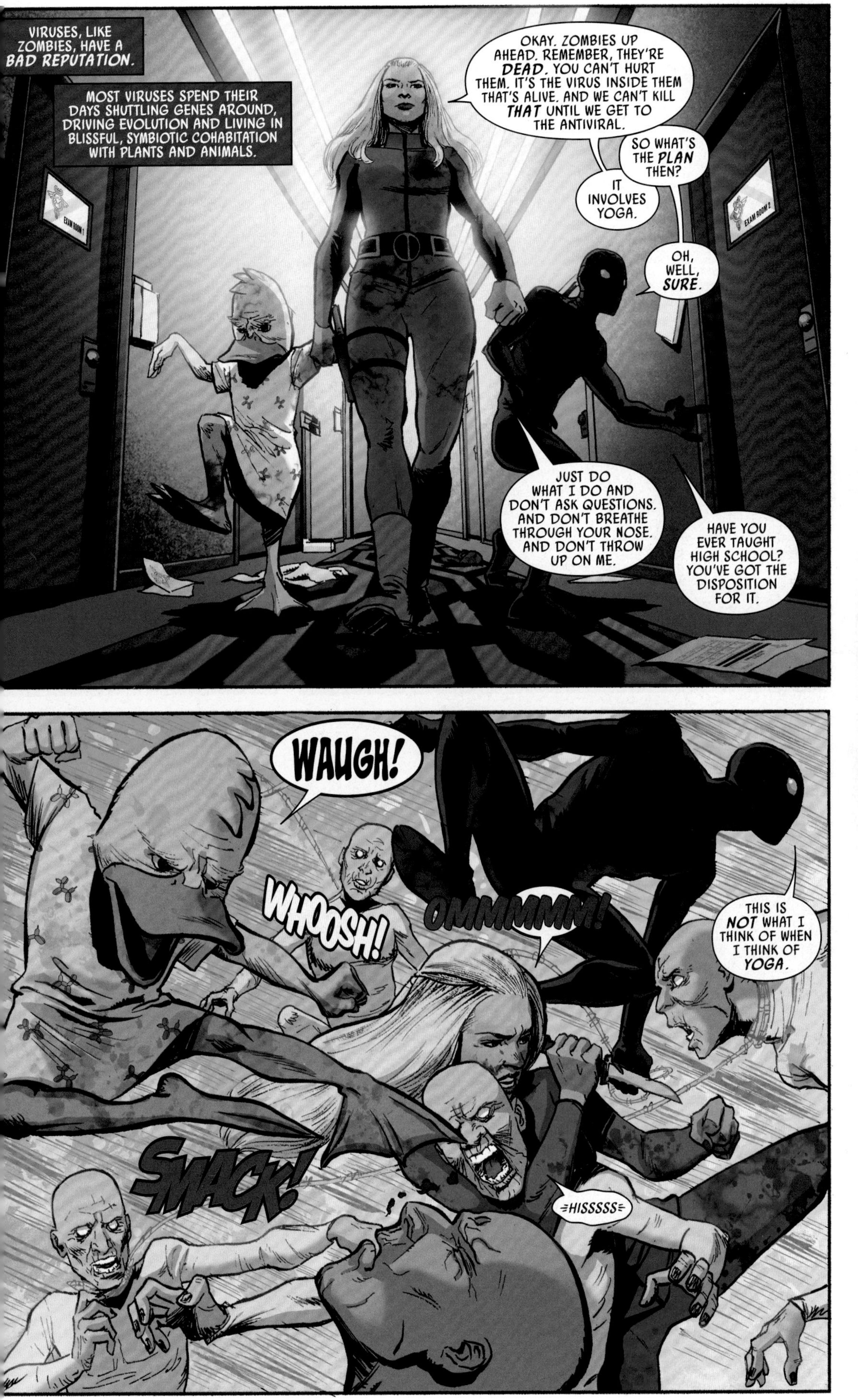
VIRUSES, LIKE ZOMBIES, HAVE A BAD REPUTATION.
MOST VIRUSES SPEND THEIR DAYS SHUTTLING GENES AROUND, DRIVING EVOLUTION AND LIVING IN BLISSFUL, SYMBIOTIC COHABITATION WITH PLANTS AND ANIMALS.
EXAM ROOM 1
EXAM ROOM 2
OKAY. ZOMBIES UP AHEAD. REMEMBER, THEY'RE DEAD. YOU CAN'T HURT THEM. IT'S THE VIRUS INSIDE THEM THAT'S ALIVE. AND WE CAN'T KILL THAT UNTIL WE GET TO THE ANTIVIRAL.
SO WHAT'S THE PLAN THEN?
IT INVOLVES YOGA.
OH, WELL, SURE.
JUST DO WHAT I DO AND DON'T ASK QUESTIONS. AND DON'T BREATHE THROUGH YOUR NOSE. AND DON'T THROW UP ON ME.
HAVE YOU EVER TAUGHT HIGH SCHOOL? YOU'VE GOT THE DISPOSITION FOR IT.
WAUGH!
WHOOSH!
OMMMMMM!
THIS IS NOT WHAT I THINK OF WHEN I THINK OF YOGA.
SMACK!
HISSSSS

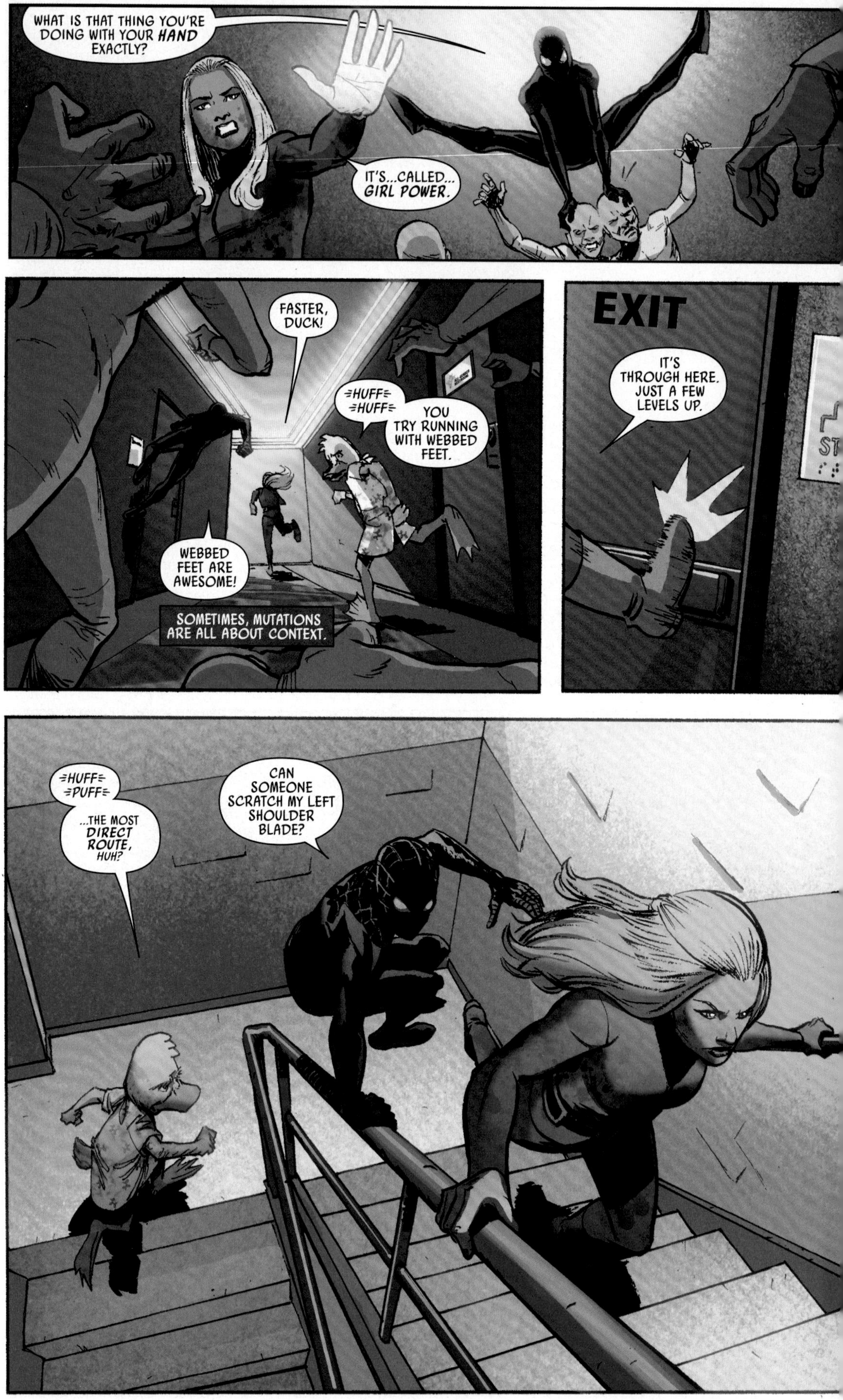
WHAT IS THAT THING YOU'RE DOING WITH YOUR HAND EXACTLY?
IT'S...CALLED... GIRL POWER.
FASTER, DUCK!
HUFF HUFF
YOU TRY RUNNING WITH WEBBED FEET.
WEBBED FEET ARE AWESOME!
SOMETIMES, MUTATIONS ARE ALL ABOUT CONTEXT.
EXIT
IT'S THROUGH HERE. JUST A FEW LEVELS UP.
HUFF PUFF
...THE MOST DIRECT ROUTE, HUH?
CAN SOMEONE SCRATCH MY LEFT SHOULDER BLADE?

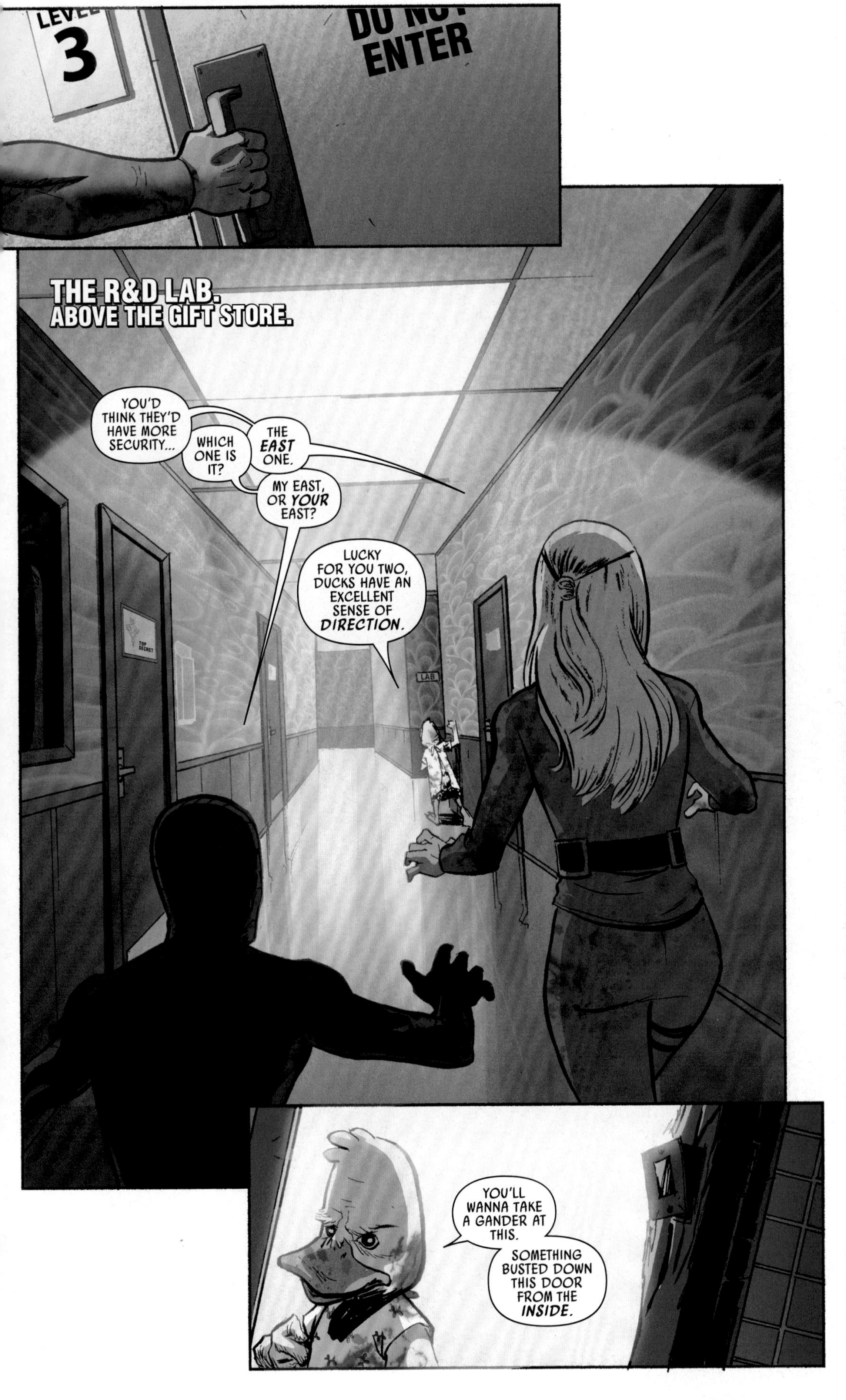
LEVEL 3
DO NOT ENTER
THE R&D LAB.
ABOVE THE GIFT STORE.
YOU'D THINK THEY'D HAVE MORE SECURITY...
WHICH ONE IS IT?
THE EAST ONE.
MY EAST, OR YOUR EAST?
LUCKY FOR YOU TWO, DUCKS HAVE AN EXCELLENT SENSE OF DIRECTION.
LAB
YOU'LL WANNA TAKE A GANDER AT THIS.
SOMETHING BUSTED DOWN THIS DOOR FROM THE INSIDE.

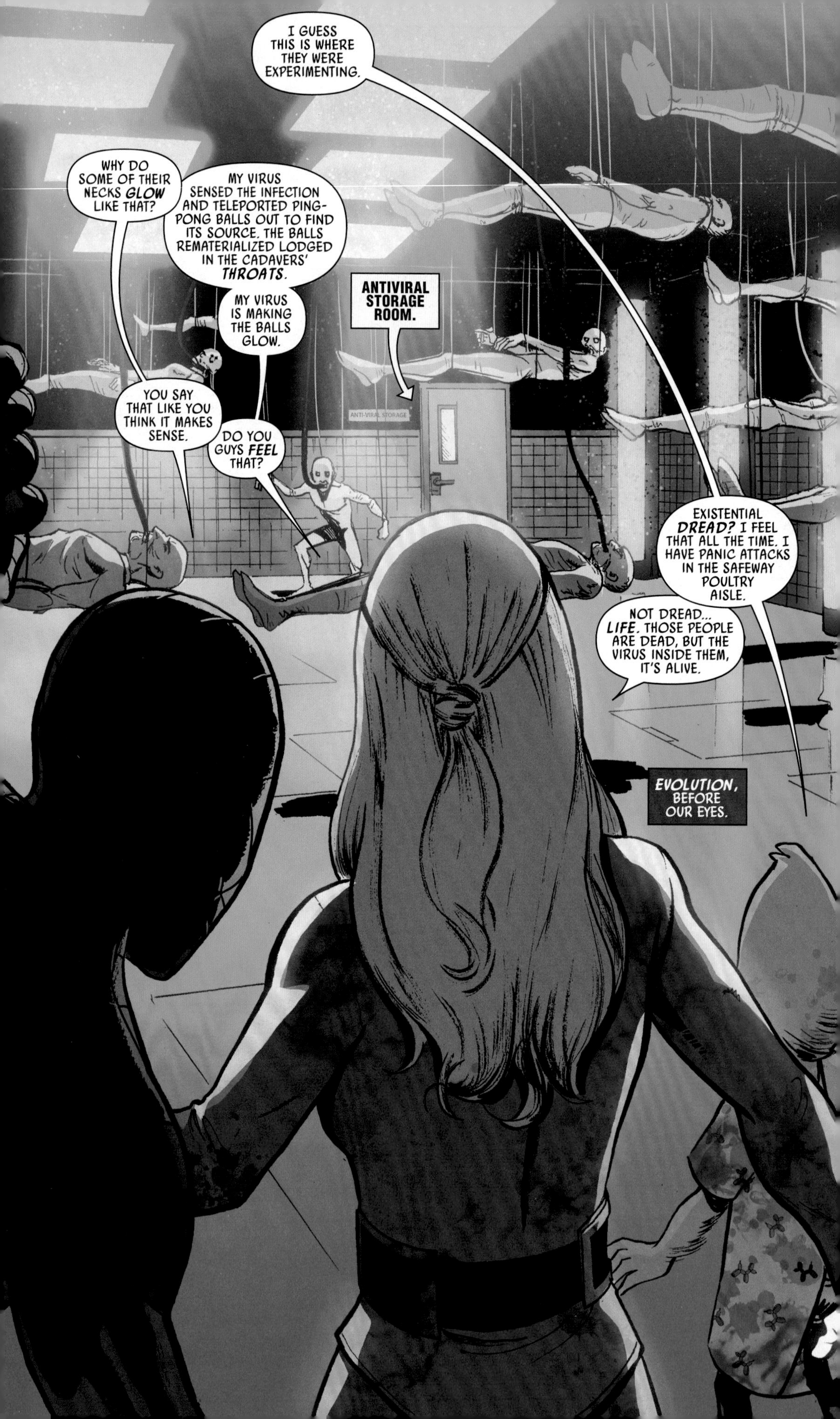
I GUESS THIS IS WHERE THEY WERE EXPERIMENTING.
WHY DO SOME OF THEIR NECKS GLOW LIKE THAT?
MY VIRUS SENSED THE INFECTION AND TELEPORTED PING-PONG BALLS OUT TO FIND ITS SOURCE. THE BALLS REMATERIALIZED LODGED IN THE CADAVERS' THROATS.
MY VIRUS IS MAKING THE BALLS GLOW.
ANTIVIRAL STORAGE ROOM.
ANTI-VIRAL STORAGE
YOU SAY THAT LIKE YOU THINK IT MAKES SENSE.
DO YOU GUYS FEEL THAT?
EXISTENTIAL DREAD? I FEEL THAT ALL THE TIME. I HAVE PANIC ATTACKS IN THE SAFEWAY POULTRY AISLE.
NOT DREAD... LIFE. THOSE PEOPLE ARE DEAD, BUT THE VIRUS INSIDE THEM, IT'S ALIVE.
EVOLUTION, BEFORE OUR EYES.

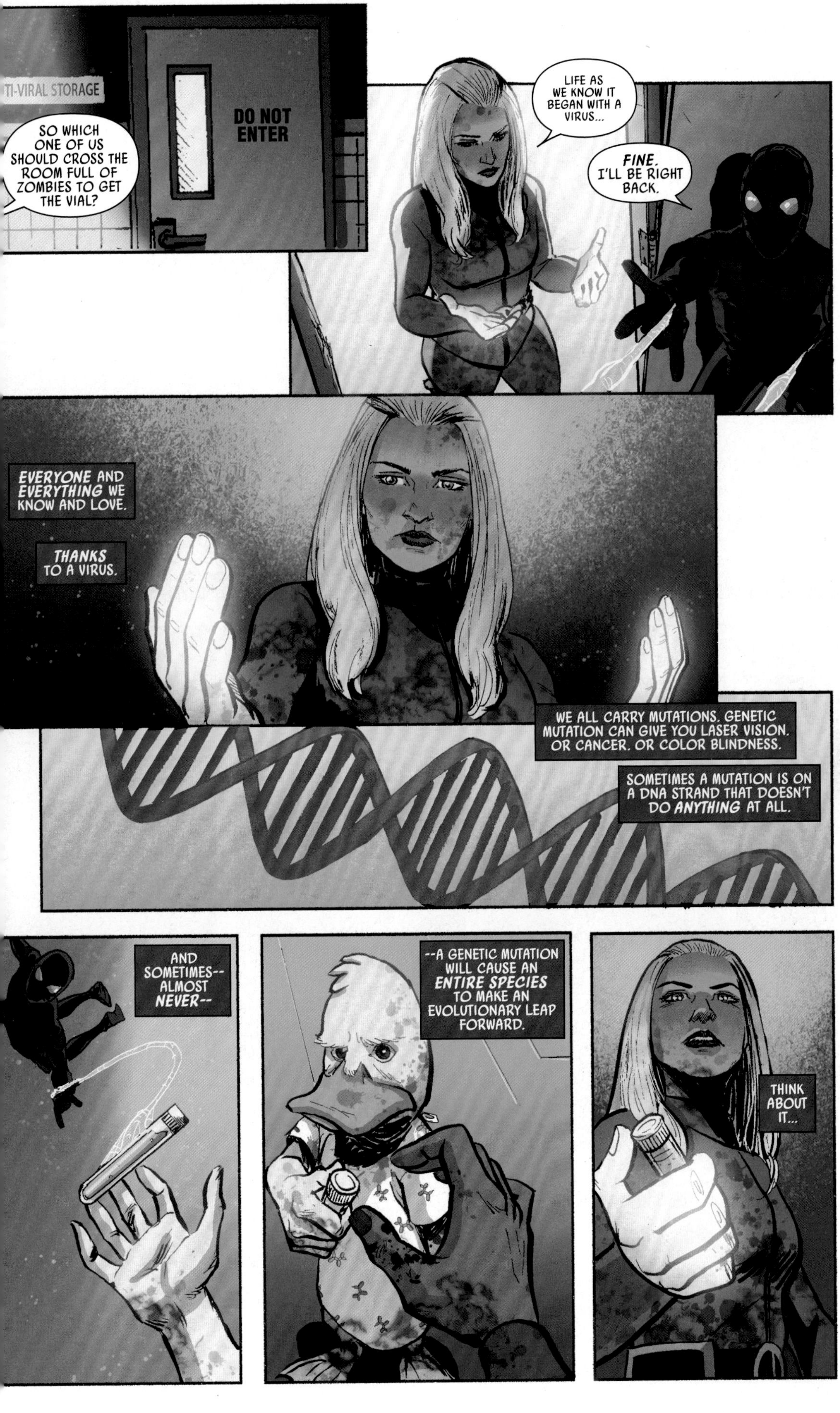

TI-VIRAL STORAGE
DO NOT ENTER
SO WHICH ONE OF US SHOULD CROSS THE ROOM FULL OF ZOMBIES TO GET THE VIAL?
LIFE AS WE KNOW IT BEGAN WITH A VIRUS...
FINE. I'LL BE RIGHT BACK.
EVERYONE AND EVERYTHING WE KNOW AND LOVE.
THANKS TO A VIRUS.
WE ALL CARRY MUTATIONS. GENETIC MUTATION CAN GIVE YOU LASER VISION. OR CANCER. OR COLOR BLINDNESS.
SOMETIMES A MUTATION IS ON A DNA STRAND THAT DOESN'T DO ANYTHING AT ALL.
AND SOMETIMES-- ALMOST NEVER--
--A GENETIC MUTATION WILL CAUSE AN ENTIRE SPECIES TO MAKE AN EVOLUTIONARY LEAP FORWARD.
THINK ABOUT IT...

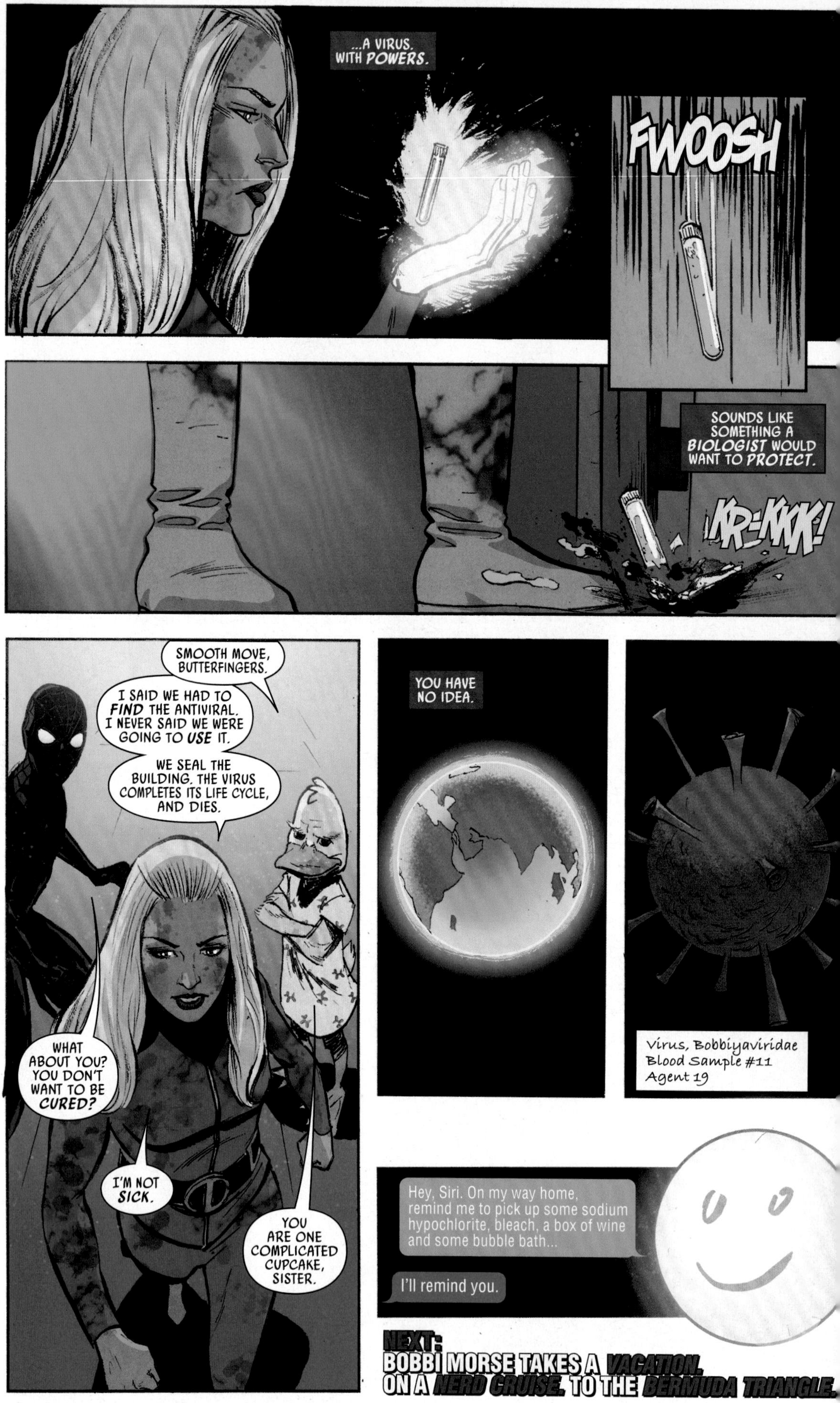
...A VIRUS. WITH POWERS.
FWOOSH
SOUNDS LIKE SOMETHING A BIOLOGIST WOULD WANT TO PROTECT.
KR-KKK!
SMOOTH MOVE, BUTTERFINGERS.
I SAID WE HAD TO FIND THE ANTIVIRAL. I NEVER SAID WE WERE GOING TO USE IT.
WE SEAL THE BUILDING. THE VIRUS COMPLETES ITS LIFE CYCLE, AND DIES.
WHAT ABOUT YOU? YOU DON'T WANT TO BE CURED?
I'M NOT SICK.
YOU ARE ONE COMPLICATED CUPCAKE, SISTER.
YOU HAVE NO IDEA.
Virus, Bobbiyaviridae
Blood Sample #11
Agent 19
Hey, Siri. On my way home, remind me to pick up some sodium hypochlorite, bleach, a box of wine and some bubble bath...
I'll remind you.
NEXT:
BOBBI MORSE TAKES A VACATION.
ON A NERD CRUISE. TO THE BERMUDA TRIANGLE.

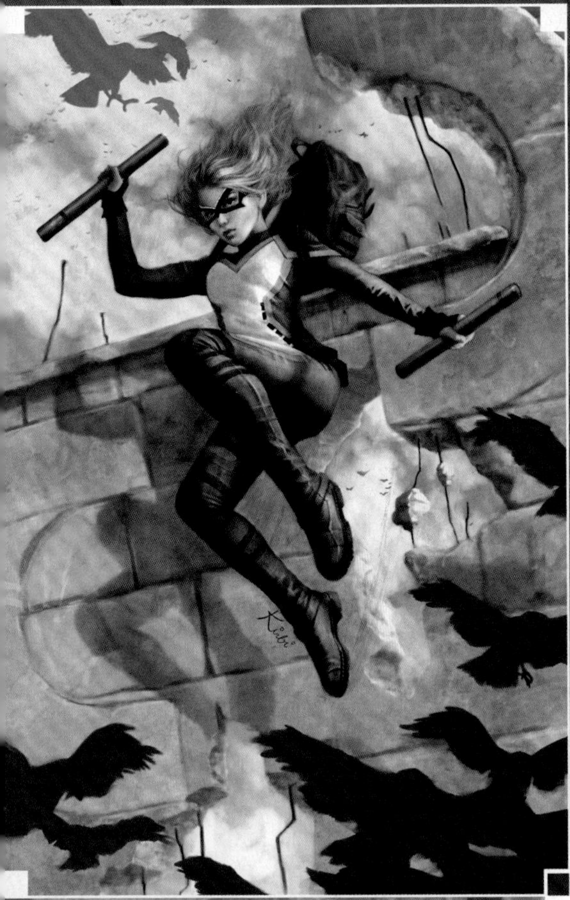

#1 WOMEN OF POWER VARIANT BY
Kirbi Fagan

#1 VARIANT BY
Skottie Young

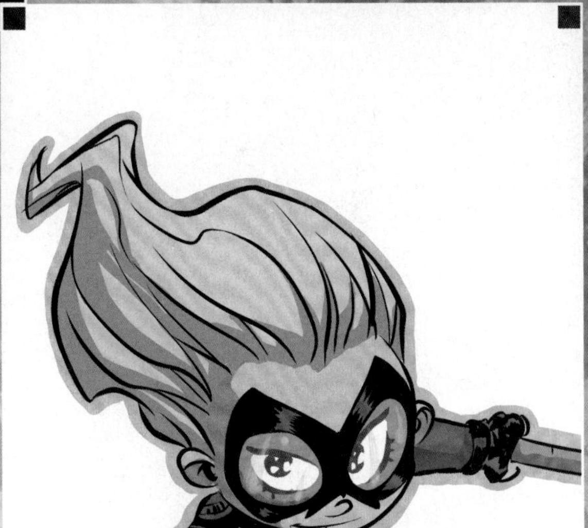

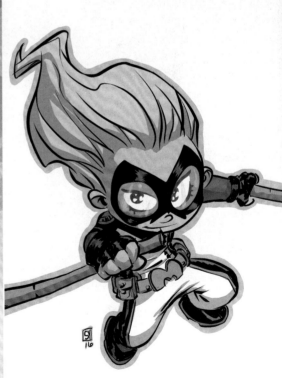

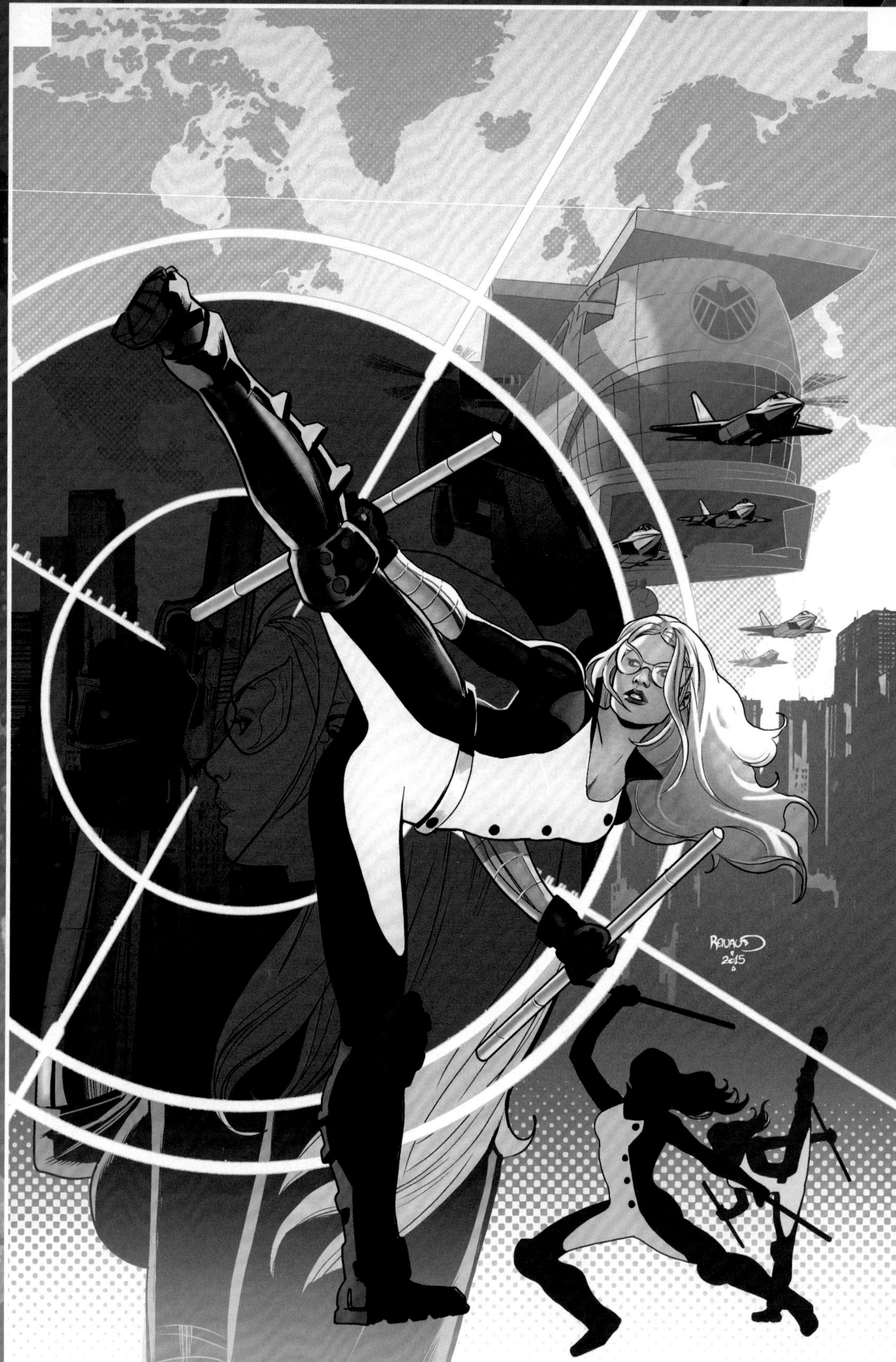
RAVAUD
2015

Mockingbird: S.H.I.E.L.D. 50TH Anniversary #1

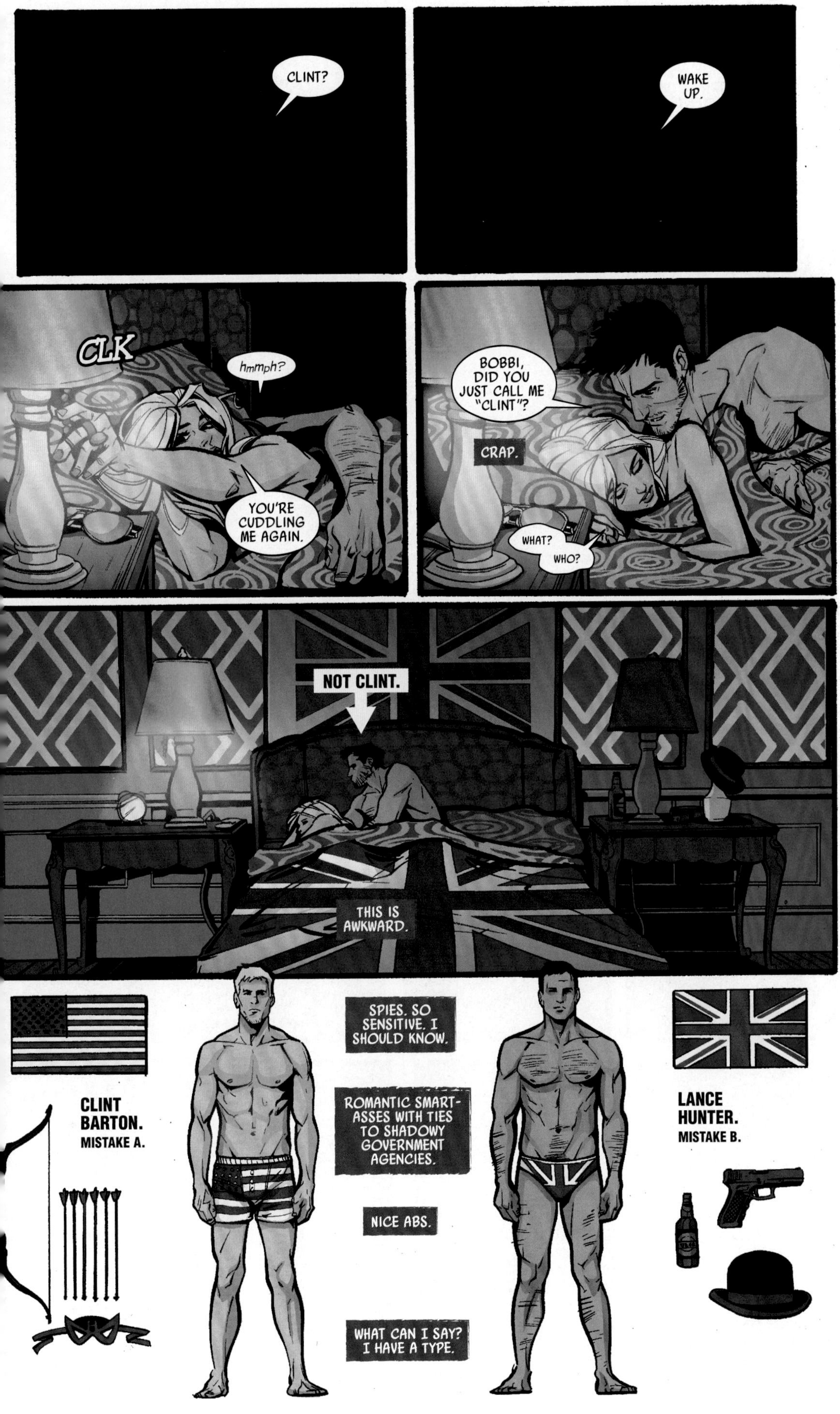

CLINT?
WAKE UP.
CLK
hmmph?
YOU'RE CUDDLING ME AGAIN.
BOBBI, DID YOU JUST CALL ME "CLINT"?
CRAP.
WHAT? WHO?
NOT CLINT.
THIS IS AWKWARD.
SPIES. SO SENSITIVE. I SHOULD KNOW.
CLINT BARTON.
MISTAKE A.
ROMANTIC SMART-ASSES WITH TIES TO SHADOWY GOVERNMENT AGENCIES.
LANCE HUNTER.
MISTAKE B.
NICE ABS.
WHAT CAN I SAY? I HAVE A TYPE.

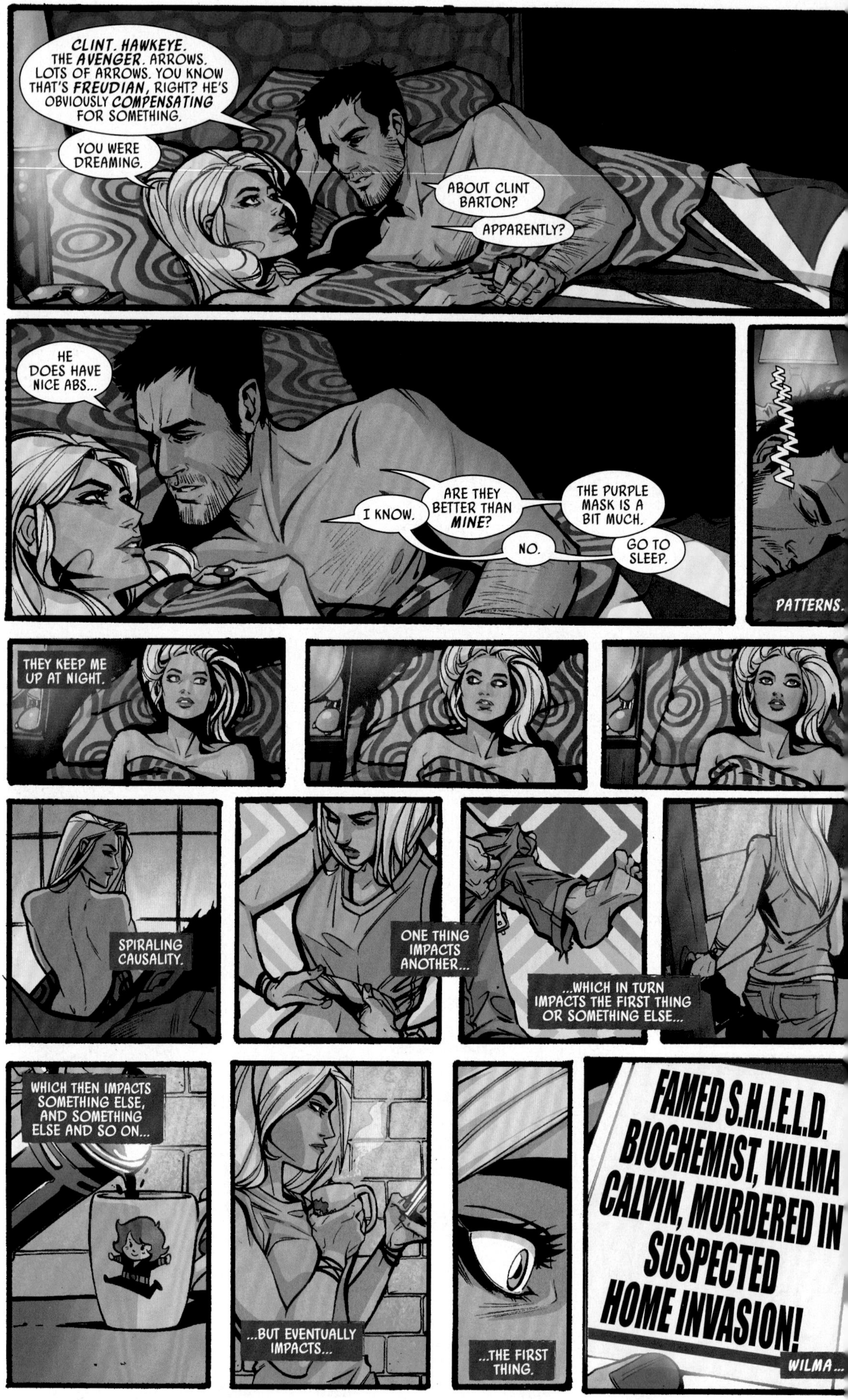

CLINT. HAWKEYE. THE AVENGER. ARROWS. LOTS OF ARROWS. YOU KNOW THAT'S FREUDIAN, RIGHT? HE'S OBVIOUSLY COMPENSATING FOR SOMETHING.
YOU WERE DREAMING.
ABOUT CLINT BARTON?
APPARENTLY?
HE DOES HAVE NICE ABS...
I KNOW.
ARE THEY BETTER THAN MINE?
THE PURPLE MASK IS A BIT MUCH.
NO.
GO TO SLEEP.
NNNNNNNN
PATTERNS.
THEY KEEP ME UP AT NIGHT.
SPIRALING CAUSALITY.
ONE THING IMPACTS ANOTHER...
...WHICH IN TURN IMPACTS THE FIRST THING OR SOMETHING ELSE...
WHICH THEN IMPACTS SOMETHING ELSE, AND SOMETHING ELSE AND SO ON...
...BUT EVENTUALLY IMPACTS...
...THE FIRST THING.
FAMED S.H.I.E.L.D. BIOCHEMIST, WILMA CALVIN, MURDERED IN SUSPECTED HOME INVASION!
WILMA...

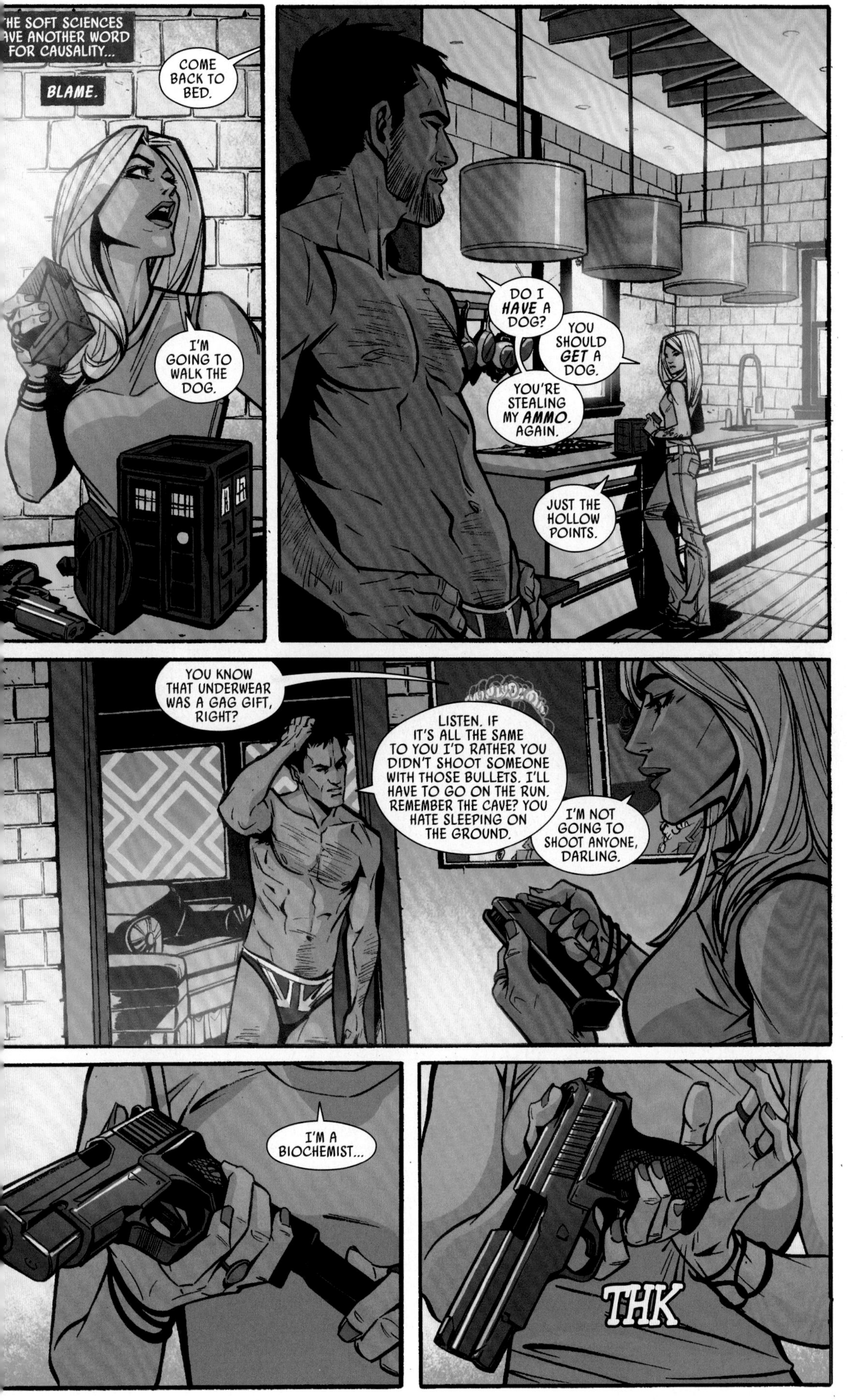

THE SOFT SCIENCES
AVE ANOTHER WORD
FOR CAUSALITY...
BLAME.
COME BACK TO BED.
I'M GOING TO WALK THE DOG.
DO I HAVE A DOG?
YOU SHOULD GET A DOG.
YOU'RE STEALING MY AMMO. AGAIN.
JUST THE HOLLOW POINTS.
YOU KNOW THAT UNDERWEAR WAS A GAG GIFT, RIGHT?
LISTEN. IF IT'S ALL THE SAME TO YOU I'D RATHER YOU DIDN'T SHOOT SOMEONE WITH THOSE BULLETS. I'LL HAVE TO GO ON THE RUN. REMEMBER THE CAVE? YOU HATE SLEEPING ON THE GROUND.
I'M NOT GOING TO SHOOT ANYONE, DARLING.
I'M A BIOCHEMIST...
THK

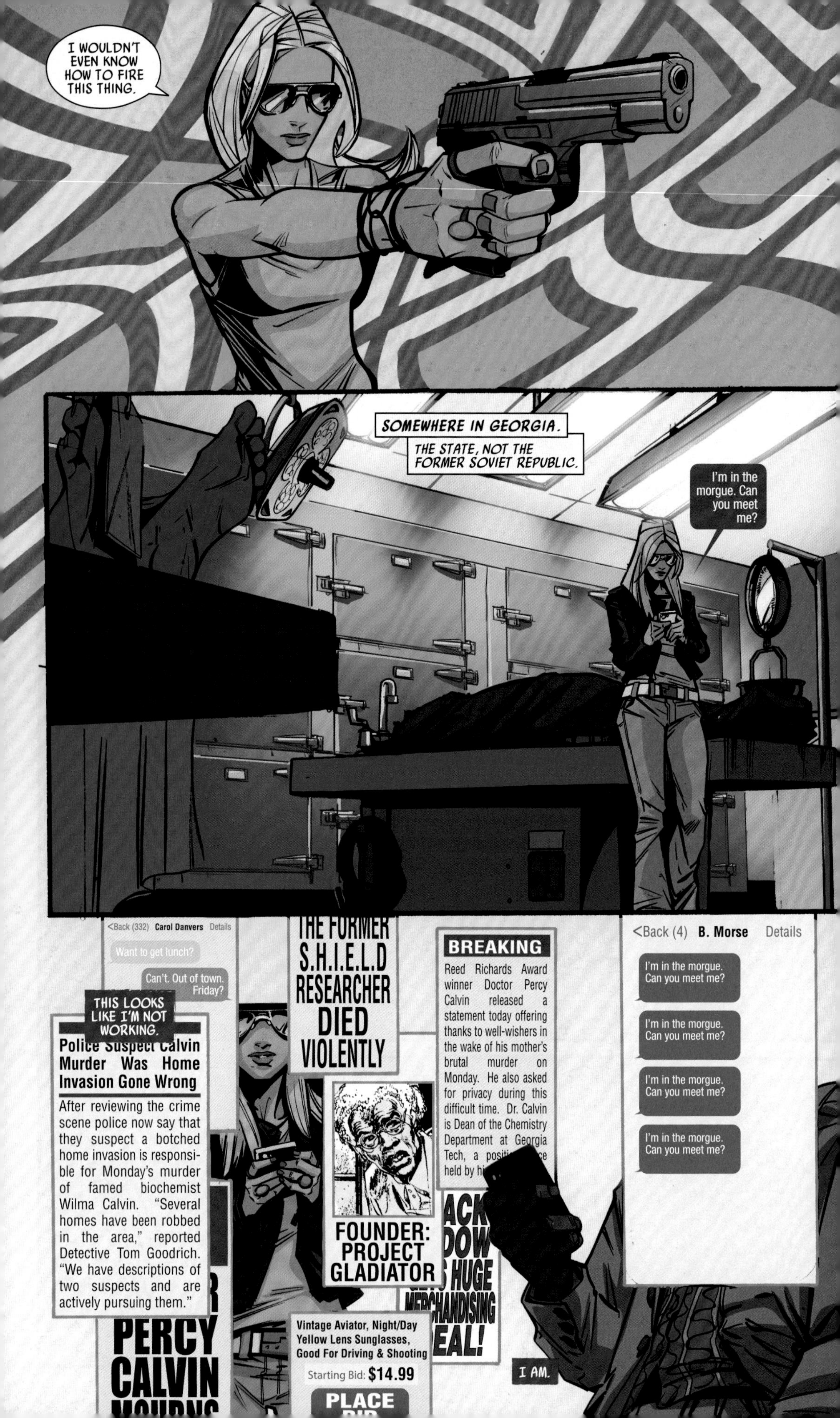
I WOULDN'T EVEN KNOW HOW TO FIRE THIS THING.
SOMEWHERE IN GEORGIA.
THE STATE, NOT THE FORMER SOVIET REPUBLIC.
I'm in the morgue. Can you meet me?
<Back (332) Carol Danvers Details
Want to get lunch?
Can't. Out of town. Friday?
THIS LOOKS LIKE I'M NOT WORKING.
Police Suspect Calvin Murder Was Home Invasion Gone Wrong
After reviewing the crime scene police now say that they suspect a botched home invasion is responsible for Monday's murder of famed biochemist Wilma Calvin. "Several homes have been robbed in the area," reported Detective Tom Goodrich. "We have descriptions of two suspects and are actively pursuing them."
PERCY CALVIN
THE FORMER S.H.I.E.L.D RESEARCHER DIED VIOLENTLY
FOUNDER: PROJECT GLADIATOR
BREAKING
Reed Richards Award winner Doctor Percy Calvin released a statement today offering thanks to well-wishers in the wake of his mother's brutal murder on Monday. He also asked for privacy during this difficult time. Dr. Calvin is Dean of the Chemistry Department at Georgia Tech,
Vintage Aviator, Night/Day Yellow Lens Sunglasses, Good For Driving & Shooting
Starting Bid: $14.99
PLACE
<Back (4) B. Morse Details
I'm in the morgue. Can you meet me?
I'm in the morgue. Can you meet me?
I'm in the morgue. Can you meet me?
I'm in the morgue. Can you meet me?
I AM.

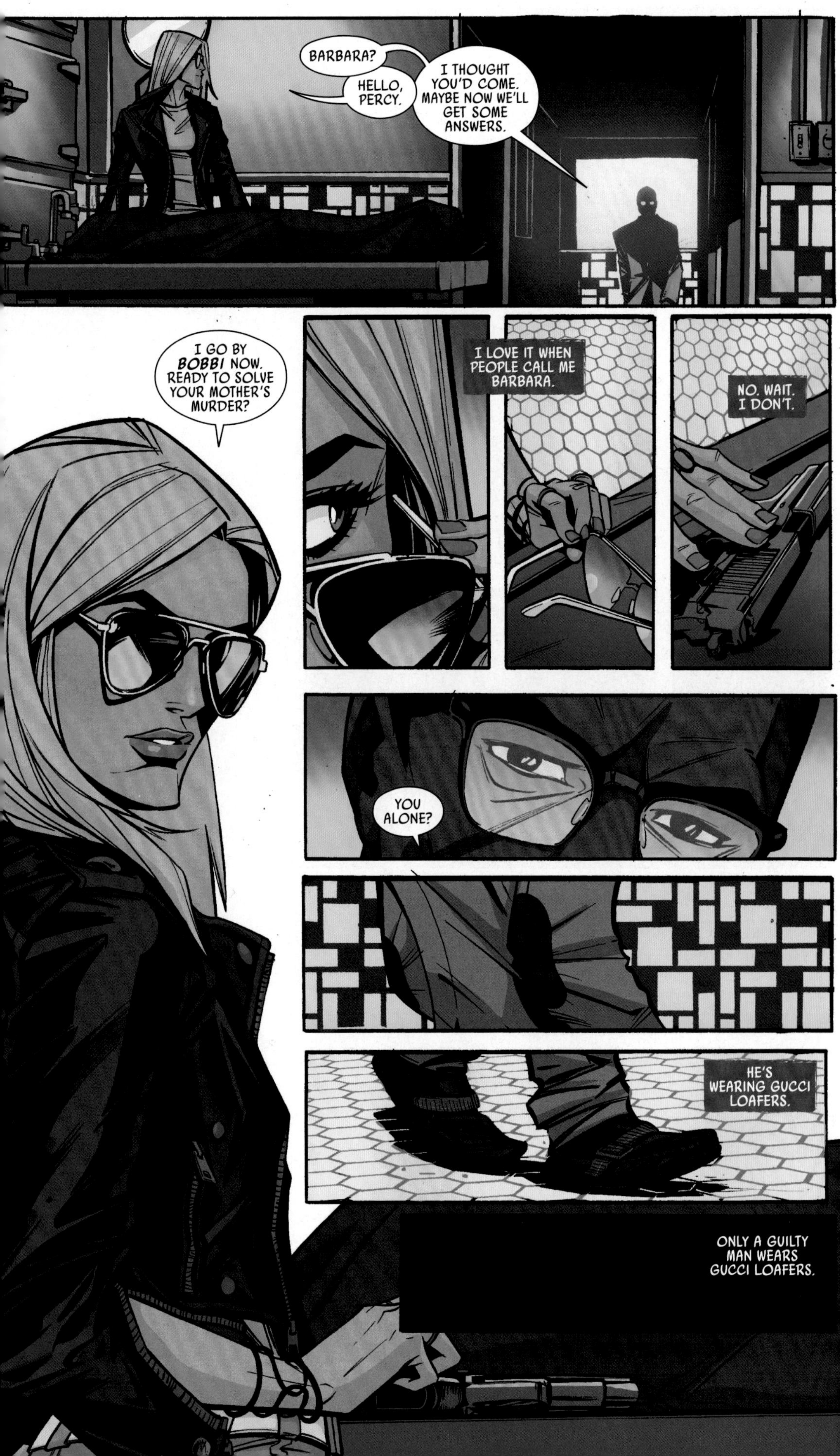

BARBARA?
HELLO, PERCY.
I THOUGHT YOU'D COME. MAYBE NOW WE'LL GET SOME ANSWERS.
I GO BY BOBBI NOW. READY TO SOLVE YOUR MOTHER'S MURDER?
I LOVE IT WHEN PEOPLE CALL ME BARBARA.
NO. WAIT. I DON'T.
YOU ALONE?
HE'S WEARING GUCCI LOAFERS.
ONLY A GUILTY MAN WEARS GUCCI LOAFERS.

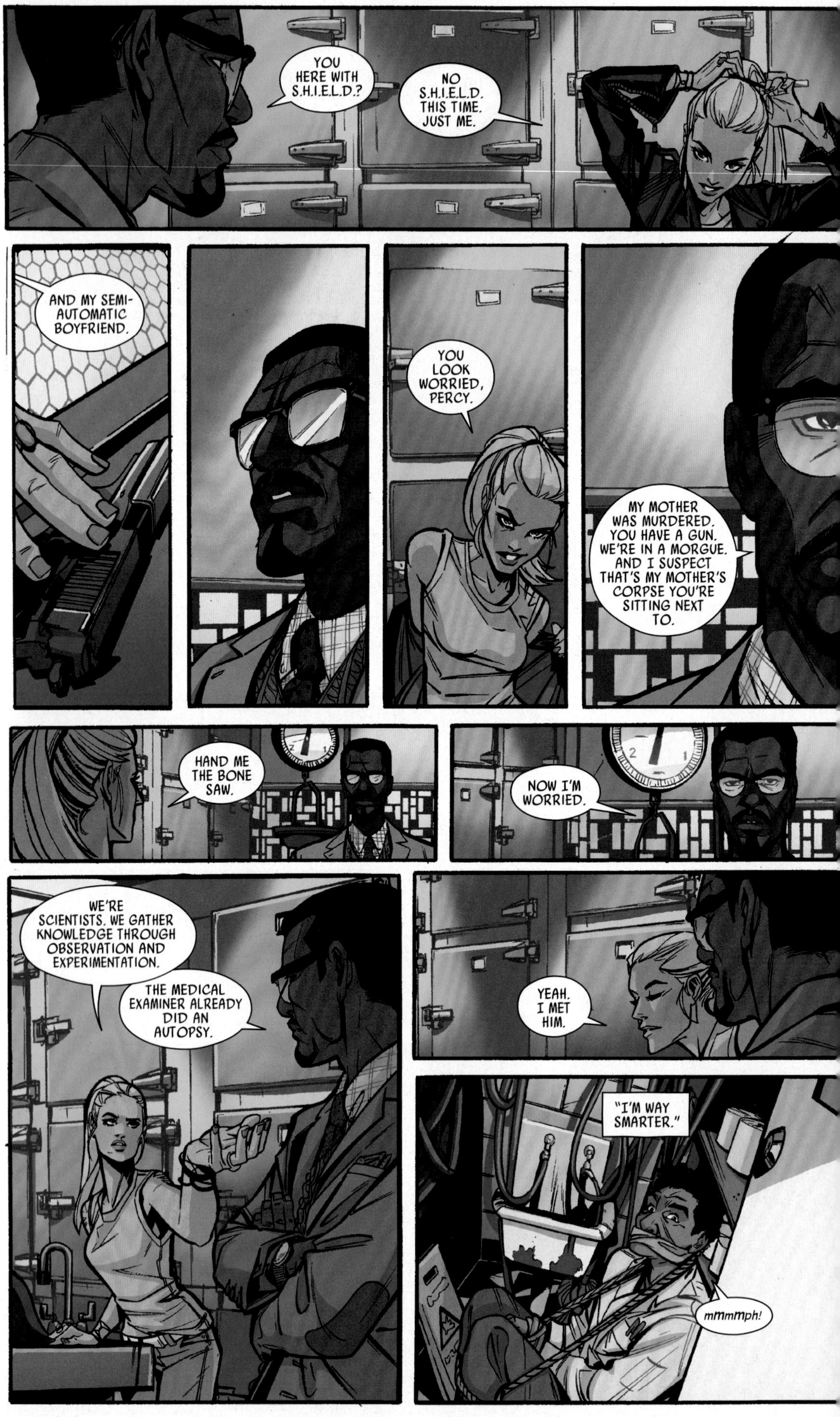
YOU HERE WITH S.H.I.E.L.D.?
NO S.H.I.E.L.D. THIS TIME. JUST ME.
AND MY SEMI-AUTOMATIC BOYFRIEND.
YOU LOOK WORRIED, PERCY.
MY MOTHER WAS MURDERED. YOU HAVE A GUN. WE'RE IN A MORGUE. AND I SUSPECT THAT'S MY MOTHER'S CORPSE YOU'RE SITTING NEXT TO.
HAND ME THE BONE SAW.
NOW I'M WORRIED.
WE'RE SCIENTISTS. WE GATHER KNOWLEDGE THROUGH OBSERVATION AND EXPERIMENTATION.
THE MEDICAL EXAMINER ALREADY DID AN AUTOPSY.
YEAH. I MET HIM.
"I'M WAY SMARTER."
mmmmph!

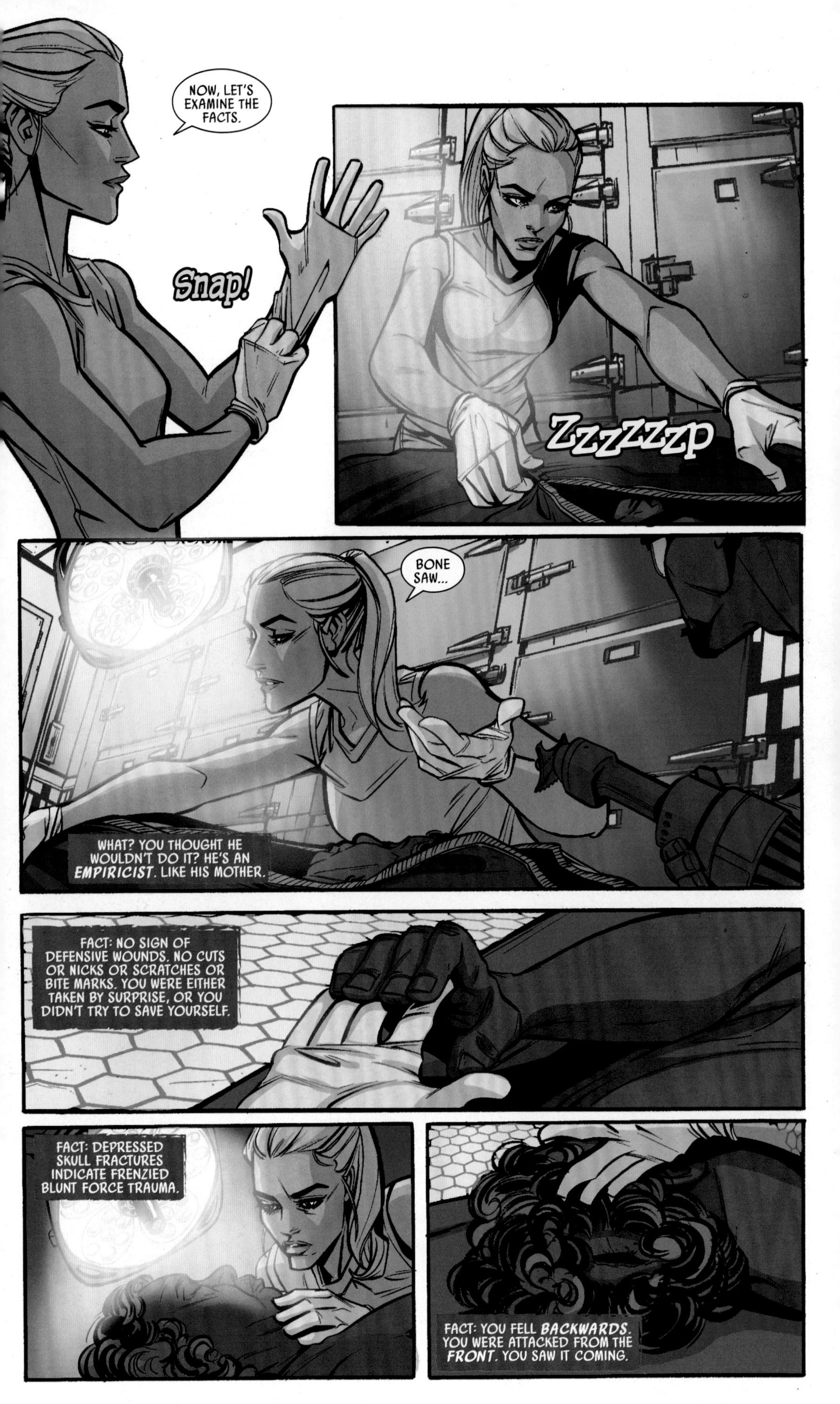
NOW, LET'S EXAMINE THE FACTS.
Snap!
Zzzzzzp
BONE SAW...
WHAT? YOU THOUGHT HE WOULDN'T DO IT? HE'S AN *EMPIRICIST*. LIKE HIS MOTHER.
FACT: NO SIGN OF DEFENSIVE WOUNDS. NO CUTS OR NICKS OR SCRATCHES OR BITE MARKS. YOU WERE EITHER TAKEN BY SURPRISE, OR YOU DIDN'T TRY TO SAVE YOURSELF.
FACT: DEPRESSED SKULL FRACTURES INDICATE FRENZIED BLUNT FORCE TRAUMA.
FACT: YOU FELL *BACKWARDS*. YOU WERE ATTACKED FROM THE *FRONT*. YOU SAW IT COMING.

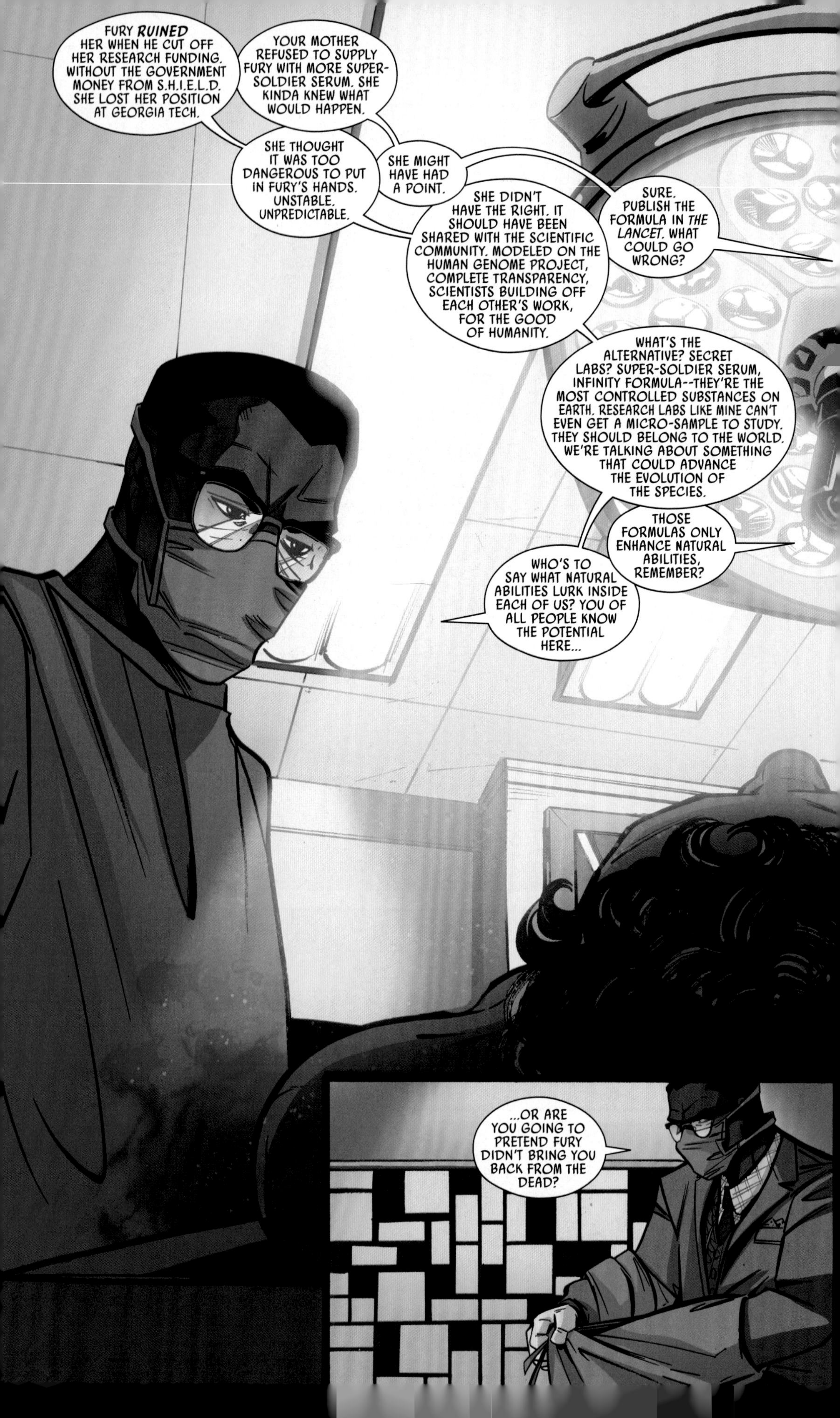
FURY *RUINED* HER WHEN HE CUT OFF HER RESEARCH FUNDING. WITHOUT THE GOVERNMENT MONEY FROM S.H.I.E.L.D. SHE LOST HER POSITION AT GEORGIA TECH.
YOUR MOTHER REFUSED TO SUPPLY FURY WITH MORE SUPER-SOLDIER SERUM. SHE KINDA KNEW WHAT WOULD HAPPEN.
SHE THOUGHT IT WAS TOO DANGEROUS TO PUT IN FURY'S HANDS. UNSTABLE. UNPREDICTABLE.
SHE MIGHT HAVE HAD A POINT.
SHE DIDN'T HAVE THE RIGHT. IT SHOULD HAVE BEEN SHARED WITH THE SCIENTIFIC COMMUNITY. MODELED ON THE HUMAN GENOME PROJECT, COMPLETE TRANSPARENCY, SCIENTISTS BUILDING OFF EACH OTHER'S WORK, FOR THE GOOD OF HUMANITY.
SURE. PUBLISH THE FORMULA IN *THE LANCET*. WHAT COULD GO WRONG?
WHAT'S THE ALTERNATIVE? SECRET LABS? SUPER-SOLDIER SERUM, INFINITY FORMULA--THEY'RE THE MOST CONTROLLED SUBSTANCES ON EARTH. RESEARCH LABS LIKE MINE CAN'T EVEN GET A MICRO-SAMPLE TO STUDY. THEY SHOULD BELONG TO THE WORLD. WE'RE TALKING ABOUT SOMETHING THAT COULD ADVANCE THE EVOLUTION OF THE SPECIES.
THOSE FORMULAS ONLY ENHANCE NATURAL ABILITIES, REMEMBER?
WHO'S TO SAY WHAT NATURAL ABILITIES LURK INSIDE EACH OF US? YOU OF ALL PEOPLE KNOW THE POTENTIAL HERE...
...OR ARE YOU GOING TO PRETEND FURY DIDN'T BRING YOU BACK FROM THE DEAD?

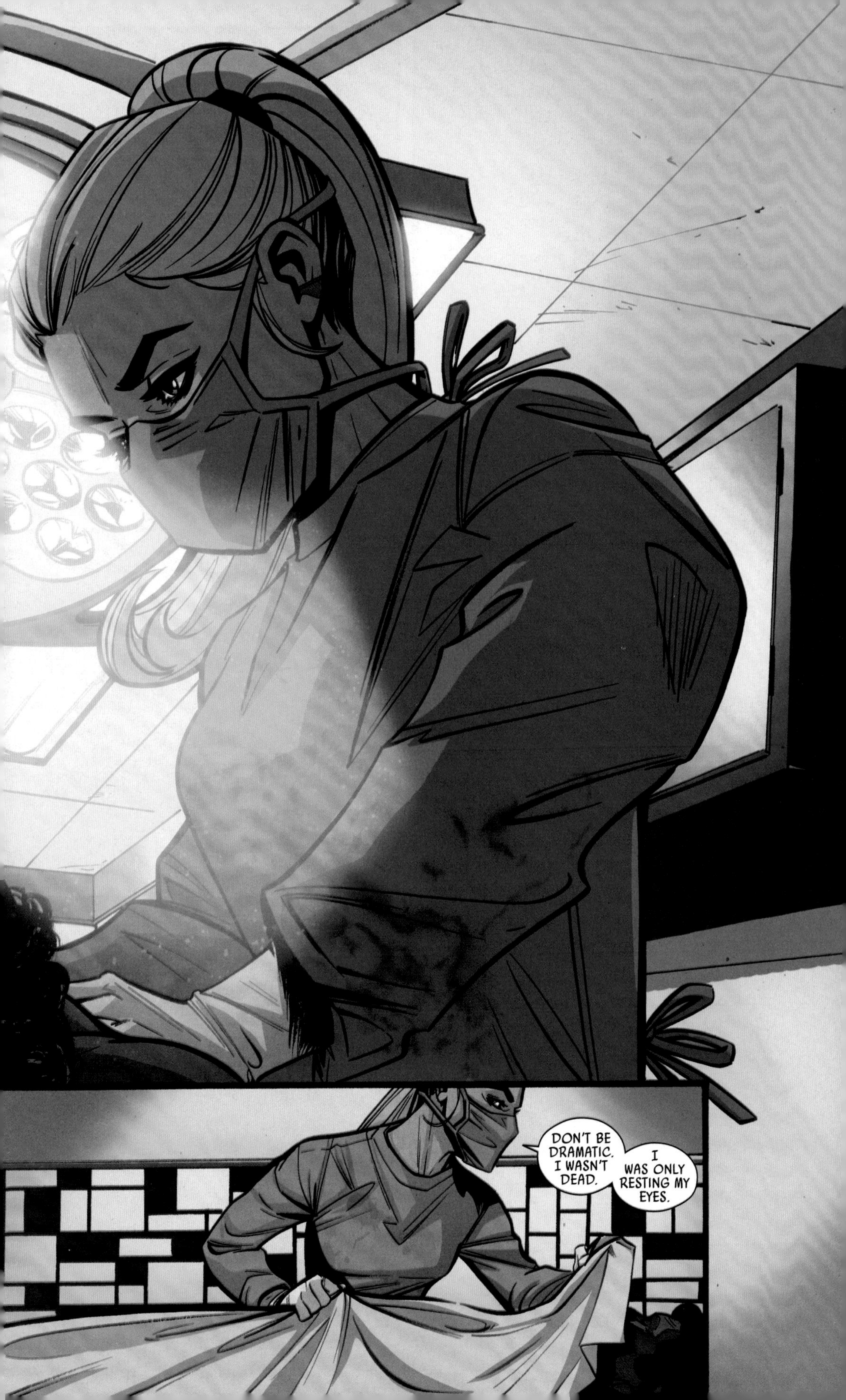
DON'T BE DRAMATIC. I WASN'T DEAD.
I WAS ONLY RESTING MY EYES.

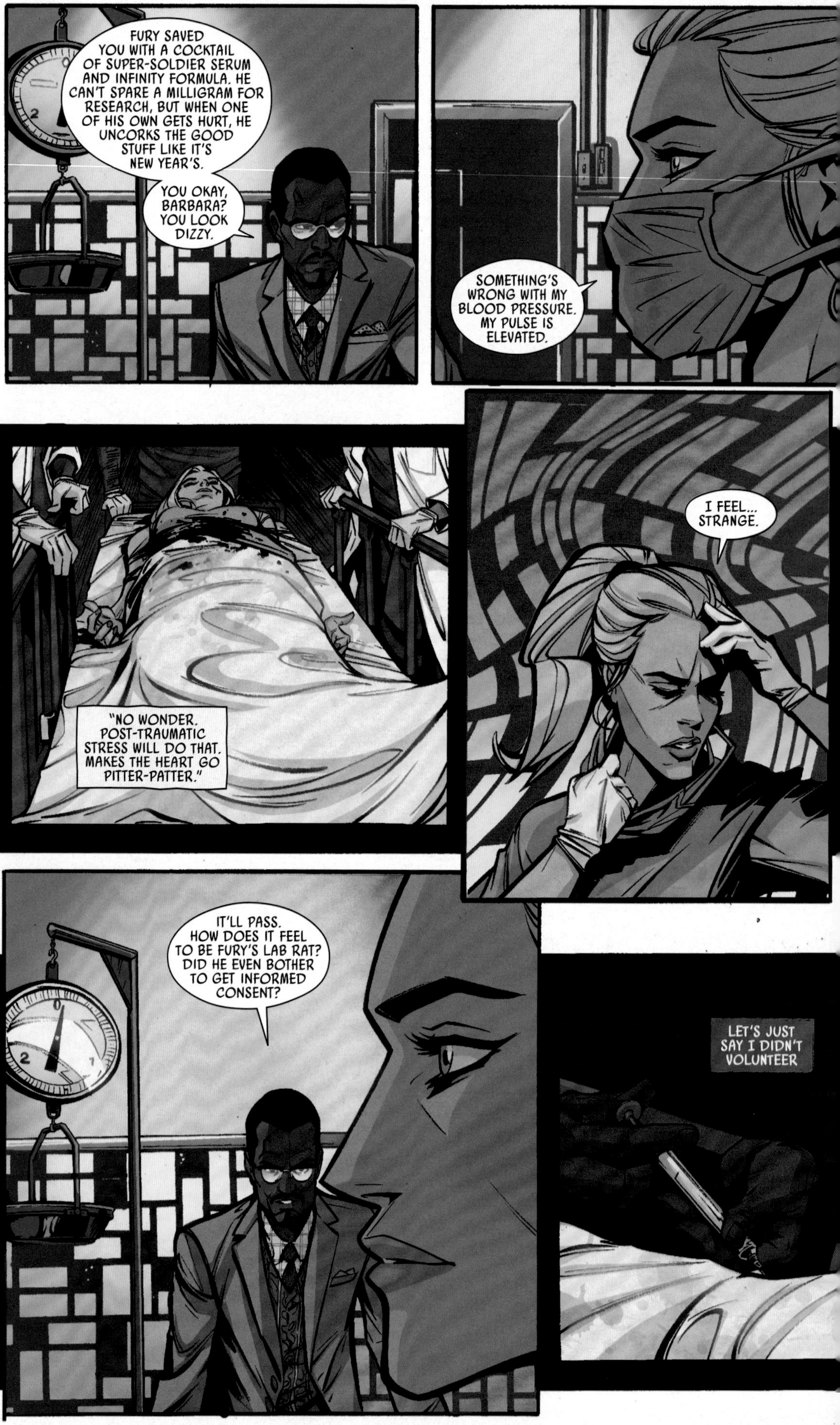
FURY SAVED YOU WITH A COCKTAIL OF SUPER-SOLDIER SERUM AND INFINITY FORMULA. HE CAN'T SPARE A MILLIGRAM FOR RESEARCH, BUT WHEN ONE OF HIS OWN GETS HURT, HE UNCORKS THE GOOD STUFF LIKE IT'S NEW YEAR'S.
YOU OKAY, BARBARA? YOU LOOK DIZZY.
SOMETHING'S WRONG WITH MY BLOOD PRESSURE. MY PULSE IS ELEVATED.
"NO WONDER. POST-TRAUMATIC STRESS WILL DO THAT. MAKES THE HEART GO PITTER-PATTER."
I FEEL... STRANGE.
IT'LL PASS. HOW DOES IT FEEL TO BE FURY'S LAB RAT? DID HE EVEN BOTHER TO GET INFORMED CONSENT?
LET'S JUST SAY I DIDN'T VOLUNTEER

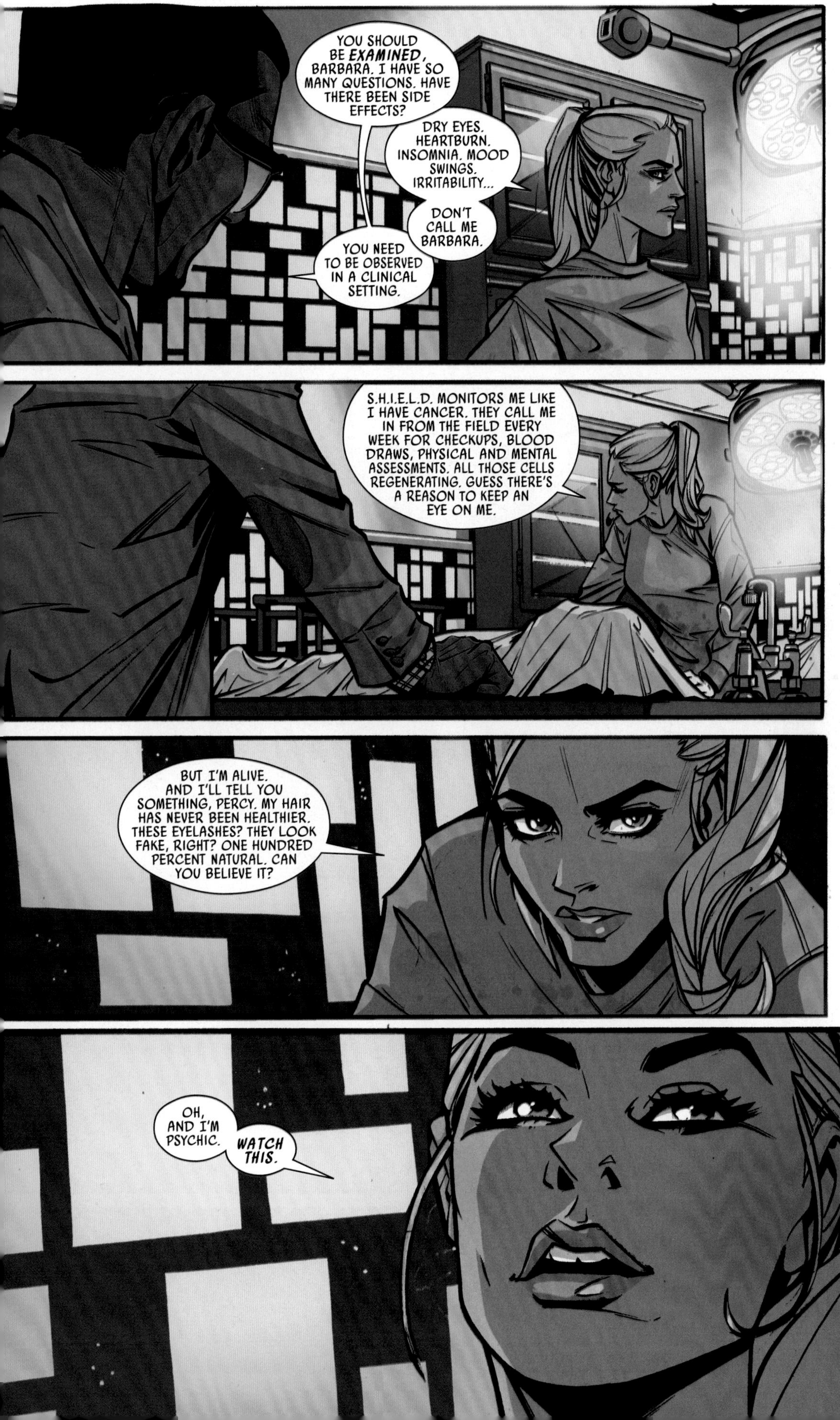
YOU SHOULD BE *EXAMINED*, BARBARA. I HAVE SO MANY QUESTIONS. HAVE THERE BEEN SIDE EFFECTS?
DRY EYES. HEARTBURN. INSOMNIA. MOOD SWINGS. IRRITABILITY...
DON'T CALL ME BARBARA.
YOU NEED TO BE OBSERVED IN A CLINICAL SETTING.
S.H.I.E.L.D. MONITORS ME LIKE I HAVE CANCER. THEY CALL ME IN FROM THE FIELD EVERY WEEK FOR CHECKUPS, BLOOD DRAWS, PHYSICAL AND MENTAL ASSESSMENTS. ALL THOSE CELLS REGENERATING. GUESS THERE'S A REASON TO KEEP AN EYE ON ME.
BUT I'M ALIVE. AND I'LL TELL YOU SOMETHING, PERCY. MY HAIR HAS NEVER BEEN HEALTHIER. THESE EYELASHES? THEY LOOK FAKE, RIGHT? ONE HUNDRED PERCENT NATURAL. CAN YOU BELIEVE IT?
OH, AND I'M PSYCHIC.
WATCH THIS.

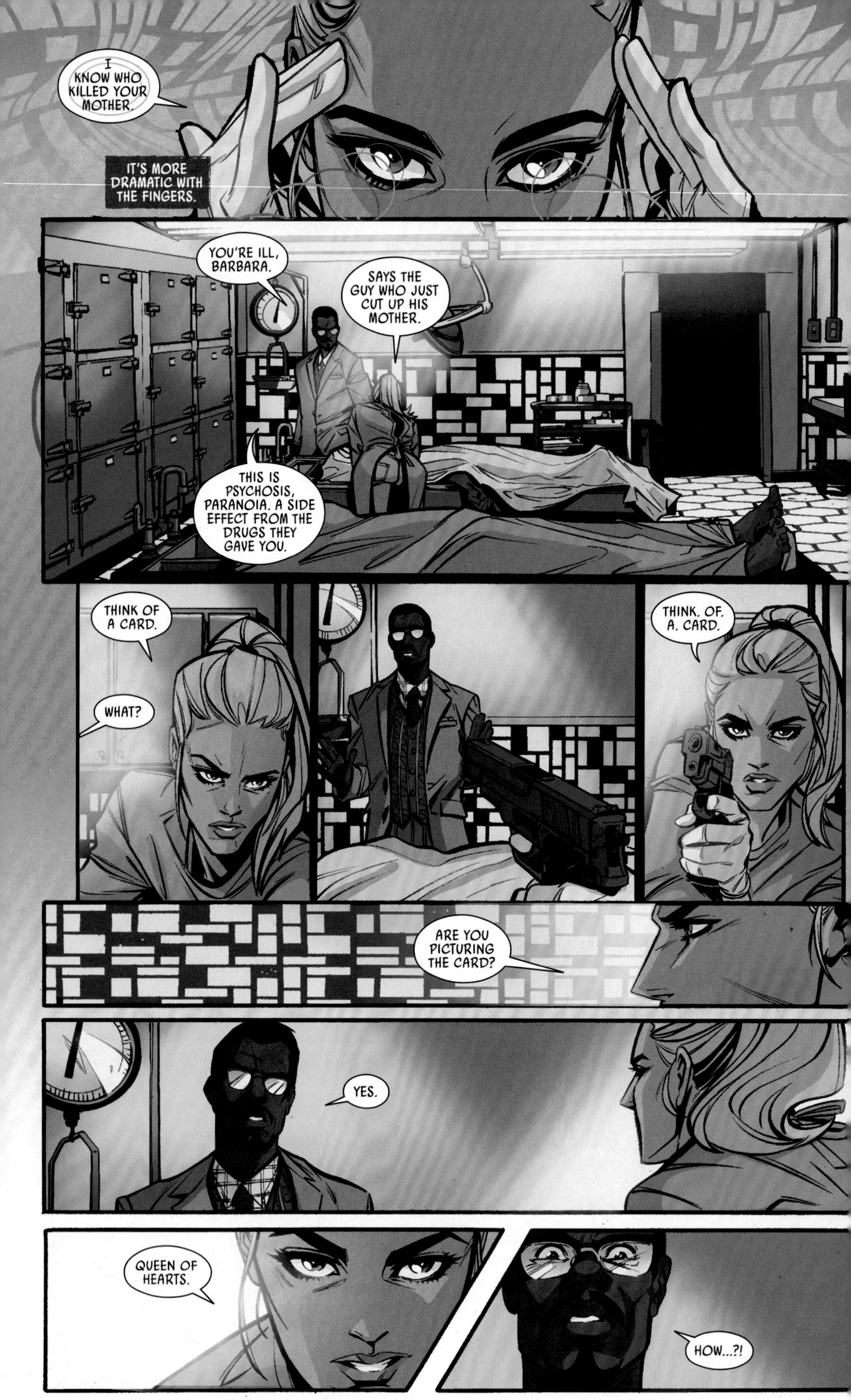
I KNOW WHO KILLED YOUR MOTHER.
IT'S MORE DRAMATIC WITH THE FINGERS.
YOU'RE ILL, BARBARA.
SAYS THE GUY WHO JUST CUT UP HIS MOTHER.
THIS IS PSYCHOSIS, PARANOIA. A SIDE EFFECT FROM THE DRUGS THEY GAVE YOU.
THINK OF A CARD.
WHAT?
THINK. OF. A. CARD.
ARE YOU PICTURING THE CARD?
YES.
QUEEN OF HEARTS.
HOW...?!

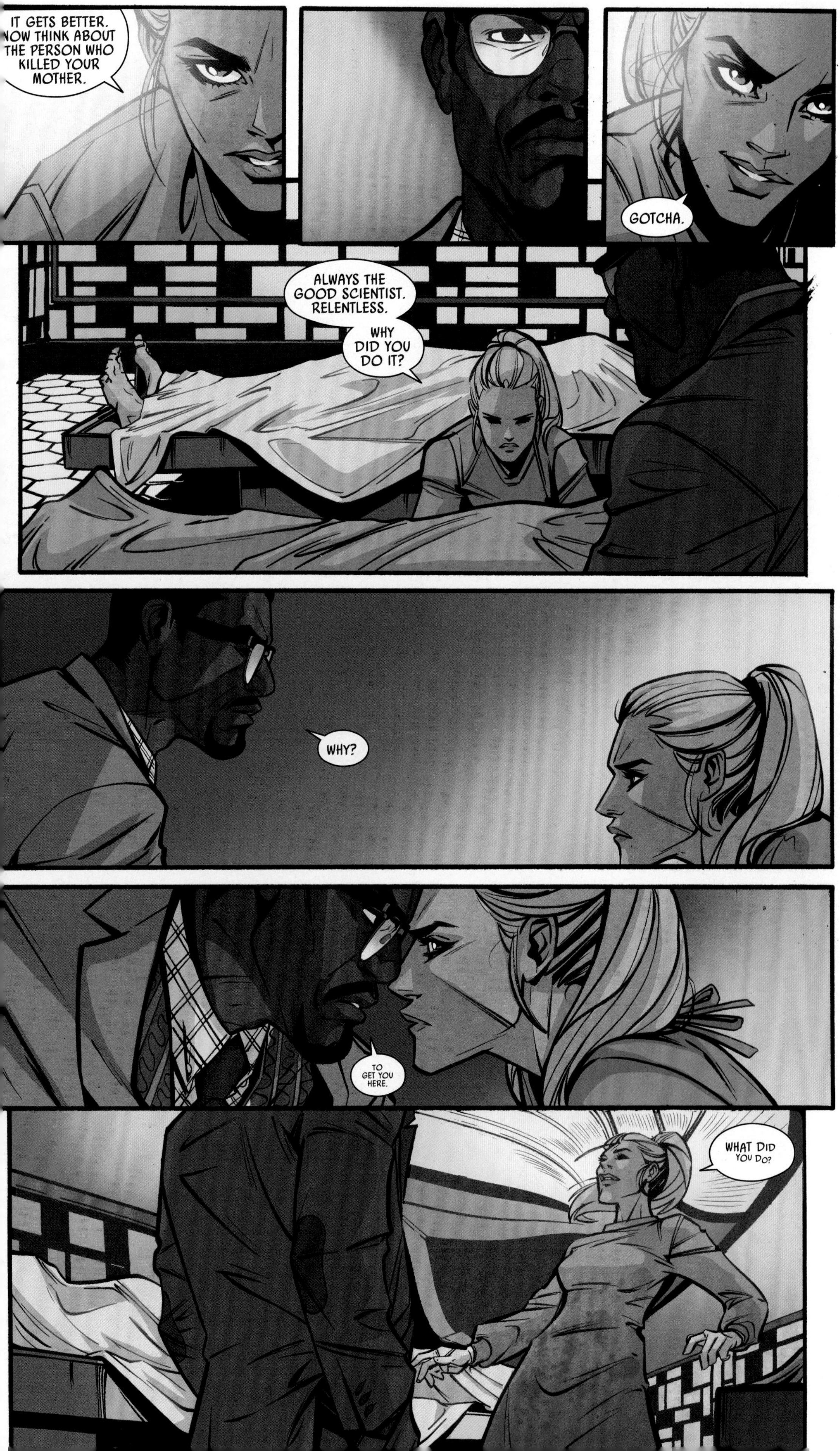

IT GETS BETTER. NOW THINK ABOUT THE PERSON WHO KILLED YOUR MOTHER.
GOTCHA.
ALWAYS THE GOOD SCIENTIST. RELENTLESS.
WHY DID YOU DO IT?
WHY?
TO GET YOU HERE.
WHAT DID YOU DO?

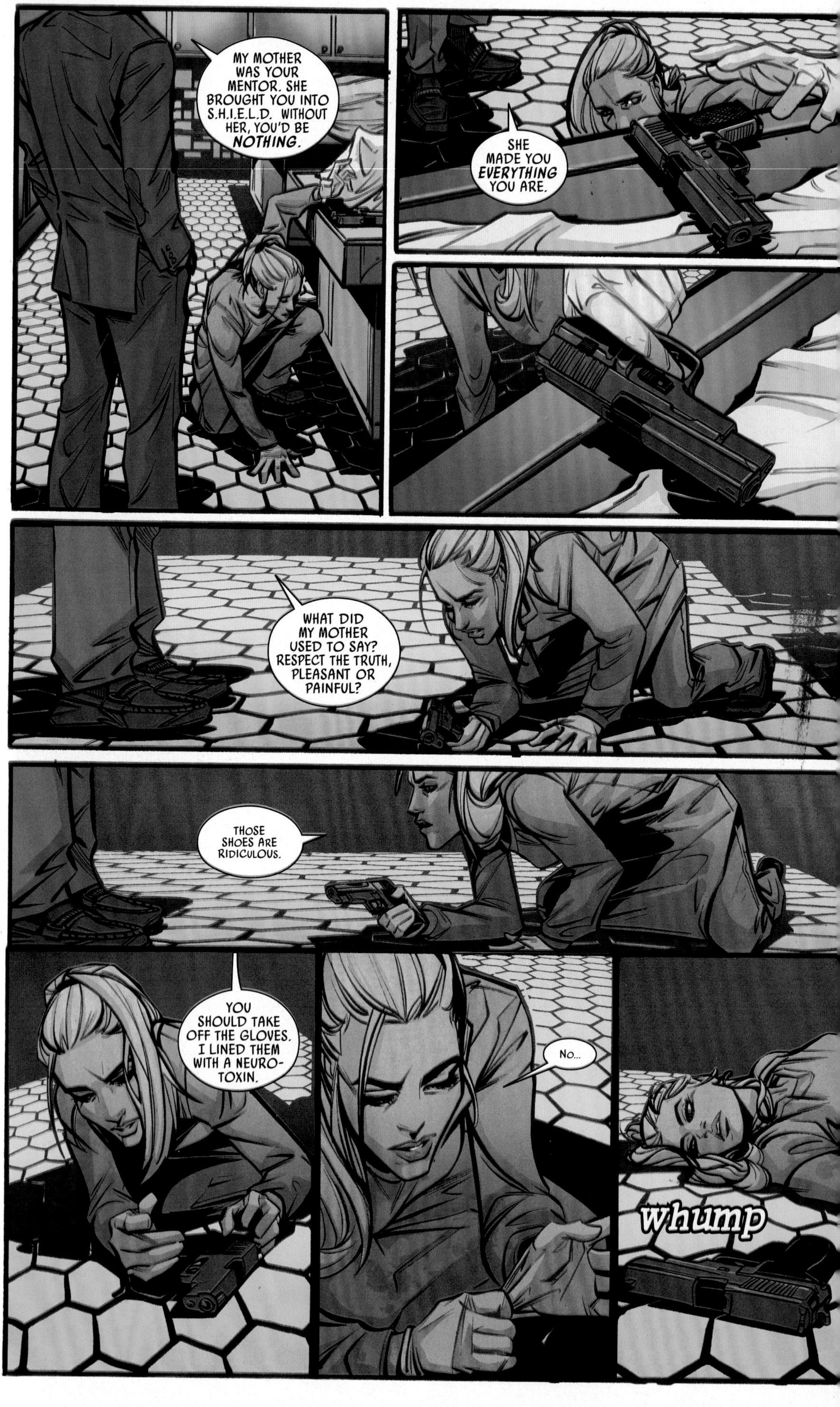
MY MOTHER WAS YOUR MENTOR. SHE BROUGHT YOU INTO S.H.I.E.L.D. WITHOUT HER, YOU'D BE NOTHING.
SHE MADE YOU EVERYTHING YOU ARE.
WHAT DID MY MOTHER USED TO SAY? RESPECT THE TRUTH, PLEASANT OR PAINFUL?
THOSE SHOES ARE RIDICULOUS.
YOU SHOULD TAKE OFF THE GLOVES. I LINED THEM WITH A NEURO-TOXIN.
NO...
whump

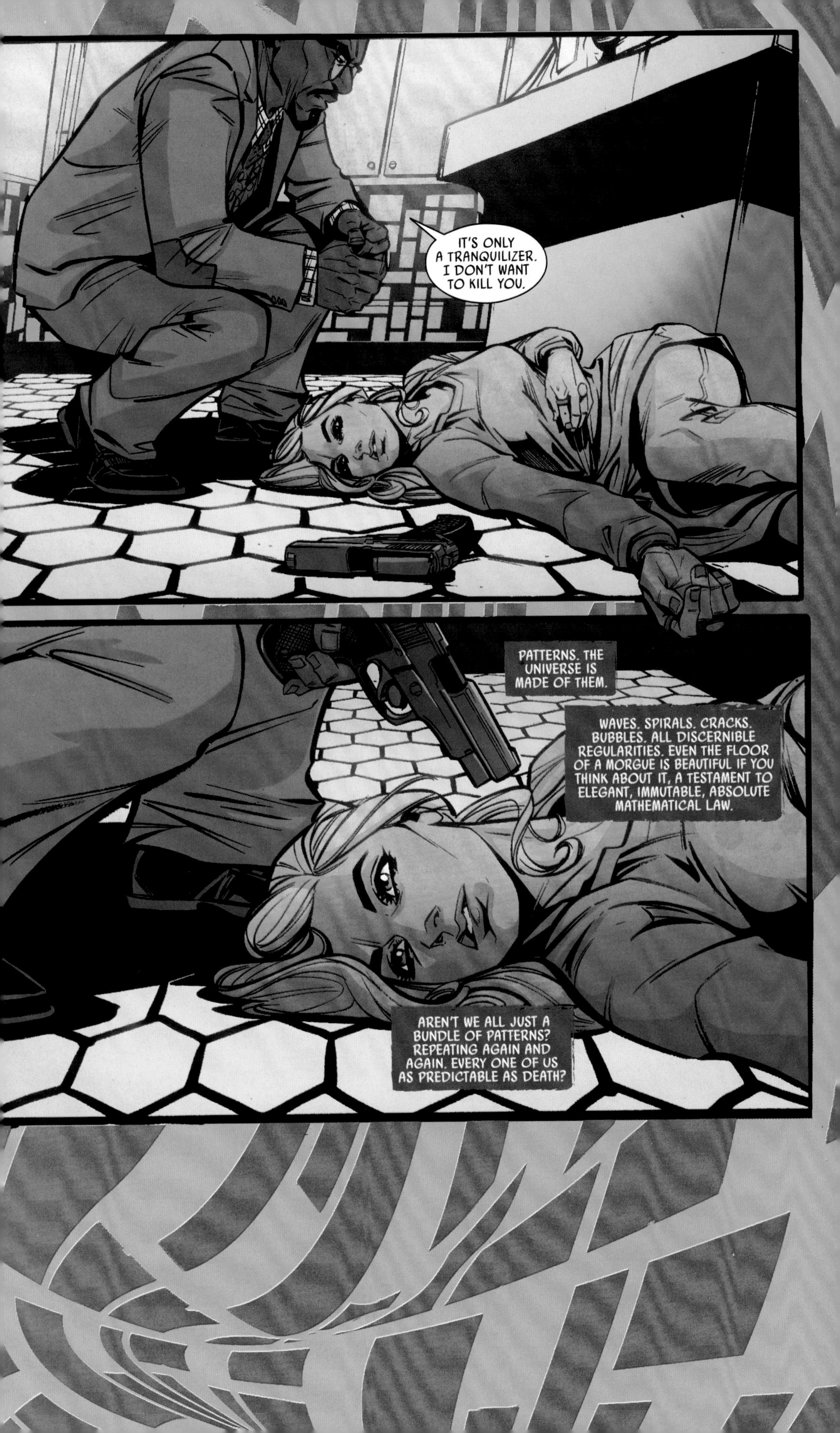
IT'S ONLY A TRANQUILIZER. I DON'T WANT TO KILL YOU.
PATTERNS. THE UNIVERSE IS MADE OF THEM.
WAVES. SPIRALS. CRACKS. BUBBLES. ALL DISCERNIBLE REGULARITIES. EVEN THE FLOOR OF A MORGUE IS BEAUTIFUL IF YOU THINK ABOUT IT, A TESTAMENT TO ELEGANT, IMMUTABLE, ABSOLUTE MATHEMATICAL LAW.
AREN'T WE ALL JUST A BUNDLE OF PATTERNS? REPEATING AGAIN AND AGAIN. EVERY ONE OF US AS PREDICTABLE AS DEATH?

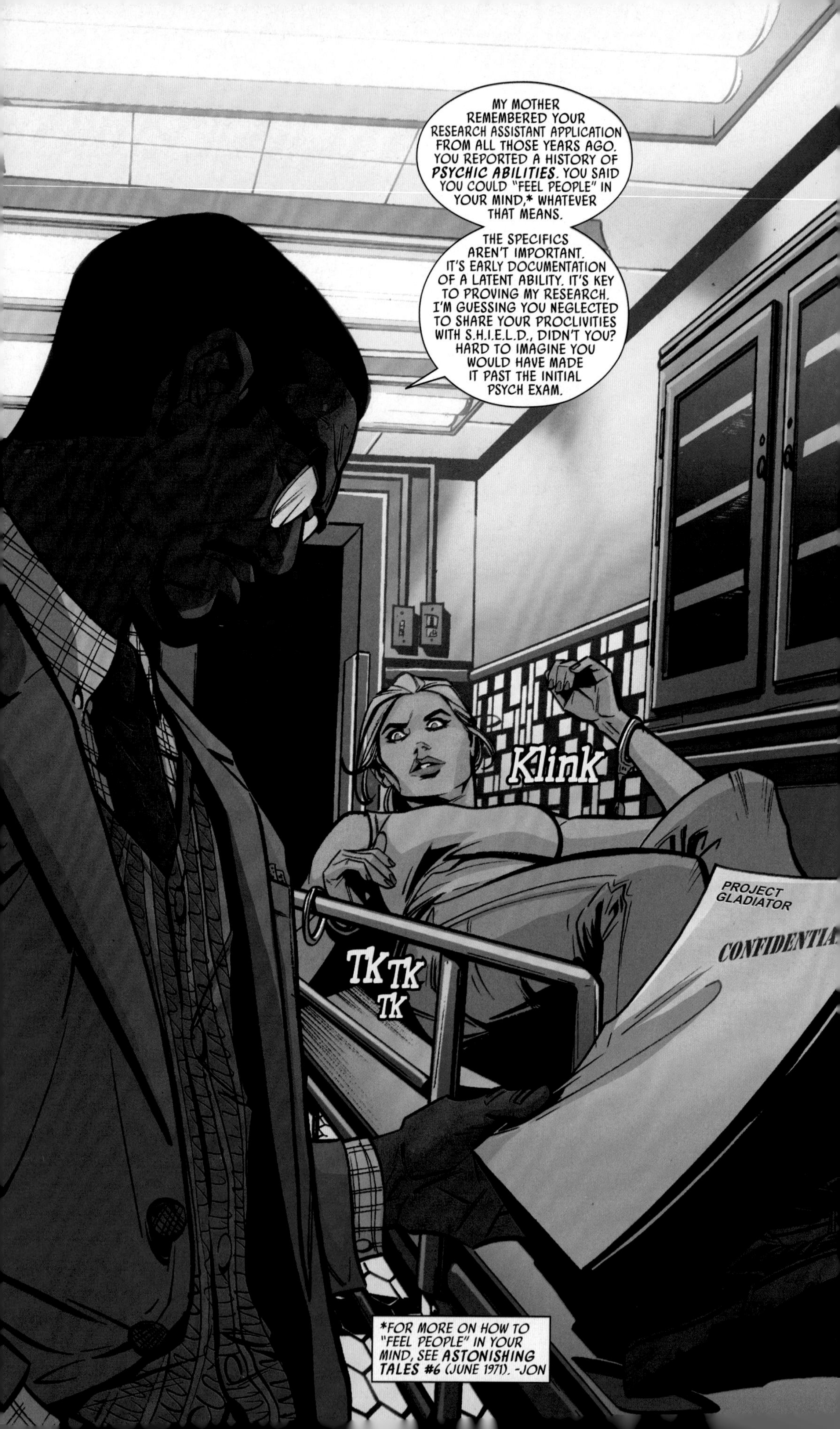
MY MOTHER REMEMBERED YOUR RESEARCH ASSISTANT APPLICATION FROM ALL THOSE YEARS AGO. YOU REPORTED A HISTORY OF PSYCHIC ABILITIES. YOU SAID YOU COULD "FEEL PEOPLE" IN YOUR MIND,* WHATEVER THAT MEANS.
THE SPECIFICS AREN'T IMPORTANT. IT'S EARLY DOCUMENTATION OF A LATENT ABILITY. IT'S KEY TO PROVING MY RESEARCH. I'M GUESSING YOU NEGLECTED TO SHARE YOUR PROCLIVITIES WITH S.H.I.E.L.D., DIDN'T YOU? HARD TO IMAGINE YOU WOULD HAVE MADE IT PAST THE INITIAL PSYCH EXAM.
Klink
PROJECT GLADIATOR
CONFIDENTIA
TK TK TK
*FOR MORE ON HOW TO "FEEL PEOPLE" IN YOUR MIND, SEE ASTONISHING TALES #6 (JUNE 1971). -JON

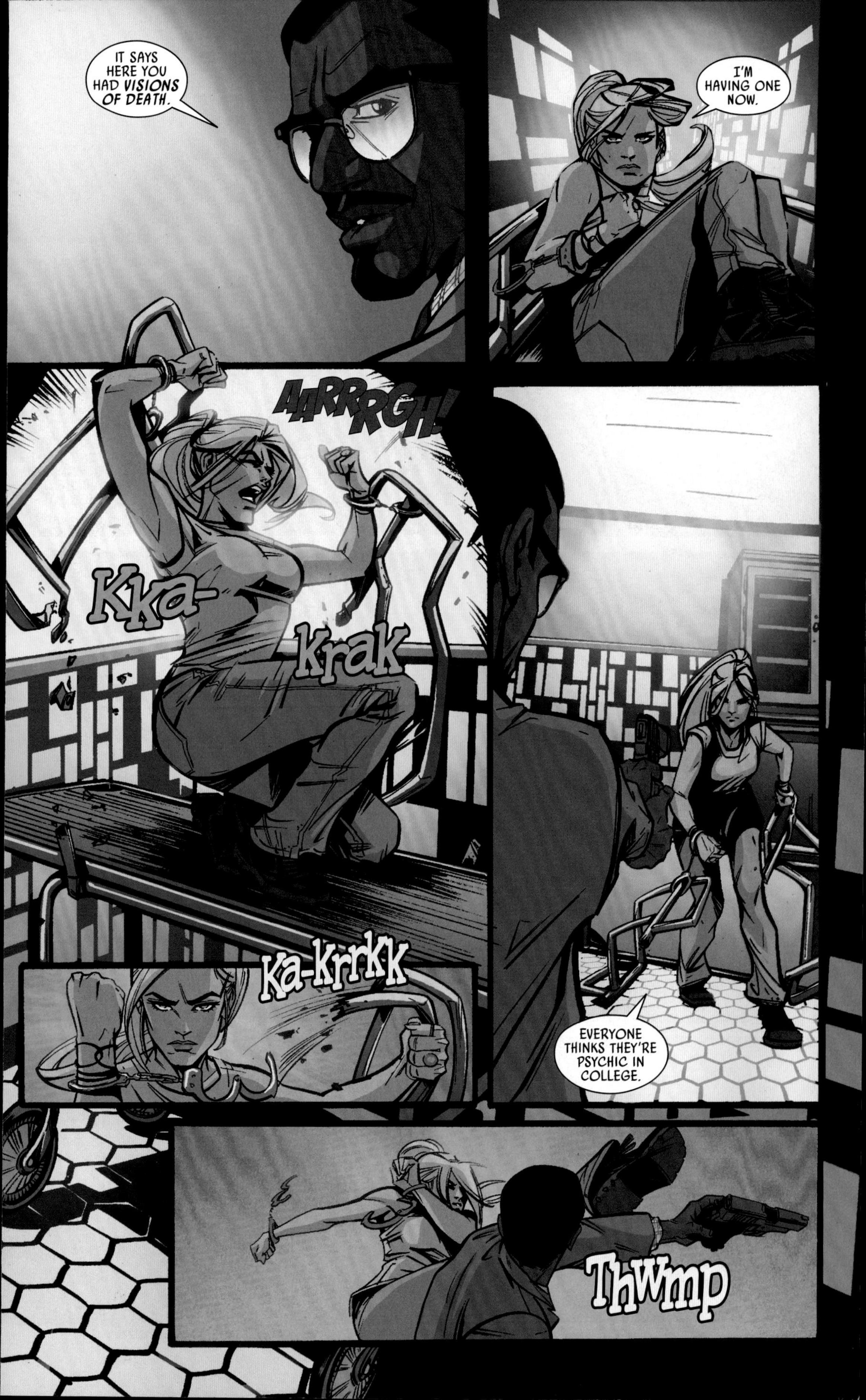
IT SAYS HERE YOU HAD VISIONS OF DEATH.
I'M HAVING ONE NOW.
AARRRGH!
Kka-
krak
Ka-KrrKK
EVERYONE THINKS THEY'RE PSYCHIC IN COLLEGE.
ThWmp

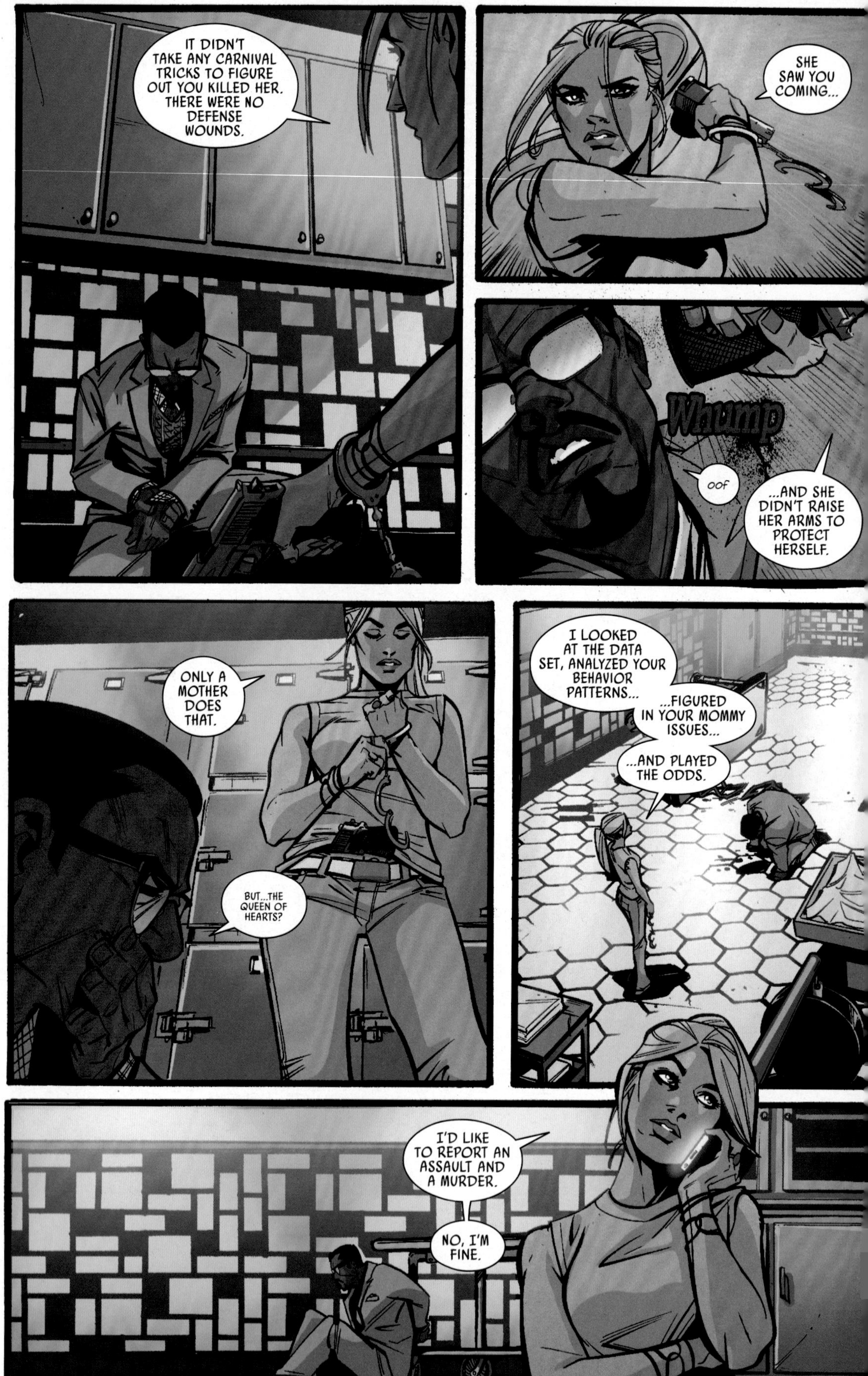
IT DIDN'T TAKE ANY CARNIVAL TRICKS TO FIGURE OUT YOU KILLED HER. THERE WERE NO DEFENSE WOUNDS.
SHE SAW YOU COMING...
Whump
OOF
...AND SHE DIDN'T RAISE HER ARMS TO PROTECT HERSELF.
ONLY A MOTHER DOES THAT.
BUT...THE QUEEN OF HEARTS?
I LOOKED AT THE DATA SET, ANALYZED YOUR BEHAVIOR PATTERNS...
...FIGURED IN YOUR MOMMY ISSUES...
...AND PLAYED THE ODDS.
I'D LIKE TO REPORT AN ASSAULT AND A MURDER.
NO, I'M FINE.

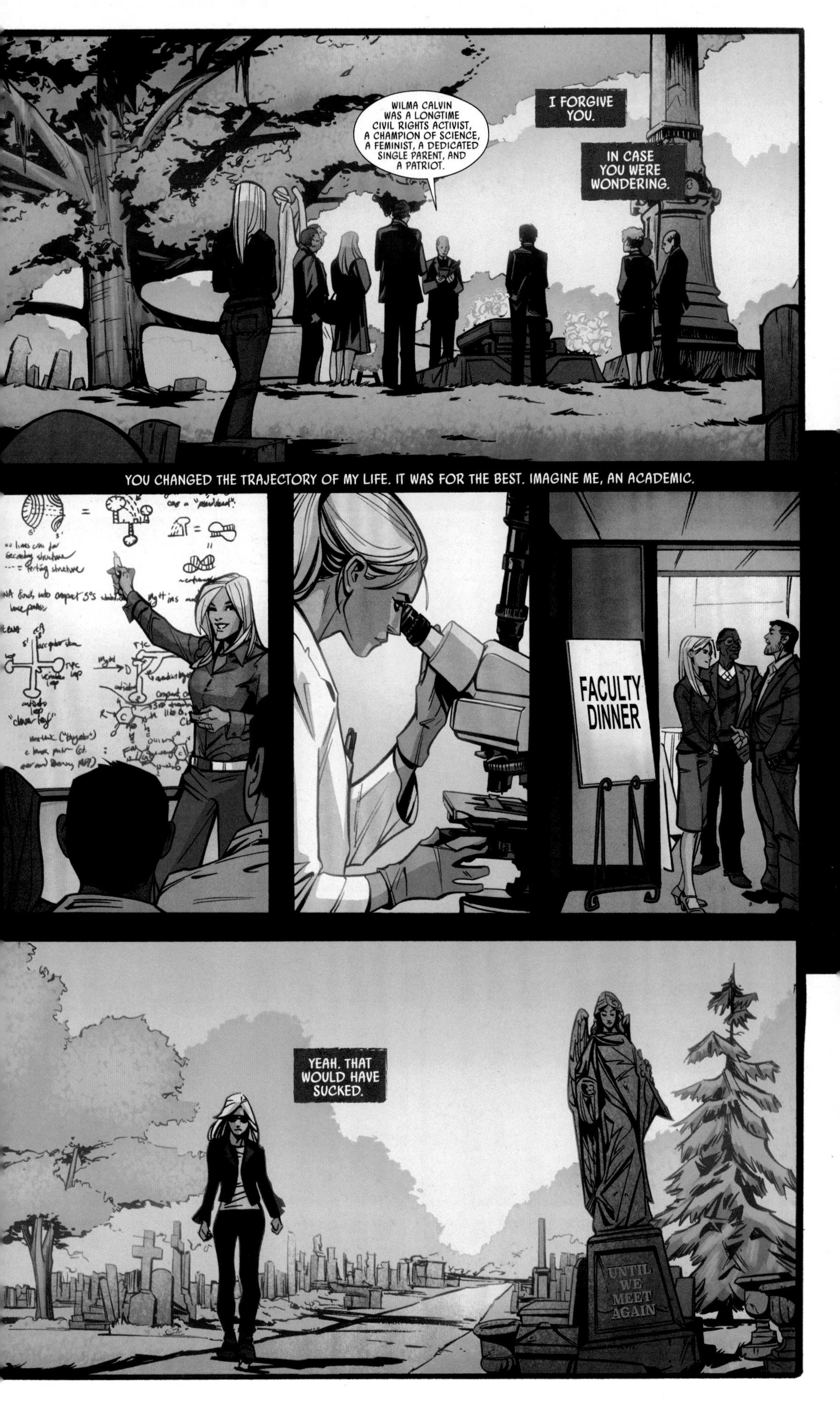
WILMA CALVIN WAS A LONGTIME CIVIL RIGHTS ACTIVIST, A CHAMPION OF SCIENCE, A FEMINIST, A DEDICATED SINGLE PARENT, AND A PATRIOT.
I FORGIVE YOU.
IN CASE YOU WERE WONDERING.
YOU CHANGED THE TRAJECTORY OF MY LIFE. IT WAS FOR THE BEST. IMAGINE ME, AN ACADEMIC.
FACULTY DINNER
YEAH. THAT WOULD HAVE SUCKED.
UNTIL WE MEET AGAIN

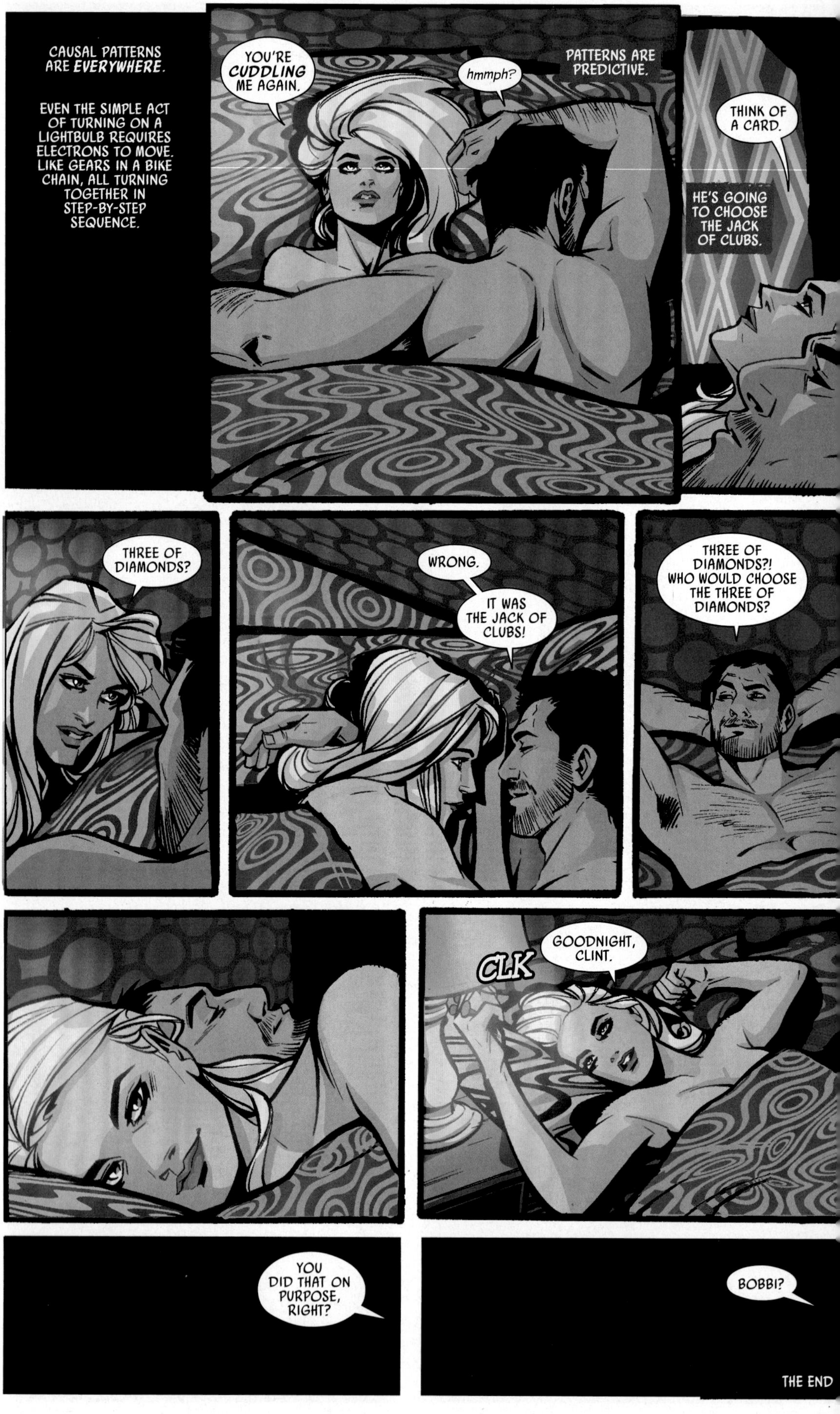

CAUSAL PATTERNS ARE *EVERYWHERE*.
EVEN THE SIMPLE ACT OF TURNING ON A LIGHTBULB REQUIRES ELECTRONS TO MOVE. LIKE GEARS IN A BIKE CHAIN, ALL TURNING TOGETHER IN STEP-BY-STEP SEQUENCE.
YOU'RE *CUDDLING* ME AGAIN.
hmmph?
PATTERNS ARE PREDICTIVE.
THINK OF A CARD.
HE'S GOING TO CHOOSE THE JACK OF CLUBS.
THREE OF DIAMONDS?
WRONG.
IT WAS THE JACK OF CLUBS!
THREE OF DIAMONDS?! WHO WOULD CHOOSE THE THREE OF DIAMONDS?
CLK
GOODNIGHT, CLINT.
YOU DID THAT ON PURPOSE, RIGHT?
BOBBI?
THE END

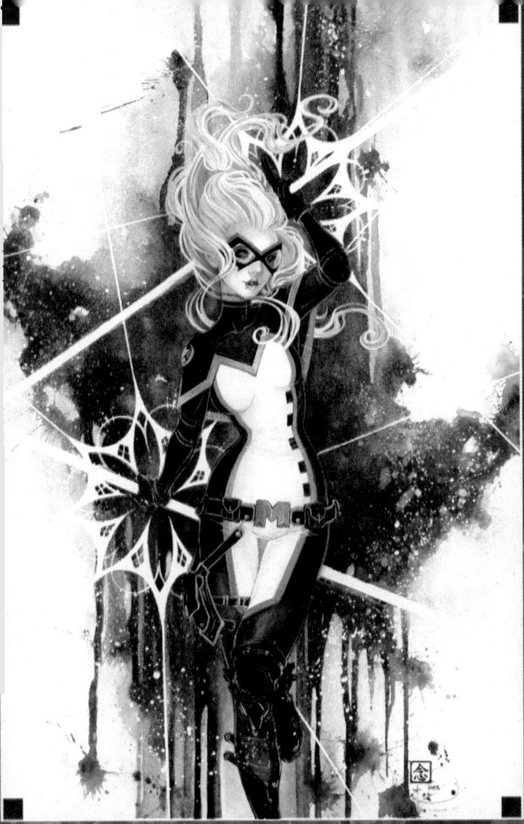

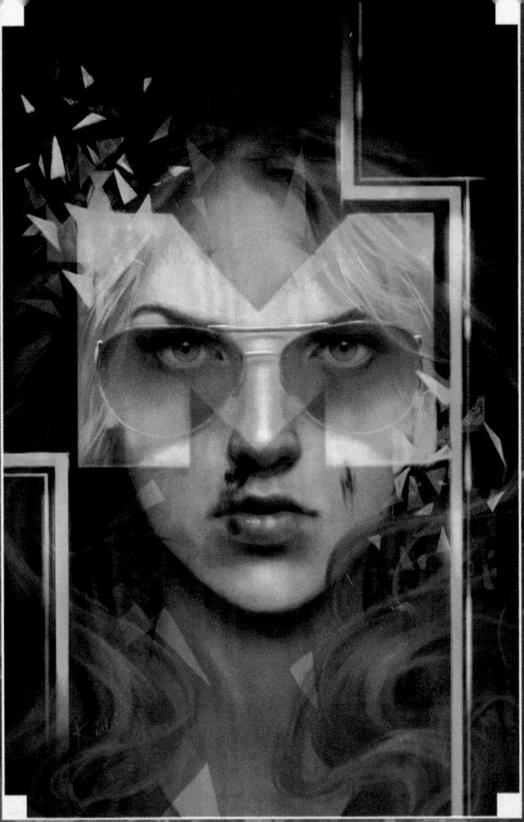

#2 VARIANT BY
Nen Chang

#2 VARIANT BY
Kirbi Fagan

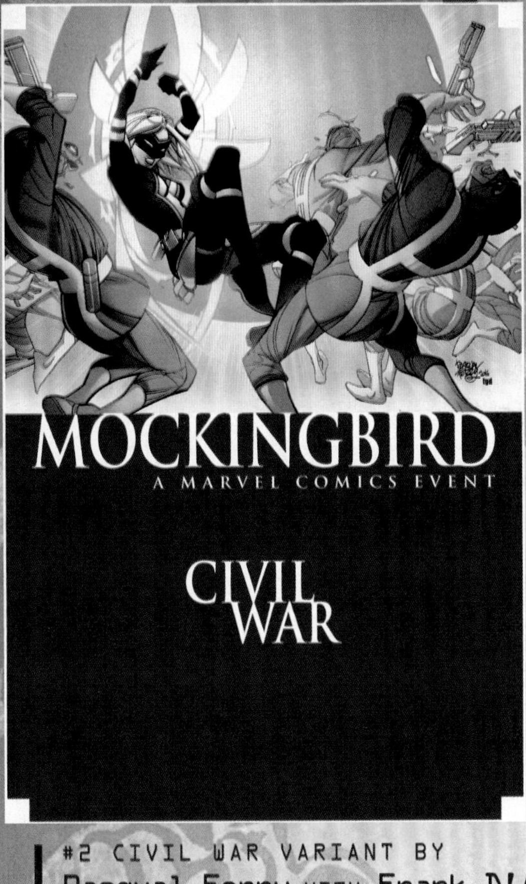
MOCKINGBIRD
A MARVEL COMICS EVENT
CIVIL WAR

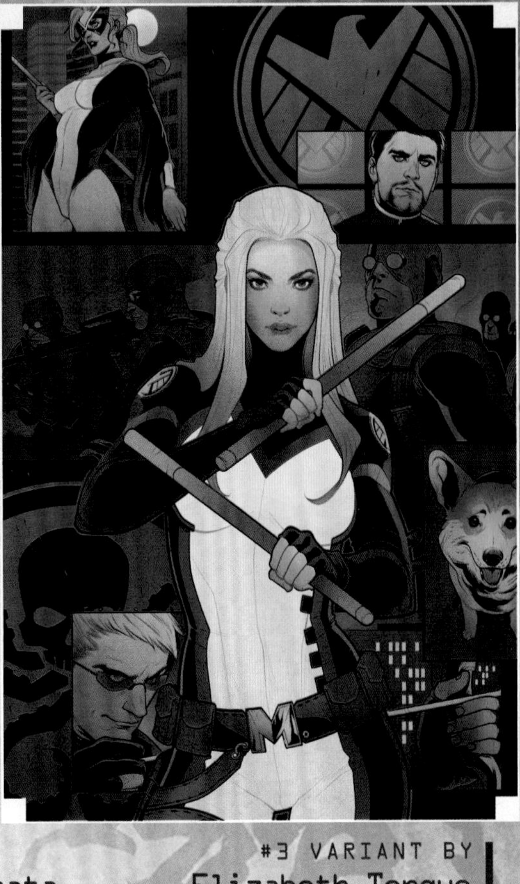

#2 CIVIL WAR VARIANT BY
Pasqual Ferry WITH Frank D'Armata

#3 VARIANT BY
Elizabeth Torque

You might have some questions. Because, what the heck? None of that made
any sense at all. Or did it? Do black holes make sense? Do cats make sense?
Does Joan Crawford make sense? No. But these things are still awesome.

I present to you, smart MOCKINGBIRD fans, the first issue of a five-issue puzzle
box. I did not know it was called that until I pitched it to Tom Brevoort and he
said, "Oh, yeah, a puzzle box," and that seemed to please him so I went along with
it and looked it up later. He is so smart! Like Bobbi.

This first issue makes no sense. It's not really supposed to, though it certainly
plants a lot of fun clues. Each of the next three issues will fill in what happened
between appointments and then the fifth issue will pick up where this one leaves
off. The next issues are all linear, by the way, and much more episodic. We'll se
Bobbi on various missions. My goal is that you will read this issue, read the next
four, and then come back and read this one again, and it will be a completely
different experience. It's like two for one.

Heady, right?

I am here because of you.   Because the S.H.I.E.L.D. 50TH ANNIVERSARY
MOCKINGBIRD one-shot (the clumsiest title ever) was met with such
enthusiasm and you guys were like, more of that please. Are you mad with power

I promise this: I promise science, I promise math. I promise competence and
confidence. I promise a Bobbi who is the smartest person in the room and
capable of taking down everyone in it.   I promise barbed wit and dro
punchlines. I promise Lance Hunter and Clinton Barton. Shirtless.

I get to work with an amazing team on this book. Kate Niemczyk did the ar
which took a leap of faith on her part because I kept telling her to draw thing
and that they'd make sense later. (Artists love that.) Because of our nine-hou
time difference I can tell you that we have literally been working o
MOCKINGBIRD for you around the clock. Our collected emails could be
200-page compendium. Right now Kate is happily drawing away in a Hellfi
dungeon--where Bobbi has gone on a mission to rescue Hunter. (You know wh
happens when you let us ladies near the Hellfire Club? The men serve t
drinks.) Issue #2! Order it today!

Joëlle Jones did the cover art. She is brilliant. I hope to live up to this cover
future issues.

Tom Brevoort, Katie Kubert and Alanna Smith have been such terrific (a
patient) editors. They have looked at outlines for all five issues in this puzz
box, so know that we have our eyes on the big picture.

Our colorist, Rachelle Rosenberg is the best. I'm consistently amazed by wh
she's able to add to the page. The wallpaper in this issue makes me swoon.

I want MOCKINGBIRD to look different than other comics. To take risks.
rather fail big and have tried something, you know? So I'll screw up sometim
I'm new here. I still haven't gotten over the thrill of seeing emails from Mar
in my in-box.

Thanks for letting me go on this ride with you.

Please get in touch at MHEROES@MARVEL.COM and let us know what you thi
of this first issue. (She says, nervously.) Thanks!

~ Chel

For anyone who has ever felt dismissed, undervalued, fourth tier, "too Eighties," unworthy, unheard, lightweight, thinly sketched -- for anyone who has ever felt two-dimensional or too blond -- this Bobbi Morse paper doll is for you. New clothes, accessories, and puzzle box clues in every issue!

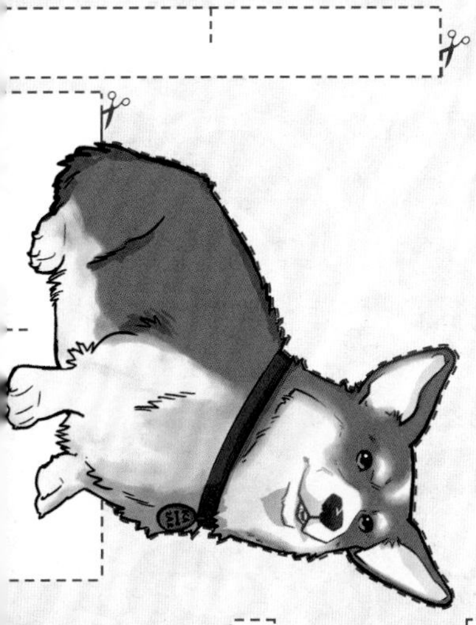

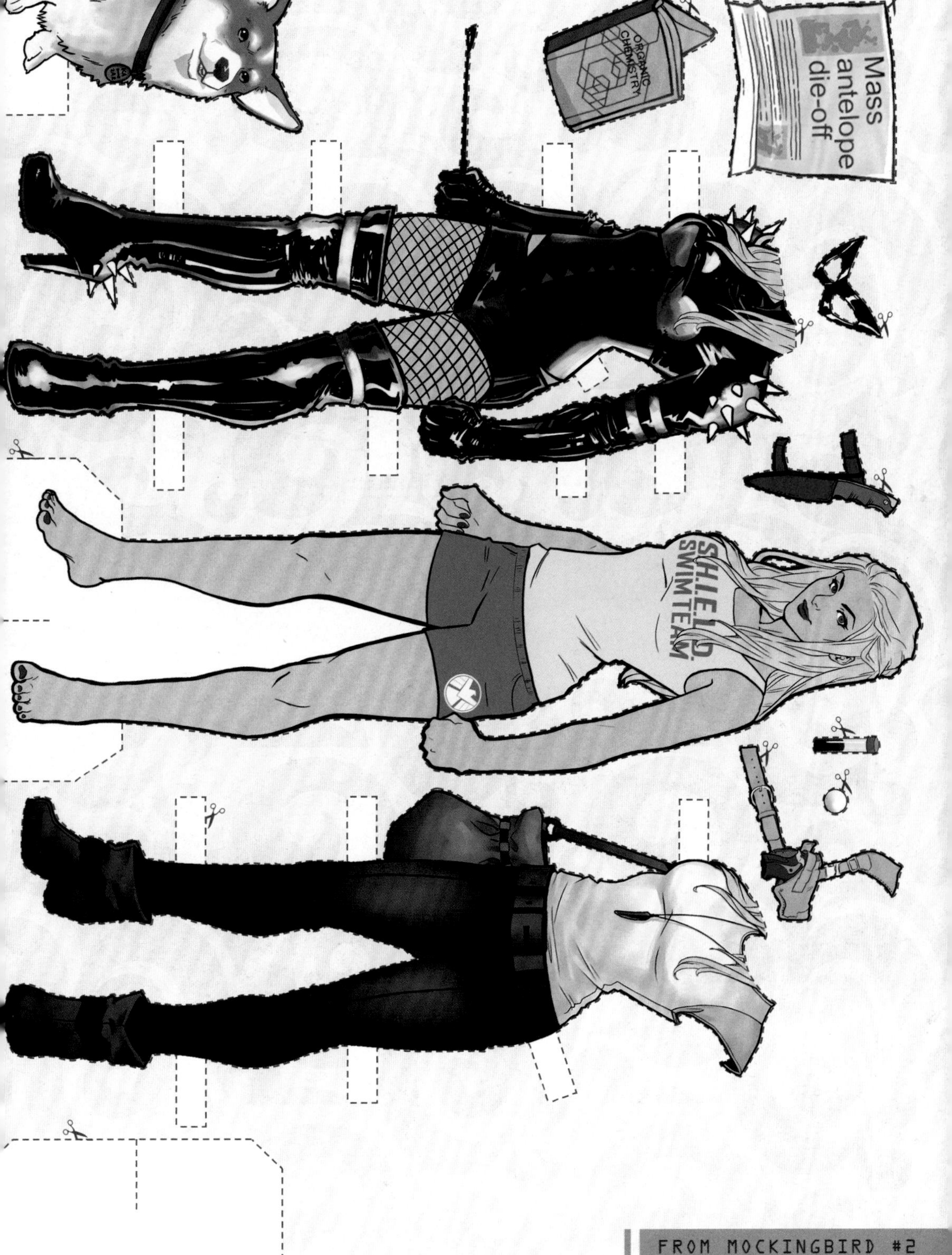

ORGANIC CHEMISTRY
Mass antelope die-off
S.H.I.E.L.D. SWIM TEAM

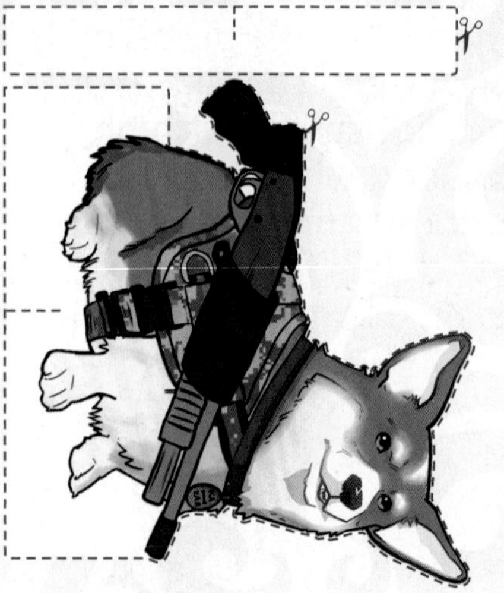

What does Mockingbird wear under her costume? Deadly weapons. She also has five tattoos. (Tequila, Hunter, Barton, long story.) Can you tel which is which? Can the Marvel continuity lawyers? Stay tuned for this and other reveals as the MOCKINGBIRD #puzzlebox continues.

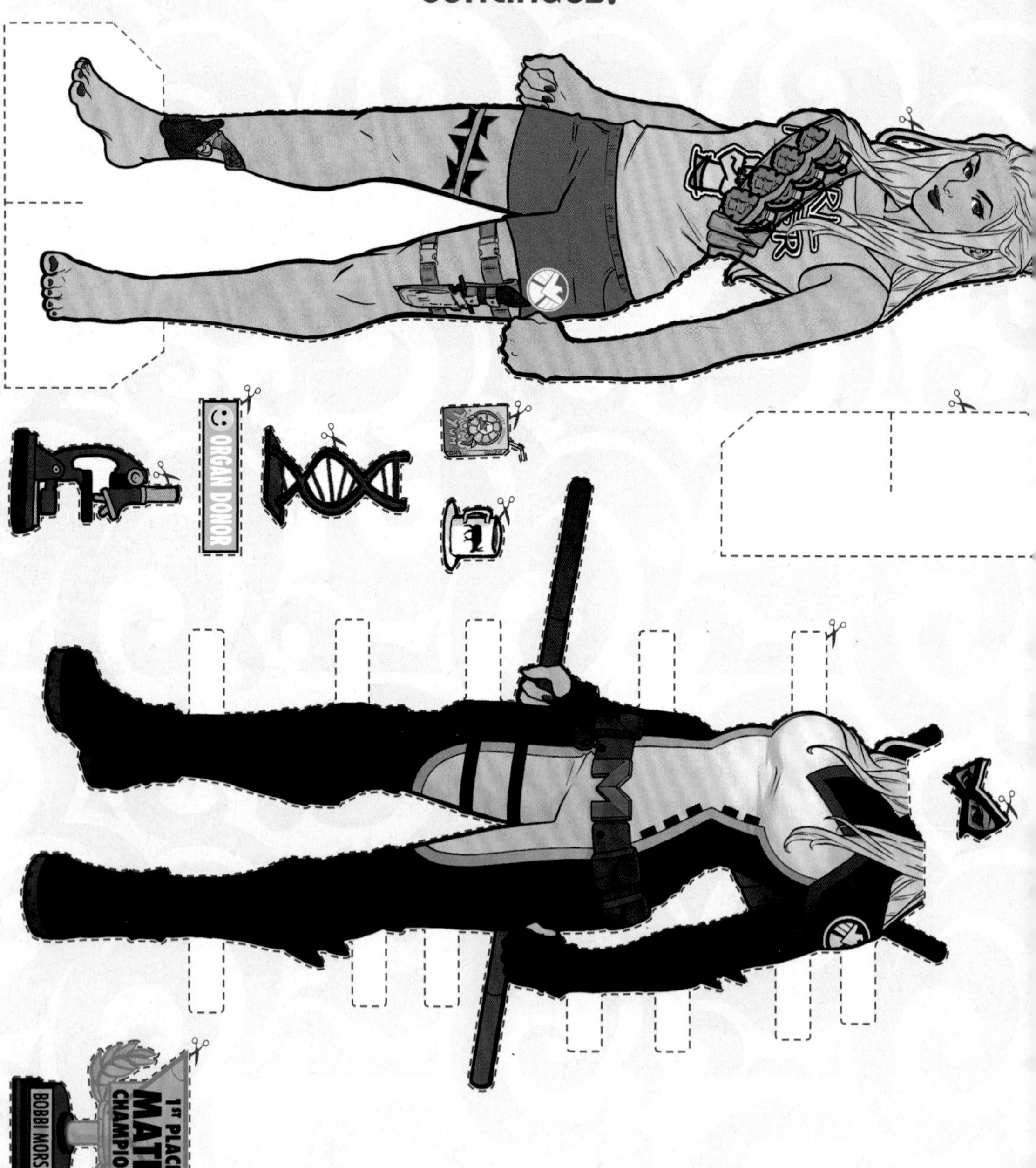
ORGAN DONOR

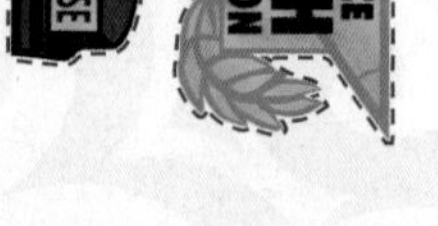
1ST PLACE
MATH
CHAMPION
BOBBI MORSE

BOBBI MORSE, ON ACCESSORIES:

"Ex-husbands are like old purses. You can replace them. But it's nice to keep the old ones around on the shelf, just in case. Because you never know when one will match your outfit."

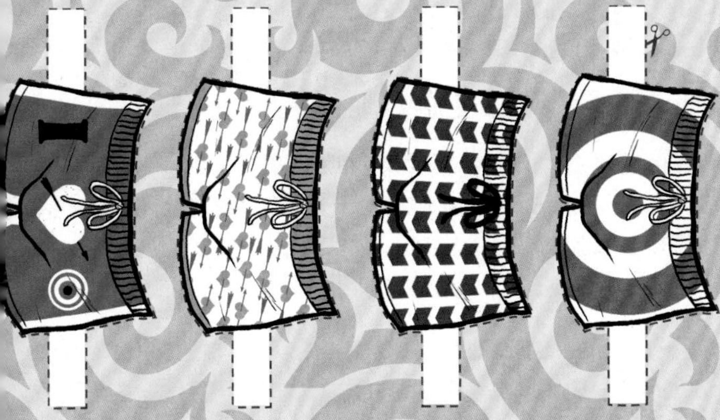

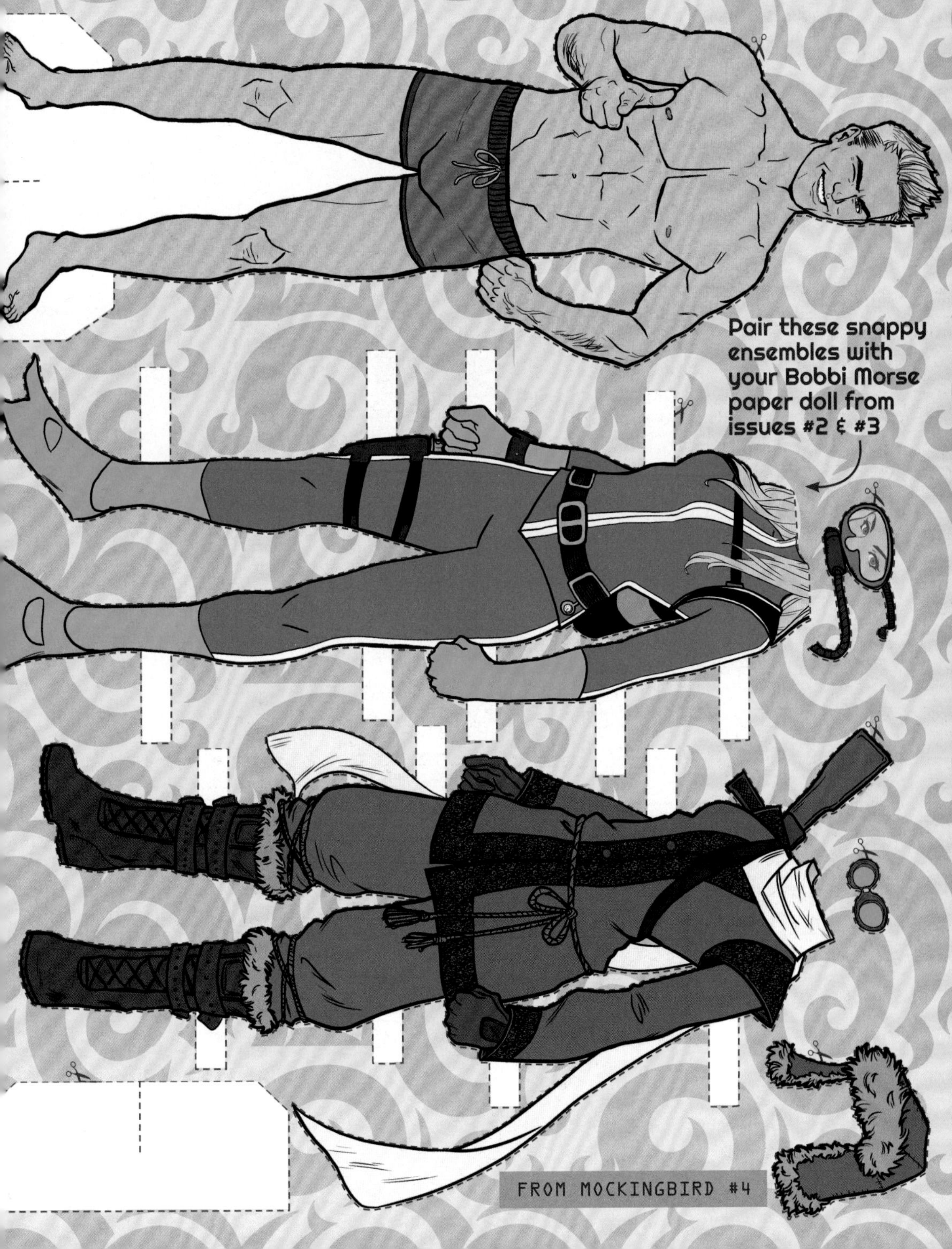
Pair these snappy ensembles with your Bobbi Morse paper doll from issues #2 & #3
FROM MOCKINGBIRD #4

BOBBI MORSE, HOUSEHOLD TIP #1 CORPSE JUICE STAIN REMOVAL

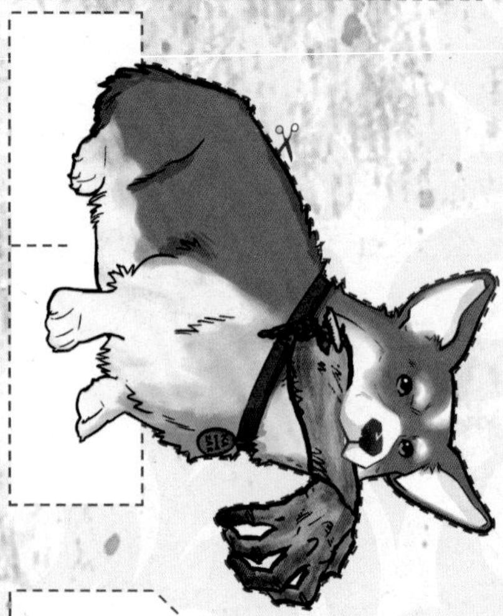

Fighting zombies is dirty work. But you can't throw away an outfit just because o a little corpse juice. Try removing the stair instead, using these simple steps:

1. Pre-soak for three hours in cold water mixed with a product containing enzyme
2. Hand wash with sodium hypochlorite bleach.
3. Repeat.
4. Repeat.
5. Repeat.
6. Have a glass of wine.
7. Line-dry.

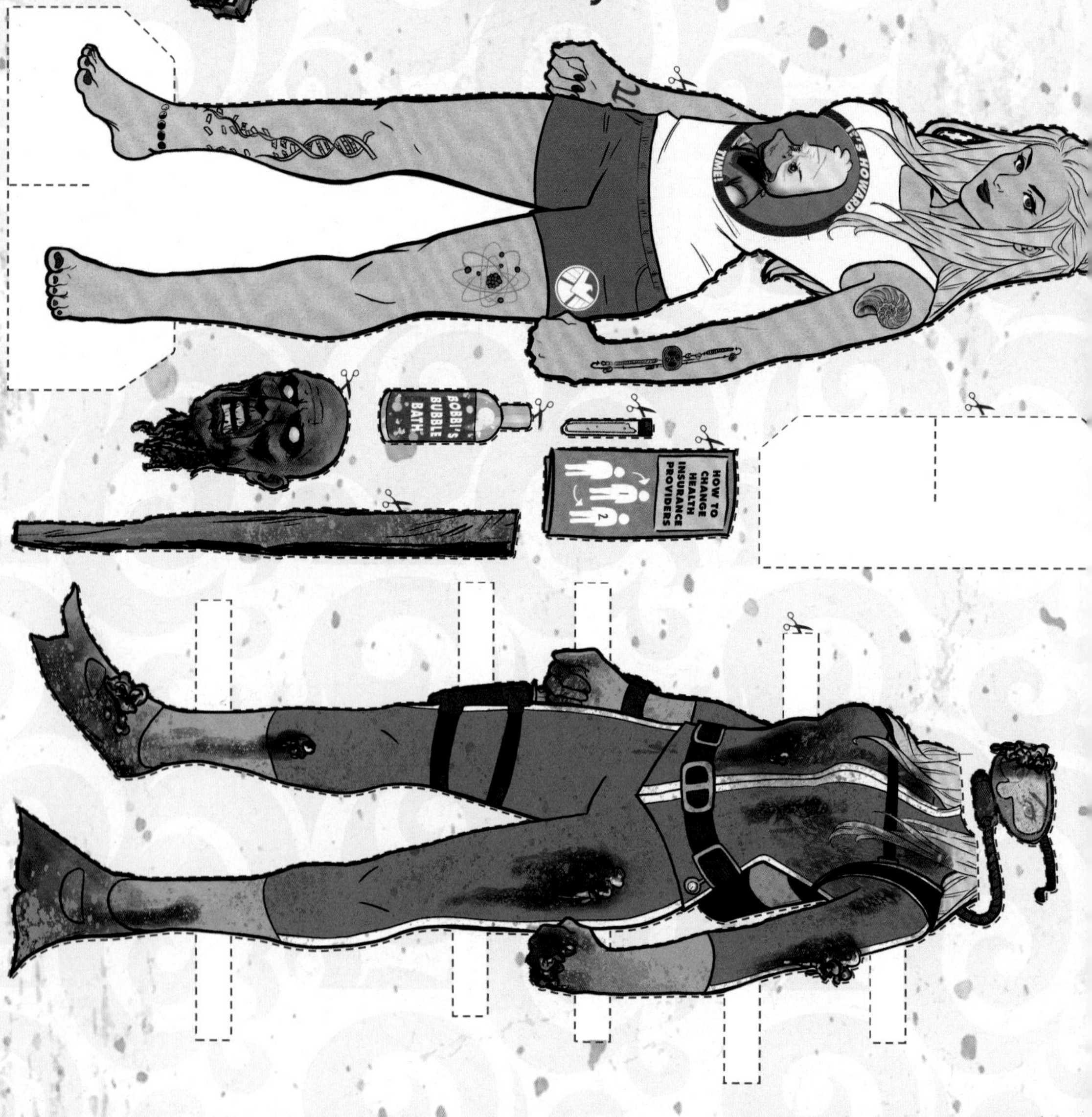
BOBBI'S BUBBLE BATH
HOW TO CHANGE HEALTH INSURANCE PROVIDERS

FROM MOCKINGBIRD #5